Sound Effect

Performance + Design is a series of monographs and essay collections that explore understandings of performance design and scenography, examining the potential of the visual, spatial, material and environmental to shape performative encounters and to offer sites for imaginative exchange. This series focuses on design both for and as performance in a variety of contexts including theatre, art installations, museum displays, mega-events, site-specific and community-based performance, street theatre, design of public space, festivals, protests and state-sanctioned spectacle.

Performance + Design takes as its starting point the growth of scenography and the expansion from theatre or stage design to a wider notion of scenography as a spatial practice. As such, it recognizes the recent accompanying interest from a number of converging scholarly disciplines (theatre, performance, art, architecture, design) and examines twenty-first- century practices of performance design in the context of debates about postdramatic theatre, aesthetic representation, visual and material culture, spectatorship, participation and co-authorship.

Series Editors
Stephen Di Benedetto, Joslin McKinney and Scott Palmer

Contemporary Scenography: Practices and Aesthetics in German Theatre, Arts and Design
Edited by Birgit Wiens
978-1-3500-6447-8

The History and Theory of Environmental Scenography: Second Edition
Arnold Aronson
978-1-4742-8396-0

Scenography Expanded: An Introduction to Contemporary Performance Design
Edited by Joslin McKinney and Scott Palmer
978-1-4742-4439-8

The Model as Performance: Staging Space in Theatre and Architecture
Thea Brejzek and Lawrence Wallen
978-1-4742-7138-7

Forthcoming titles
Consuming Scenography: The Theatricality of the Shopping Mall
Nebojša Tabacki
978-1-3501-1089-2

Digital Scenography: 30 Years of Experimentation and Innovation in Performance and Interactive Media
Neill O'Dwyer
978-1-3501-0731-1

Immersion and Participation in Punchdrunk's Theatrical Worlds
Carina E. I. Westling
978-1-3501-0195-1

Sites of Transformation: Applied and Socially Engaged Scenography in Rural Landscapes
Louise Ann Wilson
978-1-3501-0444-0

Sound Effect

The Theatre We Hear

ROSS BROWN

methuen | drama
LONDON • NEW YORK • OXFORD • NEW DELHI • SYDNEY

METHUEN DRAMA
Bloomsbury Publishing Plc
50 Bedford Square, London, WC1B 3DP, UK
1385 Broadway, New York, NY 10018, USA
29 Earlsfort Terrace, Dublin 2, Ireland

BLOOMSBURY, METHUEN DRAMA and the Methuen Drama logo are trademarks of
Bloomsbury Publishing Plc

First published in Great Britain 2020
This paperback edition published in 2021

Copyright © Ross Brown, 2020

Ross Brown has asserted his right under the Copyright, Designs and Patents Act, 1988, to be identified as the author of this work.

For legal purposes the Acknowledgements on p. ix constitute an extension of this copyright page.

Series design by Burge Agency
Cover photograph by Ross Brown

All rights reserved. No part of this publication may be reproduced or transmitted in any form or by any means, electronic or mechanical, including photocopying, recording, or any information storage or retrieval system, without prior permission in writing from the publishers.

Bloomsbury Publishing Plc does not have any control over, or responsibility for, any third-party websites referred to or in this book. All internet addresses given in this book were correct at the time of going to press. The author and publisher regret any inconvenience caused if addresses have changed or sites have ceased to exist, but can accept no responsibility for any such changes.

A catalogue record for this book is available from the British Library.

A catalog record for this book is available from the Library of Congress.

ISBN: HB: 978-1-3500-4590-3
PB: 978-1-3502-3600-4
ePDF: 978-1-3500-4592-7
eBook: 978-1-3500-4591-0

Series: Performance and Design

Typeset by RefineCatch Limited, Bungay, Suffolk

To find out more about our authors and books visit www.bloomsbury.com and sign up for our newsletters

For Alan Brown
1939–2017

Contents

Acknowledgements ix
Now hear this (A preface) xiii

PART ONE Theatrical hearing

1 It's obviously an effect (An introduction) 3
   Splat 3
   By design 15

2 Dispositions 23
   The god sound 23
   Auditory space and its dramaturgy 34
   The scenography of sound 38

3 Auditorium 47
   A space in process 47
   A fictional ontology 60

PART TWO Reconfigurations

4 Present (A theatre about our person) 67
   Inscape 67
   Personal audio/immersive theatre 72
   The hi-fi cell 74

5 A sound from the suburbs (The curious story of Colonel Gouraud) 83
   An electric house 85
   A baby cries 87
   Anathema maranatha! 88

6 Picturing the scene   93

  The scenic reconfiguration   93
  The picturesque of sound   101
  The Eidophusikon   110

PART THREE 'Our thunder is the best' (Living in the audio world)

7 Arty, exotic and gothic   119

  Pop, art and the theatre of hearing   119
  The theatre we daydream   125
  Thunder on the ear   134

8 Inside out (Symbolism, cinema and *The Bells*)   143

  The soundtrack, its prehistory and audiovisual morphology   143
  My God, it's coming out of your ears!   150
  The free ear   158

9 Audio drama   165

  The sound effect in its widest sense (the stuff of radio)   165
  The theatre Corwin heard   173
  Common sound   182
  The Anatomy of Sound, by Norman Corwin   183

10 Conclusion   191

  Audimus: the theatre we hear   191

References   199
Index   207

Acknowledgements

Thanks to the American Radio Archives, Thousand Oaks Library, and the Norman Corwin Estate for permission to reproduce extracts from *The Anatomy of Sound*. Parts of Chapters 6 and 7 have been reworked, in English, from my chapter 'Bruit pittoresque / Cadres musicaux' in *Le Son du Théâtre*, edited by J. M. Larrue and M. M. Mervant-Roux (Paris: CNRS Éditions, 2016: 135–62). Parts of Chapter 9 have been reworked from my chapter 'Fix your eyes on the horizon and swing your ears about: Corwin's Theatre of Sound' in *Anatomy of Sound: Norman Corwin and Media Authorship*, edited by Jacob Smith and Neil Verma (Oakland: University of California Press, 2016: 171–94). Parts of Chapter 4 build on my paper 'Theatron Immersed', presented at the International Federation of Theatre Research, 14 June 2016, Stockholm. Thanks to Mark Dudgeon and Lara Bateman at Methuen Drama and my colleagues at the Royal Central School of Speech and Drama who supported me in the writing of this book, especially Maria Delgado, Catherine McNamara, Joshua Abrams, John Sibley, Debbie Scully and Heather Akif. Thanks also to Karin Bijsterveld for recommending me to Neil Verma, who introduced me to the genius of Norman Corwin, and to Jonathan Sterne who cooked me pizza in Montreal and encouraged me to carry on writing and not be subsumed by my administrative role as Dean. Thanks to Mike Roberts, John Harman and Matthew Diamond for useful conversations about art, pop and novelty records, to Lynne Kendrick for reading drafts, Deirdre McLaughlin for reading and proofing, and Farokh Soltani, whose PhD research into radio dramaturgy gave me ideas. Special thanks to Simon Shepherd for all his past encouragement and mentorship, to Anthony Dean for the vision to introduce theatre sound design as a degree subject at Central in 1993 and for employing me to teach it, and lastly and always, to Kate Atkins and Eliza Brown.

Space is the extent of things.
ELSIE FOGERTY, *Rhythm*, 1936: 32

Now hear this
(A preface)

Theatre sounds but first it must hear. The ancient theatron was an instrument for seeing and theorizing, but theatre begins with people entering an aural apparatus – then, a giant marble ear on a hillside turned up to a cosmos whose inaudible music accounted for all; now, an auditorium, an instrument for hearing, turned inwards on the people, their auditory culture and sounds.

This is a book about drama, entertainment, modernity and the theatre of their audibility. It addresses the cultural frames of resonance that supply coordinates to our understanding of SOUND as the rubric of, and a figure in, the world we inhabit through our ears. It addresses how mythologies, pop culture, art and commerce have shaped hearing as a sense of theatre. Garrick, De Loutherbourg, Brecht, Dracula, Jekyll, Hyde, Spike Milligan, John Lennon, James Bond, Scooby-Doo and Edison will make cameo appearances as a history of modern hearing is woven together with an argument that sound is a story, audibility has a dramaturgy, hearing is scenographic, and the auditoria of drama (in theatres, cinemas, homes and headphone spaces) provide a definitive frame of reference for the aurality of life.

In this book, theatre is approached as the convening of a hearing, or audience. Audience, in turn, is described as a dialectic between first-person singular and plural; between I and we; between the personal intimacy of the intracranial, auratic space that surrounds the voice at the epicentre of our sense of self, and the socially produced space of the *audimus*, a collective conversance in the memes, tropes and clichés of the sonically theatrical or picturesque.

Locating the subject: academic and cultural contexts

I approach this history from a British perspective and a disciplinary context with which I declare a personal involvement. I began working with theatre music and sound as a recent art school graduate around 1985, moving quickly from the Fringe and small-scale tours to large and international work. This progress was rapid because of a fashionable demand for a more filmic use of sound in stage drama, but also because of the burgeoning of the 'theatre of states and of scenically dynamic formations' that Hans-Thies Lehmann subsequently identified as postdramatic (2006: 68). The work that was needed involved technical engineering and content creation or composition, but more importantly, a participation in, and contribution to, the collaborative process of creating theatre in rehearsals. This process constituted a new kind of dramaturgy, which attended to the workings of the production's aesthetics rather than the textual mechanics of the written play. Sound was central to this, but at the time there was no training for it. We were making it up as we went along.

Between 1994 and 2002, I became the first academic in theatre sound design in the UK, developing the first degree programmes in the subject. Still making it up as I went along, I established a training methodology and put together a historical and conceptual framework within which the practice of Theatre Sound could be discussed as a scenographic discipline (the basis of my first book, *Sound*, 2009). Meanwhile, sound design (as a billing, a job, a budget line and an agenda item in design and planning meetings) continued to find its footing within the professional theatre industry. This period has subsequently been considered a sonic turn in theatre practice, but it was also a theatrical turn, the senses of theatre and sound being closely linked.

The theatrical turn

There were technology and labour-related reasons for sound design appearing, in the 1980s, as a regular specialist seat at theatre's creative top table, and these are described in *Sound* (2009: 9–46). However, the demand for more sound also accompanied a renewed public and academic interest in theatre and theatricality. This was at a time of cultural and aesthetic eclecticism characterized variously as postpunk or 'designer', and a *Zeitgeist* encapsulated by MTV and the hyping of the music video as the artform of the times. A new spirit of romanticism spread across the arts. This extended beyond the flamboyant celebrations of gender fluidity usually associated with the term 'New Romantic', to a wide range of culturally knowing picturesques, from Goth culture to, for example, the neo-noir of David Lynch's films or Tom Waits' trilogy of albums, *Swordfishtrombones*

(1983), *Rain Dogs* (1985) and *Franks Wild Years* (1987), the latter subtitled 'Un Operachi Romantico'. Painterliness, expressionism and figuration returned to the fine arts. In theatre, international touring productions, from Lev Dodin's Maly Theatre of St Petersburg to Japan's Yukio Ninagawa, brought a less literary-based *regie* or director-led theatre to world stages, while musicals like *Les Misérables* (1985) and *Miss Saigon* (1985) turned to an operatic, romantic, European tradition, and away from American musical comedy.

Meanwhile, new opera and experimental music theatre began to use audio technologies and radio mics not for vocal reinforcement, but for aesthetic reasons (e.g., Robert Wilson and Hans Peter Kuhn; Peter Sellars). In the UK, new Fringe companies like Théâtre de Complicité, DV8, Red Shift, The Shadow Syndicate, and others in the Arts Council's small-scale touring funding bracket, along with more progressive regional repertory theatres, began to integrate a combination of domestic and professional audio and video technologies in hybrid forms of drama, dance, music and mime. Besides the political drama the 1980s is remembered for, in the latter part of the decade there was a fashion for slick, expressionistic theatre that carried some of the do-it-yourself ethos of punk and new-wave music, whose exponents often cited New York's Wooster Group as an influence.

This period constituted a waning of the mid-twentieth-century hegemony of literary theatre. In production terms, the process of transferring artistically unimpeachable plays from the page to the stage in a rehearsal room closed to all but the director, actor and deputy stage manager, while the design was worked out separately in scale models and schematic drawings, only to be introduced to the performance in the technical rehearsal, now seemed at odds with the new *Zeitgeist*. A more holistically scenographic process began to take shape, in which the theatre, rather than the play, became the thing.

As the digital revolution happened and the media network wrapped itself ever more densely around each waking moment from the ringing to the setting of the digital radio alarm clock, theatre became perhaps uniquely placed to explore the materiality, rather than the mystique, of *presence* and the constitution of *liveness*. Counterintuitively perhaps, amid all the hype for personal computing, videoconferencing, mobile telephony, multichannel cable TV and personal audio, theatre began to seem more modern and relevant, where only a dozen or so years earlier it had seemed the opposite. From the living room, to the nightclub, the high street and the City of London after the financial Big Bang of 1986, signals and sign-systems proliferated to the point where they seemed to become an immersive environment of audiovisual noise. An aural rather than a visual logic seemed to be required to make sense of it all, and aural logic (or analogic) has a theatrical, scenographic character, as I shall describe in Chapter 2. Terms like 'resonance' and 'noise' began to become tropes across the social sciences, while within the academic discourses of drama and performance, theatre and theatricality became words uttered again without equivocation, proviso or apology.

The noise of the dense media sign-forest was not merely a metaphor. Many of these new sign systems had sonified user interfaces. The world bleeped, blooped, buzzed and glitched with all manner of new sound effects, from ATMs to electronic car keys. Of all the time-based arts, theatre offered a plastic space to explore the audibility of contemporary life and its scenes – an audibility now conditioned by the ubiquity of audio in the acoustic world – whether attended to or overheard. The structures of audibility became destabilized. The hearing of sounds (words, actions, music, events) now seemed predicated on ever-changing binaries of engagement and distraction, figure and ground, signal and noise. In each of these pairs, the latter was as likely to consist of a babble of audio reproductions or synthetic sounds where once it might have been limited to the urban permadrone of combustion engines or the weather. Across the time-based arts, in theatre rehearsal rooms and auditoria, recording studios or film-editing suites, sound design acquired a meta-purpose of negotiating, configuring, and literally making sense of, this jumbled field of acoustic data. It was in the context of all this that theatre sound staff became busy again.

It should be remembered that during the mid-twentieth century, what one might still think of as the 'legitimate' theatre of spoken plays had become unusually quiet and reserved. The process of producing drama had become an exercise in minimalism, whose objective was to 'eliminate background noise (set, and lighting design, the actor's charisma, and indeed [. . .] directorial decisions) to let the play speak for itself' (Rebellato, 1999: 88). Music had been all but excluded from the drama auditorium in a way that David Mayer describes as a brief 'aberration' of theatre history (1976: 122). It is perhaps unsurprising that there was no extant framework in the early 1990s for discussing theatre's aurality, because it was during this anomalously noiseless period of literary minimalism that the dedicated university study of Drama had emerged from English Literature departments (Shepherd and Wallis, 2004: 7–14). Thus, at the moment drama was instituted as a university subject, sound effects, perhaps more than anything else, epitomized the noisy theatricality that literary modernism had sought to eradicate from its production processes. Such theatricality tended either to be equated with the crassness of melodrama or the sensory excesses of spectacular (as twentieth-century modernism characterized them, not kindly). Otherwise, it was dealt with in relation to Brechtian or Artaudian principles, whereby it was something to be 'excised' from dramatic representation in the pursuit of an unmitigated present-ness (ibid.: 229), and served-up separately, in order dialectically to estrange the audience from the insidious, empathetic effect of mimetic drama. Repertory theatres in the UK, in the early 1980s, had tape recorders and some still played sound effects from records on panatropes, but they were rarely used aside from the Christmas panto. The common experience of working with sound at that time was that it usually got cut, because it just didn't 'work' (which meant that it didn't feel right).

Perfunctory references to thundersheets, rumble-carts and technical processes aside, the history of theatre's sonic practices and the auditory materiality of drama were hardly considered at all in the twentieth-century drama curriculum. The idea that one might discuss theatre's sound without reference to sound effects technologies seemed not to have occurred. Where theatre's phenomenal materiality was discussed, it tended to be equated with visibility, and theorized in a way that imparted on Theatre Studies much of the ocularcentric bias of the modern philosophical tradition (Levin, 1993; Jay, 1994). Such was this bias that theatre's primordial, ontological concern with sound, resonance and aural affect had been completely obscured from theatre history. The 'discoveries' that sound had a theatrical materiality and theatre had a sonic materiality were associated with the twentieth-century modernist avant-garde (e.g., Kahn, 1999; Curtin, 2014), while the realization that sound might be 'an actor in the drama of things' would be attributed to 'postdramatic' theatre (Ovadija, 2013: 9). I shall be arguing against both of these assumptions in this book.

In the UK, the university study of drama changed when, in 1992, the Higher Education Act brought an influx of former art colleges and conservatories into the higher education sector. Subjects such as stage design, acting and other theatre crafts became degree subjects and demanded more accommodation within the academic discourses of drama and performance. One conservatoire, the Central School of Speech and Drama (Central), took advantage of the opportunity for additional funded student numbers in 1993 by launching a practical Theatre Studies degree where students could specialize in, among other things, Sound Design (which is where I came in). A decade later, when an intercollegiate London Theatre Seminar was formed and its early meetings set about taking stock of the changes I describe above, I was invited to present the second of the series. I called it *Theatre Noise* (13 October 2003).

The sonic turn

Beyond the arts and humanities, aurality, sound and noise had also started to become metaphors for ordering, structuring and criticizing the complexity of intermedial subjectivity, across the social sciences. The arrival of the interdisciplinary discourse of sound studies (see Sterne, 2012) also seemed to be connected with the jumbled, hypertextual, non-linearly structured aurality of the new millennium, and the dialectics of subjectivity within the multimedia matrix, between liveness and life, narrative and truth, realistic and the real, and so on. Where films such as *The Matrix* (1999) addressed these as pop ontology, sound studies became an intersectional space between disciplines that considered them in terms of auditory modalities and acoustic models of spatial data interface.

Slowly, the emerging discourse of theatre sound found a place in this intersectional discourse. The *Theatre Noise* seminar became the first of a number of provocations to the subject areas of Drama, Performance and Theatre Studies, to think of theatre sound in a broader frame than that of 'technical theatre', and indeed, of theatre *per se*. Still the only full-time academic in the field in the UK, I spoke at the inaugural conference of the Theatre and Performance Research Association (Manchester, 2004) and wrote an article called 'The Theatre Soundscape and the End of Noise' in *Performance Research: On Technē* (2005). Chapters on staged sound in edited volumes on scenography, bodies, performance and mediatized cultural heritage followed, as well as the book *Sound* (2009), structured around ways in which theatre's sound has historically been organized in relation to the dramaturgy and space of its physical and conceptual resonance. A Theatre Sound Colloquium convened at the National Theatre in 2002 (and again in 2016), and the OISTAT Sound Design Working Group that formed at the first of these drew together practitioners and academics from around the globe, most of whom, like me, were lone voices on the subject in their home countries.

By the mid-2000s, this had changed. I was no longer the only UK teacher-researcher specializing on sound within Theatre Studies. A major international conference, also called *Theatre Noise*, was held at Central in April 2009, comprising performances, installations, residencies, round-table discussions, presentations and workshops from around the world, with keynotes from the Wooster Group/ERS's John Collins and the music theatre-maker Heiner Goebbels. The American Shakespearian scholar Bruce R. Smith, whose book *The Acoustic World of Early Modern England* (1999) made seminal connections between theatre and sound studies, joined me as co-respondent in leading the plenaries. The third keynote was from the legendary Royal Shakespeare Company voice teacher Cicely Berry (who sadly passed away while I was writing this book). Cicely provided a living link to Central's founder, Elsie Fogerty, who trained her, and who will make several cameo appearances in this book as one of the many unsung historical figures who changed the audibility of theatre.

Through that conference, the discourse of theatre sound came into conversation with the international sound studies community. The networks formed there are still driving the conversation forward. The academy can no longer be accused of being deaf to theatre's principal phenomenal encounter (which precedes the opening of its curtain and its eyes). The seminal edited volume *Theatre Noise* derived from that conference (Kendrick and Roesner, 2011), and recent books such as Bennett's *Sound* (2019), Kendrick's *Theatre Aurality* (2017), Roesner's *Sound Design* (2017) and Home-Cook's *Theatre and Aural Attention* (2015) – as well as many journal articles and PhD theses – continue to broaden and diversify the discourse that began in those twin theatrical and sonic turns.

Terminology

In this book, *auditory* and *audibility* differ from *aural* and *aurality* in that the former pair relate to processes of hearing, whereas the latter relate to the subjectivities of the acoustic world. Thus, a person has an aurality that is an auditory subjectivity, but an object or stage prop has an aurality that is a sonic subjectivity – a relationship to its sonic environment (the definition of *sound* is to be discussed at greater length).

Diegetic means pertaining to a pictorially framed, cellular narrative structure of scenes, typically using theatrical devices as well as words to tell a story. Diegetic forms, like epic theatre, present or tell a story, whereas *mimetic* forms pretend *to be* in order to show something about human being.

In auditory terms, *disposition* relates to a detached (*dis*), yet placed or configured (*position*-ed), way of hearing. It thus describes an attitudinal relationship between hearer and sounds, but it can also mean a detached attitudinal relationship between sounds. This is different from *composition* because it describes a unity of parts that are related yet remain separate like an encircled set of objects. In this, it is like the architectural term 'disposition', which is a collection of separate schematic aspects. I argue that the aesthetic unity of a soundscape or sound design is dispositional rather than compositional.

I use *dispositive* after Baudry's 'cinema *dispositif*' and Schultze's 'auditory dispositive' (in Bijsterveld, 2014) to mean an apparatus for social hearing comprising the dramaturgy, design concepts, architectures, institutional structures and terminologies, politics, discourses, conventions and publicity materials that structure theatre as a material space and cultural activity.

Dramaturgy means the rules, index and criteria according to which a drama, scenographic arrangement or diegetically framed everyday situation is made to work, or be effective.

Noise tends to mean the acoustic background, whose audibility is not identified by the dramaturgical processes of hearing (which I will explain) as sounds, music, voices, words or, indeed, particular noises, which in scenographic terms might constitute significant auditory figures.

Ontology is used after Peter Sellars' use of the term (in Kaye and LeBrecht, 1992: vii), when discussing tropes or aurality or aesthetic uses of sound that address (or seem to address) the metaphysics of being. In a not unconnected way, an *ontology* can also mean a relational framework that defines a closed system of truth or knowing, such as Feld's *acoustemology* (see below), or the relational programming logic that constitutes 'the world' of a computer game or children's make-believe play.

Throughout the book, I suggest that the ways in which drama in the theatre and the media hears, sounds, distributes, and then re-hears and redistributes its hearing, constitute a *way of knowing*. By *way of knowing*, I refer to Feld's anthropological concept of *acoustemology* (*passim*, but summarized concisely by Feld in Novack and Sakakeeny, 2015: 12–14), within which the audibility of environmental acoustic phenomena, the social production and reproduction of sounds, and cultural or art products, performances and ritual practices, are all ecologically and reiteratively related.

The book uses the word *we* deliberately in its title and as a pronoun and is never intended to co-opt the reader into the author's way of thinking. I shall put it in italics where I want to flag that in using the word, the identity of *we* is being addressed.

I also have used my first-person voice and experience in this book deliberately, for reasons that I hope will become clear. I am conscious of the social privilege involved in some of the personal history I use, and that the history in this book centres on London, which also contributes a psycho-geography to the acoustemological way of knowing described. I am also conscious that this is only one history, and a predominantly white, northern hemispheric one, whose global hegemony has probably silenced other ways of knowing. The word *we* therefore opens an uncomfortable space that *I* have decided not to avoid in the traditional academic way with passive phrasing and third-person pronouns. During the course of the book, I point to examples of how theatre's *we* structures an aurality of inclusion and exclusion – for example, in the characterization of certain approximately heard or wilfully misheard 'foreign' sounds as 'exotic', and in the way the marketing of certain audiophile products has targeted men in an overtly sexist way, characterizing women as noisy audiophilistines. Stoever (2016) has published work on the cultural politics of audibility, and Tan (2012) on cultural appropriation within the intercultural utopianism of sound in performance, but there is much more to be done about the structures of exclusion in the dramaturgy of sound. These histories of privilege and exclusion run through the scripts, tropes and dramaturgy of the colonized canon, and the aesthetics of theatre production, and continue to condition audible space and auditory knowing.

Associated with this problematized *we* is one of this book's new terms: the *audimus*, which takes the first-person plural of *audire*, to hear, to describe the collective auditory habitus (set of learned auditory techniques, dispositions and habits) of the *we* which theatre convenes.

Structure

Part One is theoretical and introduces the terms *audio meme* and *audimus*. I use Sterne, Serres, Lefebvre and others to argue that the audimus produces (rather than occupies) audible spaces. I suggest that the term 'sound' in its singular form is both a theatrical figure and space; an auditory disposition, and a sonic disposition. The theatrical meaning of sound, I propose, now lies principally in a relationship between sound effects, which constitutes an aesthetic, and not in the semantic link between effect and cause. Drawing on Rancière, I describe this dispositional meaningfulness as a fictional ontology.

Part Two begins with a consideration of diegetic space, the head(-phone) auditorium and Complicite's 2016 production *The Encounter*, but is then largely historical, moving from Edison back in time to the modern foundations of the audimus in the relationship between the reconfiguration of the legitimate English playhouse and of the sensible everyday environment as the 'scenery' of Romantic subjectivity.

Part Three looks at another reconfiguration of the sensible, by electroacoustic sound or audio. It examines some pioneering work in radio and film audio, and is about audio space, microphonics, amplification, psychology, symbolism and psychedelia. It concludes with an essay, 'Audimus: the Theatre We Hear', that draws together the threads of the book and recapitulates its original propositions.

Style

Aside from a few exceptions, I have not geared this book around case studies of theatre productions that the reader might not have the opportunity to see. Instead, I occasionally describe imaginary or hypothetical scenarios or subjective listening experiences. These are distinguishable from the surrounding narrative by the use of italics, and by the conceit, suggested with the symbols ⏪ ⏩ ⏸ ⏹▶ • ⏭ ⏮, that the book is cutting between a narrative timeline and a set of recordings. Much of this book was drafted on an audio recorder while walking my dog in Beulah Spa and Crystal Palace park (which are near my house and feature in Part Two), and it seemed apt, given that the book concerns aural dispositions and scenic structures, to retain traces of this method.

Since another of the book's recurrent themes concerns how the scenographic use of sound in theatre since the eighteenth century reflects an aesthetic and diegetic departure from the mimetically representative regime of classical drama and acoustemology, I also use the rhetorical device 'now hear this'. This is a naval command, prefacing tannoy announcements, but I have taken it from Christopher

Logue, who uses it to begin his contemporary telling of Homer's *Iliad*, *War Music* (2001). It characterizes the theatrical rhetoric that sound often performs to convene an audience (or hearing) and condition an auditorium.

The sound effect: an extent of things

Overall, the book is a deconstruction of the term *sound effect*. The book takes Fogerty's definition of space as 'the extent of things' as its epigraph because, while the aesthetics and conceptual meaning of sound tend characteristically to suggest totalized unities, such unities are always narrativized extrapolations of the sounds of things happening. The word 'sound' itself theoretically extends the audible effects of acoustic events into an aesthetic aggregate and metaphysical frame (I will be arguing that sound does not exist, as a phenomenon). Individual effects are all we hear. It is the process of connecting them up, within conceptual or dramatic narratives (operative in human auditory perception as well as cultural discourse and processes like theatre; in the *me* as well as the *us*) that produces an effect that there is such a thing as sound or sonic space.

It was a feature of the early institution of theatre sound, in the 1980s and 1990s, as it fought for recognition as a creative art rather than a technical service, to cringe at the old-fashionedness of sound effects – to distance itself from the idea of them, as isolated, local, anecdotal objects. This was because the orthodoxy of stage design was that a 'good' design bound the disparate elements of theatre together in an aesthetic or conceptual unity. This book counters the supposition that we are beyond some old-fashioned era of obviously artificial sound effects with the argument that in an era when obviously artificial sound effects constitute reality, and when isolation and anecdote are important subjects to address, sound effects have become the topoi between which the modern state of aural being has to be mapped.

Sounds are real, sound is a fiction, whatever those words mean; but as a fiction, it is a cracking yarn, so let us begin. As Norman Corwin, one of the sound pioneers who features later in this story, said, in the midst of an earlier sonic turn, when radio promised to bring nations together and defeat tyrants through the power of its audio network:

> We have a platform regarding sound. Let it, like music, captivate the sense by metaphoric utterance; by moodstuff and far-ranging concepts. Let it say things in terms of other things, dissolve and modulate and set up new vibrations in the deepest chambers of imagination.
>
> Observe now, here is a sound effect of a crowd.
>
> From *The Anatomy of Sound*, 1941

PART ONE

Theatrical hearing

1

It's obviously an effect
(An introduction)

Splat

Now hear this. The crowd settles down as the lights dim. There is a beat of silence, and then. . .

A hazy childhood memory from the late 1960s, England. Maybe John Noakes – one of the hosts of the long-running BBC children's TV magazine programme *Blue Peter*. It is vague. It may have been another programme and another presenter, but for the sake of argument, it was Noakes. He is presenting an item on the secrets of sound effects. He is showing how to make the sounds of people being punched, by hitting a cabbage with a rolling pin. At the end of the demonstration, a watermelon is dropped for a really juicy, head-splitting splat.

These were very familiar sounds – not the sounds of cabbages and watermelons, but representations of punching. The aurality of screen violence was more known to children than those fruit and veg. Baby-boomer children heard a lot of cartoon violence in the 1960s. They mainly heard it on TV but more viscerally at 'Saturday Morning Pictures' – the variety bill of children's drama serials, cartoons and advertisements, screened weekly at the local cinema. In such auditoriums, many impressionable ears first encountered the theatrics of sound – their effect and ontology; their artifice and rhetorics. The rhetoric of commencement, for example, which has the extraordinary power to silence a crowd of excited children with the dimming of the houselights and the opening of a curtain. This is what overture means – the opening not only of a visible space, but of a hearing space beyond the here and now; beyond the ordinary. It is a rhetorical flourish that begins things. Now see this. Now hear this.

In the cinema, the curtains slowly parted to reveal the screen in the most exquisite, anticipatory silence. Soon, all the watching children knew, would come a piece of music called *Asteroid*, which began with an orchestral POW! followed by conga roll and tremolo woodwind that sucked in the silent anticipation from the auditorium, transformed it, held it for a while, built it to a crescendo, and then released it into the signature music of the cinema advertising company, Pearl and Dean (even children's theatres gather under the rubrics of commerce). Layers of framing followed. The hissing of a cartoon snake warned *us* that thieves might steal bags from under our feet. Advertisements for sugary fruit drinks and peanuts with cartoon jungle imagery and sounds, and local Indian restaurants with sitar music, clumsily edited together so as to cause loud pops from the narrow soundtrack of the worn 35mm film. A *we* formed, and felt present in a theatre, even as these frames drew us into the space beyond the curtain.

Then the programme began: heroes and villains pretending to punch each other to the sound of what those of us in the know knew were probably cabbages or watermelons. But if punches were cabbages, then what else lay behind the splats, plops, boings, thumps, bangs and crashes that accompanied the exploding bombs, ricocheting bullets and dropped anvils? What common or garden objects lay behind the haunted houses, the African jungles, and the rattlesnakes, coyotes and stampeding cattle of Wyoming or Texas? While pondering this, we were also shown the technicolour modernity of Gotham City, where big-band orchestral stabs and pop-art cartoon captions, not vegetables, stood in for punches and kicks; shown too, the black-and-white modernity of Laurel and Hardy, whose automobile sounds and police sirens we accepted as an alternative to those we heard in our streets. Silent shorts inducted us into the musical orchestration of their old-fashioned modernity: percussion and siren or swanee whistles (slapstick), woodwind and horns (sirens and the city) and strings (romance). Also on the bill were badly overdubbed melodramatic serials from abroad – *Robinson Crusoe*, *White Horses* or *Belle and Sebastien* – where the spoken voices did not match the moving faces or the acoustic of the scenic sound effects, and whose disposition of sonic oddness and melancholic music made us feel strange. Then there were the cartoons, where sound effects and musical instruments vied with one another in a harum-scarum chase, and we learned precisely what a falling anvil sounded like. It was onomatopoeic and phonically alliterative; and it had a reality of which the obvious fakeness of it all was a part.

Away from the cinema, other theatres configured a *me* rather than a *we*: listening disobediently to Pirate pop radio under the bedsheets; Ed Stewart's Junior Choice, with its swinging, sound-effect-rich novelty records. Then there were theatres of childhood *ennui* – where clocks ticked ever louder and slower as the sound of the school bell or longed-for doorbell never came. It was within the rhythms of these scenes and a framework of cabbages, swanee whistles, anvils, Stan Freberg's 'Banana Boat Song (Day O)' (1957), and the silent longueurs of anticipation, that children of this late baby-boomer generation learned to hear. It was also where *we* learned to sound. When *we* play-fought, some would mimic punching sound effects and gunfire, and others would mimic dialogue or sing theme music while they enacted domestic or romantic scenes with dolls and toys. Some put on voices or made sounds with their bodies that made others laugh; others learned to clap, sing, skip and dance in formation. This was how *we*, who were not yet sure how much we had in common, tested and agreed our aural knowing and established who *we* were.

There is nothing special about that late baby-boomer generation. Each generation learns to hear according to its own cultural circumstances. The expressive sounds and noises members of that generation then grow up to make later in life, reiterate, adapt and develop that seminal way of hearing. Its soundings reaffirm its *we* and its noise-making jams the 'unequivocal' soundings of outsiders (Lingis, 1994: 104). This becomes the way of hearing the next generation learns from, and so the audibility of the world resonates, iteratively forwards, through history, mutating slowly like an auditory genome. Children now inhabit a world of TV, films, computer games and downloadable audio products made by grown-up baby-boomers, or their grown-up Generation X offspring, and so it will go on. Do children still hear a world divided into similar scenes? The longueurs of waiting as the ticking of the clock slows down? The domestic *ennui* of windscreen wipers, boiling kettles, pinging microwaves and baby siblings crying? The solitude of lying awake at night to the creaking of the house, insulated from the weather outside within their own breathing, swallowing, sniffing bodies; sometimes scared of sounds they might have imagined? Is this kind of scenic partitioning of auditory experience innate or learned and historical?

Audio memes

The auditory genome is disseminated by performance. It is rehearsed in the playground and other theatres. It is part of an audimus, a *we hear* that treats sound effects from popular culture as repositories of aural knowledge. An example of this is the way in which, for successive generations, not only thunder, but other moments of dramatic realization, have been audible in terms of the 'Castle Thunder' effect of *Frankenstein* (1931). By the 1960s, this had become *the* definitive stock library effect by which subsequent popular TV and film quickly referenced the gothic and the index of delight, thrill and empowerment that recognition of a gothic effect instantly provides (which shall be discussed later). If you have not seen James Whale's 1931

Frankenstein, one of the earliest, genre-defining horror talkies, then you will have heard the DeLorean, or the Clock Tower, being struck by lightning in the *Back to the Future* trilogy, or the lightning and thunder in *Bambi*, or *Citizen Kane*. All three are the same recording: the Castle Thunder. If not these, then *Ghostbusters*, *Mary Poppins*, *The Sound of Music*, *The Land Before Time*, *Airplane!*, *The Jungle Book*, *The Muppet Movie*, and *Young Frankenstein* all use the same 1931 *Frankenstein* thunder clip. If you have seen none of these, and there are many others I could list, you will surely have seen episodes of *Scooby Doo* or other Hanna-Barbera cartoons. If you are a millennial, you may know it from *Spongebob Squarepants* or the *Powerpuff Girls*; from computer games such as *Oregon Trail II* and *Star Wars: Rogue Squadron*; or *The Haunted Mansion* attraction in Disney theme parks. It forms part of the sound collage in the raid of the Death Star in *Star Wars IV, A New Hope* (1977), one of the aurally defining films of Generation X. If you still cannot recall it, search online for a movie clip or gif of the Castle Thunder Sound Effect. If you grew up within the range of this kind of pop culture, you will know it.

Castle Thunder has become what I term an *audio meme*, a meme being a 'cultural element whose transmission and consequent persistence in a population, although occurring by non-genetic means (especially imitation), is considered as analogous to the inheritance of a gene' (Oxford English Dictionary, 2017). It provides an instant index of genre-based theatricality. It is a way of knowing thunder drawn not from direct sensory experience, or even from indirect representation, but from what we might term a memic index of reference sounds, whose original conditions and context might be long forgotten and are in any case irrelevant. They 'work' as alert tones on phones, apps, games and toys precisely because of this irrelevance. One can set a crash of thunder to sound when a message arrives, or a dog bark as a timer alert without confusing anyone who might overhear it. The seeming randomness acts as a kind of shibboleth or tribal password. It sends a meta-notification: I am from this play-space; I am part of that 'we' who met in one of those auditoriums and bonded through our consequent play-life. In the chapter on 'Game Audio: Virtual Reality Fundamentals' in his book *Designing Sound*, Andy Farnell writes that 'because games are written within an object framework, it is fair to say that everything in a game is an object' (2010: 316). Perhaps in life and theatre too – me, us and our aural subjectivity included.

Why do sound effects and music sound good together?

Almost from birth, children learn to hear within the artificial object framework of the sound effects repository, or memic index. Parents have probably always sung to their babies and made animal noises to teach them what animals are.

The musical box is not new, nor are sound effects devices that moo or bah or make other sounds to induct children into the epistemology of sound. In the last few decades, there have been interactive talking books or sound effect button boards that present taxonomies of common animals or machines using sampling technology. There are play phones or video game controllers with buttons built in that make sound effects. Such learning aids help children to learn language, but the play also develops an aesthetic, a sense of what they like to hear, and of the fun of making sound effects.

A point is reached when the sound effect of a cow no longer instructs the hearer in the linguistic concept of a cow but is available for scenographic functions – to suggest to the child that cows are the vicinity of the story, that the moo moo here and the moo moo there places it in a space of cows. This diegetically instructive principle becomes more complex as time progresses. The aesthetic disposition toward the sound effect perhaps does not. Children graduate to real video games and phones, and different kinds of musical box. Everyone reading this book has grown up in the audio age, wherein their relationship to music and sound effects matured in front of a loudspeaker of one kind or another (in radios, TVs, laptops or on shelves, floors or in headphones).

Let us consider music, and how it fits into the developing world of sound from a child's perspective. It begins with nursery rhymes, but as they become more aurally aware, children's understanding that music is of a different order to cows and the object framework of sounds that constitutes their everyday reality will be learned principally through these loudspeakers – the radio, if their parents have one on in the house or car, or from the soundtracks or theme tunes of TV shows or video games. Audio is not only the medium of music in these examples. It also *places* music, this different order of sounds, within the audio domain, and thus in the audio object framework, which provides coordinates to a play-space reality. It also introduces to the aural aesthetics of sound, a dispositional relationship between music and other audio objects. An aesthetic is established *between* music and sounds or audio effects. If music is the principal programme (on a record or download, for example), qualitative audio effects frame and narrate a relationship to the music. Such audio effects might be associated with formats, or terms such as high-fidelity; stereo or immersive; analogue or digital. This, in the long history of music, is a diegetic sensibility particular to the audio age, which began in earnest in the 1920s. There are now not only moo moos here and there, but commodified audio qualities or ways of sounding good.

Another memory. A phonogenic voice and a photogenic man (his picture is on the record sleeve, which is also emblazoned with the legend 'phase 4 stereo spectacular') is introducing the sections of the orchestra in Benjamin Britten's

Young Person's Guide to the Orchestra *(1966: Decca, PFS 4104). The voice is James Bond – the actor Sean Connery. He is teaching me to hear music from some unseen position, which I imagine (I must have seen football commentators in such places on TV) to be a gantry above the orchestra. The voice is startlingly clear. It has the impressive additional authority a high-quality microphone imparts, and, which, we are being invited to consider, that Phase 4 Stereo enhances. It introduces each instrument or section of the woodwind, strings and brass with Bond's stern determination. Each section obediently plays a variation of the rondeau from Purcell's incidental music to Aphra Behn's play* Abdelazer: The Moor's Revenge *(1676). Generation Xers might also know the tune as the theme from Mattel's 8-bit Intellivision console game,* Thunder Castle. *I will always think of it as music that frames James Bond's hi-fi voice. There were also popular recordings narrated by Boris Karloff and Peter Ustinov, so I suppose others will place it there. Each section of the orchestra is like a miniature scene or vignette; heard within the compass of a phonogenic celebrity. Then we arrive at the finale:*

> You have heard the whole orchestra in sections. Now for a fugue. The instruments come in one after another, in the same order you have heard beginning with the piccolo. In an exciting finale, the brass will play Purcell's fine melody, while the others play Britten's fugue.

Now hear this, James Bond says, and I do. Of course it is exciting.

Sound can be framed as music and music can be framed as sound, but it is one of the defining anthropological tenets of civilization that music and other kinds of sound are essentially different. It is also one of the founding tenets of auditory dramaturgy. Throughout human history, it has been an implicit liturgical message of the organization of theatrical events as ritual performance that the difference between music and sounds speaks to the structuring and ordering of life's materiality and spirituality – to theology or ontology. Music and sounds – even musical sounds, of somebody singing nearby or practising violin, for example – are differently audible, and this difference is what is important about music as a venerated construct (which can, indeed, exist silently on the page as notation, whereas a sound, as we shall discuss soon, is definitively audible).

For many, this fundamental difference and dramaturgical tenet is principally learned and understood in front of screens and loudspeakers (or between headphones). In such contexts, it is a difference that presents itself with a spatial architecture (implicit within the audio signal, rather than the product of stereo or surround sound). Watching dramas on TV, children learn that music comes from outside the picture: from the sky or from the sides. Listening to music on radios or records, on the other hand, the music is pictorially framed by audio – by sonic qualities and often by sound effects. But of equal importance to the architecture is the aesthetic excitement and pleasure of performed and framed dispositions of sound and music associated with the playful heuristics of audible space. A special edition of an academic journal recently posed the great question 'what sounds good?' (Curtin and Roesner, 2016). What has sounded good to me since my childhood is hearing sound effects and music collaged together, in juxtaposition to one another. The way these collages are configured is key to my understanding, as a learner-hearer of my time, of what sound is and what my relationship is to it as an actor-spectator in the contemporary theatre I hear around me. This pleasure principle – that music and sound effects sound good in each other's company – incentivizes me to attend to their interrelationship and was key to my becoming a composer and sound designer for theatre. It feels like personal taste, but there is much commercial evidence to suggest that it is, in fact, a widely shared taste.

Sound effects and pop

Pop music, I suggest, has exercised considerable agency in theatricalizing the world around us by pulling sound effects into its musically programmatic audio form and redistributing a way of hearing predicated on the aesthetics of sonic and musical juxtaposition, and on a complex ambiguity of which is framed and which is framing. The genre that has dominated the pop market for longer than any other (from the early 1990s until the present day) is hip-hop, which, formally, is based in such aurally architectural interplay. In its original form, hip-hop created an audio stage space with frameworks of audio and music effects, within which the song or rap takes place. One might say that the beat and the rap or sung voice are the content of its musical programme, and everything else is simply an expanded audio picture-frame. Music is overheard from outside the frame, sampled and pulled into a sonic tableau. The playfulness of this, the phonogenic qualities of the music's technologies (decks, records, drum-machines, synths) and the wit and the skill of the DJ or producer, all supply coordinates to the aesthetic space of the song. So do sound effects. Street noises and enacted mini-dramas (for example, between the tracks of Ice Cube's *Amerikkka's Most Wanted*, 1990, or the TV-influenced skits between tracks of De La Soul's *3 Feet High and Rising*, 1989) characterized the album form of the genre from early on. They might be intended to place the music in an imaginary soundtrack, or simply be a TV on in the room, so to speak (the sound effect of a TV on in the audio space of the song). Formally, this conceit of ambiguously placing the song in sound/sound in the song has continued to evolve. Records such Kendrick Lamar's *To Pimp a Butterfly* (2015) or Solange's *A Seat at the Table* (2016), which use counterpoints of home- and studio-recorded spoken prose and vox-pop style testimony as audio frames and cut-up-and-collaged narrative between tracks, are bound together as audio programmes. The 'concept album' has now become the default, and the eponymous concept, as it is in a theatre sound design, is expressed as an aural architecture.

In one strand of its genealogy, hip-hop can be traced to Jamaican Dance Hall culture, which has within its genealogy an African theatrical tradition of ritually performative sonic space creation. But there is also something about its space that relates specifically to the acoustemology of the audio age – a way of knowing according to records, deejays, radios or boom-boxes, answer machines, Dictaphones, voice notes, cassette mixtapes, and so on. Hip-hop represents this way of knowing-through-sampling as largely an aesthetic one that works against the beat and in counterpoint to the allusions and virtuosity of the rap. Its collaged format, however, also 'sounds good' in a tradition of progressive, studio-constructed popular music as audio theatre. The standard narrative is that this began with The Beatles' *Sgt Pepper's Lonely Hearts Club Band* (1967) or the Beach Boys' *Pet Sounds* (1966), although there are other debatable contenders earlier than that, particularly within 'easy-listening' genres that played to a marketable taste for the movie soundtrack, which we shall come to. None, though, sold as many copies and were as culturally all-pervasive as *Pepper*, nor as influential. After *Pepper*, dozens of albums were released that set their songs in sonic ambience, spot sound effects, media clips, spoken voice and vox-pop collages. From Pink Floyd's *Meddle* (1971) – built around three situationally suggestive sound effects (a theatrical wind machine, a recording of a football crowd, and a dog howling) – to Marvin Gaye's *What's Going On* (1970), which sets the music in an identifiably African-American social setting) to four 1973 albums: Stevie Wonder's *Innervisions* (sounds of street drama), Lou Reed's *Berlin* (harrowing sounds of an addict's personal and domestic crisis), The Who's *Quadrophenia* (a Mod's sonic journey from London to a confrontation with his inner nemesis against the sounds of the sea in Brighton) and Pink Floyd's *Dark Side of the Moon* (heartbeats, money, inner voices): the default album form of progressive popular music became one that played with the morphology (formal mechanics) of the soundtrack. But was the music part of a hypothetical film, or were the sound effects part of the music?

However, while characteristic of the concept album, this disposition of music and sound 'sounds good' in the still longer tradition of recorded popular music. The format of such records is influenced by radio and film, as well as by *musique concrète* and other twentieth-century forms of avant-garde sonic art. Within the discourses of progressive pop music, I suggest the latter tends to be overstated by comparison to the former, and I would suggest that much of the evident aesthetic appeal of counterposing music and sound effects derives from a popular comedy tradition. Comedy routines, 'business' or shtick around the interplay between music and sound effects is the stock-in-trade of musical hall or vaudeville. The term *slapstick* itself refers to a sound effect device. Percussion, the lewd or cheeky rasping of brass instruments, and many kinds of whistle have been part of the physical choreography of comedy for centuries, and so have vocal imitations of sounds in songs. By calling his series of animated shorts *Silly Symphonies*, Disney was referencing the musical basis of physical comedy and was copied by Warner Brothers' *Looney Tunes* (punning on the abbreviation of car-*toons*). The music, however, is intricately arranged around exquisitely funny and aesthetically satisfying sound effects, tightly synchronized to the animated picture.

Even without the picture, this slapstick-based morphology sounded good, and was replicated in radio formats, whose audio-only medium extended the possibilities for auditory punning, double-entendre (double-hearing) and irony, as I shall discuss in Part Three. From radio, it moved into pop via records that capitalized on radio's popularity. By way of example, in America in 1938, a skit of vocal imitations of the sound effects of Chicago gangster movies, *Calling All Cars*, was a hit *soundie* (a kind of early music video: a short 16mm film of a live stage act that could be viewed in penny arcades or were as a supporting feature in movie theatres) for a novelty barbershop quartet act called Four Aces. In 1940, Decca released a 78rpm record called *I'm the Sound Effects Man* by Rufe Davis, an actor known for his sound impersonations, fully illustrated with sound effects. It is a relatively genteel affair. More irreverent and frenzied in their celebration of sound effects were radio spin-off movie cameos and the soundies of Spike Jones and his City Slickers.

A pit percussionist by background, Jones made his name with a virtuosic big-band act that played at furious pace and used detuned percussion and practical sound effects as the basis of comedically rearranged orchestral classics which mimicked the sound of the *Looney Tunes* cartoons, only without the visuals. Jones had wartime hits with 'Der Fuehrer's Face' (1942) and 'Cocktails for Two' (1944), but one of the mainstays of the City Slickers' live act was the song 'The Sound Effects Man'. The shtick was of the hapless onstage sound effects man, contorting himself to play an array of elaborate contraptions, furiously chasing the lyrics with his sonic illustrations. As the references in the lyrics to Jack Benny's beloved comedy car Maxwell (which, of course, did not exist other than as a collection of sound effects) and the popular quiz Kal Kyser's *Kollege of Musical Knowledge* suggest, such records seized on the perennial fascination with the secret trickery of radio effects laid bare:

What would we do without the sound effects man that radio racketeer?
Tune your dial and wait a while and this is what you'll hear.
There's a knock upon the door (that's the sound effects man).
There's a kiss and maybe more (that's the sound effects man).
If you'd like a ring, he'll give you a ding ding ding,
And even in the early morn you'll hear him blowin' his horn
Cowboys ridin' fit to bust (that's the sound effects man).
Three more redskins bite the dust (that's the sound effects man).
He has such a very lot to do, and yet he very seldom misses a cue
He's a three-alarm fire and the fire chief too, there goes the sound effects man!
When the wind is howling
Hear the thunder growling
When the battle is raging he's right in the middle of the fray
When he blows his whistle, crime doesn't pay
Benny's old Maxwell[1] chugging right along (that's the sound effects man).
When Kay Kyser gets the answer all wrong [shout:] 'STUDENT!' (that's the sound effects man)
[. . .and so on]

> Author's transcription from a 1942 live recording on *Spike Jones, King of Corn*, Cornographic Records, C.S.J. 1001, 1975; music and lyrics uncredited

This is all harmless, mainstream, and fairly anodyne fun. But in an improbable turn after the war, particularly in Britain, the nonsense, comedic sound effect was to become the unlikely rallying point for the rebellion of a new youth subculture.

Shibboleths of sound

Ying tong . . .
[whine of bomb dropping, explosion; then as if tape played at double speed but same tempo:]
Ying tong ying tong
Ying tong ying tong
Ying tong iddle I po
Ying tong ying tong

---

[1] The comedian Jack Benny's car.

> Ying tong iddle I po
> Iddle I po.
>
> MILLIGAN / The Goons, 'Ying Tong Song', 1957, Decca

Sound effects sounded good, and after the war anything that dissented from austere establishment conventions and ethical codes tended to achieve cult-like status. In Britain, the hugely influential radio comedy series *The Goon Show* (1951–60) inflected the music hall comedic tradition of sonic comedy with a Dada surrealism and turned sonic silliness into an anti-establishment attitude. Impersonating the sonic nonsense of the Goons became a kind of rebellious shibboleth for British post-war teenagers – appropriating the old-fashionedness of sound effects of their parents' and grandparents' generations, and making it sound absurdly *ours*. Goon-like sonic silliness entered into emergent popular forms like skiffle, as an idiosyncratically British marriage of music hall shtick and American folk, blues and jazz. 'Before pop musicians discovered drugs, they made do with Spike Milligan', wrote Paul du Noyer in his obituary to the Goon Show writer (2002), a point the Beatles, who began as a skiffle group, made several times. 'We were the sons of *The Goon Show*. We were of an age. We were the extension of that rebellion in a way', said John Lennon, who, when he first met the future Beatles producer George Martin, had been particularly impressed that he had previously worked with the Goons (Stark, 2006: 108).

In fact, before the Beatles, Martin had made many other silly records, having made a success of Parlophone, the lowbrow, cut-price subsidiary label of EMI, through producing comedy and novelty singles. Where in America there was Stan Freberg, Shelly Berman, Tom Lehrer, Alan Sherman and Spike Jones, in the UK there were Martin-produced Parlophone novelty 45s by Charlie Drake, Peter Sellers, Bernard Cribbins, Flanders and Swann, and Terry Scott. All these records were loaded with sound effects reminiscent of radio comedy, and appealed to sons and daughters of the Goon Show, like Lennon, while often being consigned by baffled radio executives to BBC children's programming. Here, they infused impressionable young baby-boomer ears with an emergent, proto-psychedelic way of auditory knowing. Andy Partridge, born in 1953 and the main songwriter and leader of the neo-psychedelic, new-wave British band XTC, was one of those children, and remarked in an interview that:

> Novelty records were just psychedelia in square clothing. They use exactly the same techniques – sped-up bits, slowed-down bits, too much echo, too much reverb, that bit goes backwards. When the generation that grew up on kids' novelty records began making records for themselves, it came out as psychedelia. That genre is just grown-up novelty songs! [. . .] There was no transition to be made. You go from things like 'Flying Purple People Eater' to 'I Am the Walrus'. They go hand-in-hand. There was no rock 'n' roll

radio in England when I was a kid. It just didn't exist. And I don't think I would have liked it, because I was too young. I did like the Chipmunks records, or comedy records like those Charlie Drake singles.

PARTRIDGE and BERNHARDT, 2016: loc. 8485–97

George Martin (1926–2016) was of the ironically named 'Silent Generation'. He had grown up amid the expanding cultural horizons of inter-war radio modernity, and the new social mobility that wartime had enabled. He took elocution lessons and learned piano, but although he came across – certainly to the Beatles – as an establishment type, it is clear listening to his early Parlophone productions that this was an effect – as Partridge might say, he was a beatnik in square clothing; his novelty pop experiments might otherwise have been conducted in more avant-garde art contexts. His first 78rpm release, 'Mock Mozart'/'Phoney Folk Lore' (1952), subtitled 'The Voices and Noises of Peter Ustinov', is a surreal vocal abstraction (introduced by an auditorium murmur effect that places the music within a deliberate theatrical frame, much as it does on *Sgt Pepper*).

It is not so different from the kind of performative sonic experiments that Stockhausen, Ligeti, Cage, Kagel and Berio were undertaking in the early 1950s. Martin's production of Spike Milligan's single 'I'm Walking Out with a Mountain' (1961) is extremely surreal, with spliced-together sound effects that are as aggressive and abrupt as any Situationist piece of *musique concrète*. That same year, Martin collaborated with Maddalena Fagandini of the BBC Radiophonic Workshop to rework a piece of Latin-esque electronic Exotica (a strange subgenre of easy listening that had emerged in America in the 1950s, in part to sell hi-fi systems, which I shall return to) that she had first made as BBC TV interval music. 'Time Beat' backed by the equally space-age 'Waltz in Orbit', was released, under Martin's pseudonym Ray Cathode.

I suggested that children learn to hear in front of TV loudspeakers, so 'interval music' on television is a concept that is worth glossing. British television, until the 1970s, did not broadcast content between schools' programmes in the mid-morning, the lunchtime news and Children's Hour, and tea-time children's programmes. Instead, visual 'test-cards' were broadcast, for engineers to calibrate TV settings, or strange, hypnotic films were shown that were something like screen-savers (for example, of a clay pot being spun). These were accompanied by specially commissioned 'network opening', 'closing' and 'interval music'. Children waiting for *Watch with Mother*, or sitting in school halls, crossed-legged, watching a clock on a big cathode-ray TV mounted on a tall trolley slowly counting down to the start of a school's programme, thus found themselves in the space of some strange experimental music, often provided by the Radiophonic Workshop. The passage of time, we learned, could sound like a ticking clock, or it could transport us into an abstract and profoundly odd aural state. That strange passage-of-time music became a stock-in-trade of theatre sound design as it took shape at the hands of baby-boomers in the 1980s and 1990s may or may not be a coincidence.

By design

While there had been notable pioneering work in theatre during the early audio age, such as that of Harold Burris-Meyer in the late 1930s in America (more on him later) or David Collison in the UK in the 1950s and 1960s, theatre sound design as it is understood today – not as a process of engineering, but of scenography – really took shape during the twin theatrical and sonic turns I described in the Preface. 'Sonic turn' was retrospective nomenclature which Adrian Curtin dates to between 2006 and 2011 (2014: loc. 188–455) but whose start date I set earlier, in the 1980s. It is, however, true that most of the sonically experimental scenography of the early part of this turn was transacted as *music*. It was a little later, in the 1990s, that people began to refer to this under the rubric of sound. (My first billing as sound designer was in 1991, although the process was essentially the same as that which I had been undertaking as a composer since the mid-1980s.) For reasons that should by now be apparent, neither the term 'sound' nor 'music' is really satisfactory for a process that is in essence one of constructing attitudinal dispositions of spectators towards the audible stage, and architectural dispositions of music and sound. Usefully, then, the disciplinary rubric sound has been joined in recent years by another: aurality, which as Kendrick defines it, 'relates to many states of hearing and listening, resounding and voicing, sonance and resonance, moving and feeling [in a way that does not] necessarily preclude the other senses' (Kendrick, 2017: 1).

'The aural world of the show'

Theatre's aural reawakening was part of a *Zeitgeist*. The 1990s also saw a burst of histories, theories and exhibitions of sonic arts. Publications included *The Wireless Imagination* (Kahn and Whitehead, 1992), *Noise Water Meat* (Kahn, 1999), and reprints of seminal works such as *Silence* (Cage, 1978) and *The Soundscape* (Murray Schafer, 1994). This flurry of interest marked the beginning of sound studies – an 'interdisciplinary ferment in the human sciences that takes sound as its analytical point of departure or arrival' (Sterne, 2012: 2). Aurality, however, was not a word often used: even when I was writing *Sound* between 2007 and 2009 and defining it in relation to its ancient etymology, the search for a definition was still almost a 'googlewhack', returning only one scholarly article on Marshal McLuhan and Walter Ong, and another about jurisprudence in America. As I glossed earlier, aurality relates to the auditory subjectivity of people and the sonic subjectivity of things, but my etymological definition also related it to the atmospheric sense of place created by auras – zephyrs of scented air or gaseous emanations from Greek mountainsides (*au-* like the *atmo*, indicating air; see Brown, 2009: 214–15, 143–5).

At the time of writing, aurality is still not in the Oxford English Dictionary, but the term is in common use in the study and professional practice of theatre sound. The British Association of Sound Designers (ASD) describe the remit of the sound designer as 'the aural world of the show'. The word *aural* here might be taken simply as a synonym for auditory, but to my mind, the choice to use 'aural' instead makes another suggestion: that there is a separate world that radiates, auratically, from the show, like a halo of sound, which situates all of the scene – even its silent visible objects – within the show's matrix of audibility. This aural world, the ASD goes on, may consist in 'sound effects, atmospheres, sonic textures and filmic ambiences that will create naturalistic and abstract worlds for the show's story, as well as aid the audience's emotional and dramatic connection with the performance' (ASD, 2018). They suggest that this might involve the use of onstage or offstage props or effects, the editing or remixing of music, collaboration with a composer to make original music, or with live musicians in the theatre. They also say that sound designers may 'advise on how to best hear the performers, which may involve acoustic adjustments to the theatre and set, or the addition and configuration of radio and/or float mics for the performers'. Throughout this description, there is still a very deliberate caution about the limits to which the sound designer transgresses into the territory of music, and it is only at the end of all this that the ASD mentions the aspect of the role that many would have assumed to be its main focus, which is to 'design a sound system, bespoke to the specific production and auditorium, that will give the audience the best experience of the show' (ibid.). By putting this last, they make a rhetorical point: we are no longer the engineers, we are the architects of aurality.

Beyond the era of effects

If the distinction between music and sound was contentious within the early discourse of sound design, so was the term *sound effect*. This was nothing to do with union demarcation, and more to do with establishing a progressive identity for a new theatre art. Sound effects had become a trope for old-fashioned theatricality in the 1970s and early 1980s, and something of a laughing stock. I recall an episode of Bruce Forsyth's *The Generation Game* (season 1, episode 4, 23 October 1971), the BBC's Saturday prime-time gameshow, in which contestants had to manically keep up with the accompaniment of a melodramatic scene with practical sound effects, in the comedic fashion of Spike Jones' *Sound Effects Man*. One also thinks of the running coconut shell joke in *Monty Python and the Holy Grail* (1975) and the parallel drawn between noises-off and anachronistic theatrical bluster in the film of Ronald Harwood's *The Dresser* (1983).

As the idea of an aesthetically coherent sound design began to form, its proponents wanted to be clear that theatre's sonic turn was a new and modern way of engaging with contemporary aurality, rather than the regressive 'return' of those kinds of sound effects. Theatre sound design is now established as a very slick and modern theatre art, and while I now have no reservations about describing it as the art of sound effects, at the time many, myself included, would have flinched at this terminology.

In an important introduction to a textbook catering to the new college sound design market, the director Peter Sellars is at pains to promote sound design as a new departure and a move that would take theatre 'beyond the era of sound effects':

> Sound is no longer an effect, an extra, a garni supplied from time to time to mask a scene change or ease a transition. We are beyond the era of door buzzers and thunderclaps. Or rather, door buzzers and thunderclaps are no longer isolated effects, but part of a total program of sound that speaks to theatre as ontology. Sound is the holistic process and program that binds our multifarious experience of the world.
>
> KAYE and LEBRECHT, 1992: vii

Sellars' phrase 'total program of sound' related the subject of theatre sound design to the soundtrack, and suggested the stage be set within a continuous rather than occasional audio frame. Within this soundtrack-like continuity, music, audio effects and sounds coexisted with the spoken voice (Sellars advocated the use of microphones like Greek masks or personas, in order to separate the voice from the actor, and posit it within the mediatized, audio domain). But the phrase 'total program' also brought to the production of sound effects a modernist principle of design unity based on a musical metaphor of totality, to be discussed in Chapter 2. The realignment of sound effects like door-buzzers and thunderclaps away from isolated, semiotic functionality within the scene and towards a designed 'total program of sound', realigned its principle semantic function to that of the overarching design aesthetic. The question of what a sound meant related now firstly to its aesthetic contribution to the design concept, while its obvious, literal identity with local object or stage action became coincidental, and perhaps beside the point.

In this, Sellars is proposing that sound design becomes part of a process of aesthetic *dissensus*, or the breaking apart of the consensus of sensible phenomena and represented meaning. Instead, a detached aesthetic programme is formed that runs in parallel to the drama, which consists of the collateral realignment of effect with effect. Effects resonate with other effects, rather than their causal event-objects. Jacques Rancière has described this kind of dissensus as paradigmatic of an aesthetic regime of art that became more culturally dominant than the mimetic regime of classical representation, during and after the reconfiguring sensibility of Romanticism.

An aesthetic programme

Rancière holds that art – in a broad sense as a process of labour and participation as well as the cultural products of that labour – models and disseminates sensibility (literally, the ability to sense things). Art is responsible in a quasi-legislative way, for modelling (in its labour and products) 'the system of self-evident facts of sense perception that simultaneously discloses the existence of something in common and the delimitations that define the respective parts and positions within it' (Rancière, 2004: 7). He calls this system 'the distribution of the sensible'. Art does not merely affect, it *effects* or *produces* the common audibility and visibility of things according to several distinct regimes. It also effects a 'sensible mode of being' that structures 'an organization of "bodies"', which he calls a police (as in *polis*: a living community and its forms of exclusion, ibid.: 18, 93). Of all the arts, theatre has a special function in modernity (since Romanticism) serving, Rancière suggests, as the 'aesthetic' or 'sensible constitution' of the living community (2009: 6).

In *The Emancipated Spectator*, Rancière describes the *dissensual operation* of modern, aesthetic art using the example of the late nineteenth-century scenography of Adolphe Appia to illustrate how art broke from the *representative regime* of mimesis – the paradigm of classical drama, whose sensible mode of being is obedience to a predetermined scheme of truth (2009: 60). This scheme is represented or imitated by art (effects resonating original event-objects). The aesthetic regime breaks from a representative (or mimetic) regime in modelling a sensible mode of being where meaning (or a sense of one) can be gleaned from the collateral cohesion of artistic effects or appearances as an aesthetic, quite apart from the obvious scenario wherein they represent something else (the characteristic I ascribe to the 'total program of sound', above). In Rancière's example, he describes how the effects of Appia's lighting on performers' bodies in Wagnerian opera renders them as abstract statuesque forms. This appearance de-contextualizes them from the libretto and opens the scene to interpretations that need have nothing to do with the ostensible scenario. The stage effects gain a programmatic togetherness in their mutually apparent apartness from the specific setting referred to in the text. The result may or may not tell us something, obliquely, about Germanic mythology, but it does not show us anything that we are supposed to believe exists in that world. The stark chiaroscuro literally defaces its mimesis and casts its salient details into shadows. He terms the processing of stage figures in this way *dissensus* because it dissents from obedience to representative intent, and because it ruptures the presumption of a predetermined *consensus* between one kind of sense and the other – the sensing of phenomena, and the sense that is made of those phenomena. Effects are cut off from prescribed semantic schemes. Their meaning is laid open to the spectators, who, rather than taking instruction from the artist-sage, become auto-didacts, taking what lessons they choose from the aesthetics. They hear the pedagogic message of the art in its resonance with other art, books or discourses. Rancière refers to these as third things – resources belonging neither to the artist or the spectator – and I would add audio resources to this list (canonical audio recordings, memes, tropes and picturesques). The artist-teacher (whom he calls the 'ignorant schoolmaster') is oblivious to the meaning that is taken from the aesthetics of the intended lesson by these means. This creates a kind of open-source semiology, but also has implications for terms such as real and realistic. In a dissensual scenography, there is, as Rancière puts it, 'neither a reality concealed behind appearances nor a single regime of presentation and interpretation of the given imposing its obviousness on all' (ibid.: 49). What might be obvious about the effects, in their lateral, aesthetic cohesion with one another, becomes a matter for the audience to decide, which is the political function of dissensus in art (I have substituted *heard* for Rancière's *seen* in the following, but this does not alter the meaning):

> To reconfigure the landscape of what can be heard and what can be thought is to alter the field of the possible and the distribution of capacities and incapacities. Dissensus brings back into play both the obviousness of what can be perceived, thought and done, and the distribution of those who are capable of perceiving, thinking and altering the coordinates of the shared world.
>
> ibid.

Rancière associates the aesthetic regime with the revolution in sensory subjectivity of Romanticism, which I shall address in Part Two. Rancière's aesthetic regime breaks from *mimetic* representation, but the scenographic analogy he uses proposes theatre as a heuristic space framed by a rubrical, rehearsed and narrativized diegesis – a representation of a different kind. Let us consider what this means.

Aural representation

'Hearing is a model of understanding', says Serres, and theatre models hearing (1995: 7). This is what the auditorium is for; it should not be thought of simply as a room full of seats, but as an instrument of hearing built into the theatron's representational apparatus. Roland Barthes describes this theatre's representational apparatus in ocular terms, suggesting that the picture box auditorium/stage configuration developed by Diderot and Garrick (which models the boxed, cellular epistemology of the Enlightenment) stands as the 'Organon',[2] or model logic of non-mimetic representation in the modern era:

> Representation is not defined directly by imitation: even if one gets rid of notions of the 'real', of the 'vraisemblable', of the 'copy', there will still be representation for so long as a subject (author, reader, spectator or voyeur) casts his gaze towards a horizon on which he cuts out the base of a triangle, his eye (or his mind) forming the apex.
>
> BARTHES, 1977: 67

Representation is thus not imitation, but delimitation of the visibility of the world through a process of cutting out a part of it, and masking off the rest.

While it has a different geometry to the triangularity of cut- and masked-off sightlines that constitute the tableaux stage, the auditorium, in effect, delimits the audible world in a similar way. Where the mind is at the apex of a truncated triangle of visual representation in Barthes' ocular model, it sits at the centre-point of the spectator's sphere of auditory perception (which does not close in on the hearer, but emanates auratically outwards). The auditorium delimits this radiating auditory sphere in a number of ways: with physical architectures, but also with conventional regimes and dramaturgy that delimits that which is programmatic, or in scope, and that which is outside the theatre's interest in the scene. The delimiting geometries of theatre's Organon of auditory and

---

[2] The title given to Aristotle's collected works on logic.

visual representation seem to converge at the same spatial zero-point or singularity. If one continues the sightlines back into the intracranial space behind the eyes, they converge at the aural centre-point, which also happens to be the location of the internal monologue, the point where one can hear oneself think – or at least, when one thinks about it reflexively, one can almost hear thoughts forming themselves into language.

An auditorium is thus a delimitation of the auditory sphere that situates the spectator's point of view. It does not need to be a room. It can be any situation where audibility is delimited, by acoustic containment, speakers, or a pair of headphones (or combinations of these), or by a framing narrative or a declared set of ludic or dramaturgical rules that render things audible in certain terms and not in others. Whether aesthetic or representative, the creation of any drama involves the question: 'What is sound going to be here?' This is the question that every new piece of writing or devising asks. It is the meta-discourse behind every choice of word, voice, sound or music. Attending any piece of theatre involves learning to hear again, within the delimitations of the auditorium, at the behest of such questions.

Take Complicité's *The Encounter* (2016). The *jeu*, or play-objective, of that production was to superimpose a virtual audio reality on the visible space of the theatre. This was achieved using the conceit of lecture-demonstration of how an architectural disposition of binaural, mono and traditional stereo delivered through headphones mapped onto a stage set-up of microphones, sound-making props and speakers, and a set of precepts about the blurred line between stories and reality. The scenographic intent was to move the centre of the representational apparatus from the apex of the spectatorial triangle at the centre-point between the ears, to the stage itself, and thus to destabilize the separation of stage and auditorium. This destabilized separation was the space and the subject of the story. Helen Skiera, one of the sound team speaking at the ASD's 'Trade Secrets: A Backstage Tour of The Encounter' (The Barbican, 28 April 2016), referred to the self-imposed limitations of the show's apparatus – its stage set-up, its conceit of technical exposition and declared trickery – as its *ontology*. This suggests the representational space of the delimited auditorium as a heuristic game or set of rules. In Sellars' statement, 'a total program of sound that speaks to theatre as ontology', I take 'ontology' to relate to a Romantic notion of a unifying musical essence. I think Skiera's was a use of the word that related to the object-oriented environment used to programme the interactive first-person subjectivity of an avatar in a computer game (I shall return to each of these). In either case, ontology provides a space of working hypothesis. It is this that delimits the auditorium as a space of non-mimetic representation; this, and not necessarily a unity in 'design concept', that binds sound effects together as one aesthetic programme, with a collateral resonant integrity separate to whatever is shown on stage. We shall return to *The Encounter*.

From the examples I have considered in this chapter, we might conclude that the meaning of terms such as 'sound' or 'aurality' tends to consist in the spatial configuration of sonic or aural effects, within the delimiting compass of a narrative. When one talks of the sound of a city or scene, or indeed, of sound itself, one is talking of more than the simple collection of elements that the philosopher Liebnitz called an 'aggregate' (Serres, 1995: 2). One is talking of a diegetic, dramaturgical unity of disparates, which is what I call a *disposition*.

The next chapter considers some of the ways in which sonic and auditory dispositions have been narrativized, historically, to create the meta-sense of a singular, collective purpose or design to the audible multiplicity of the world. Now hear this.

2

Dispositions

The god sound

PLAY ▸

'What is sound?'

'The stuff we hear.'

'Be still for a moment. What do you hear?'

'Actors doing vocal warm-ups backstage. Birds. Traffic on the road outside. Drilling.'

'You have just singled out some sounds. What is sound?'

'I see. How about "an aliveness in one's ears"?'

'Arguably, but no. That describes an aural alertness in your body. The ears as an open channel; being aurally awake.'

'A sense of surrounding space when my eyes are shut.'

'Again, you describe your sensory disposition. But what do you hear? I'll tell you. Sounds: acoustic effects with specific locations: precisely here and here, or approximately over here or up there.'

'So sound is the collateral field of coincidence or correspondence between sounds?'

'You might theorize such a field, but is it sensible?'

'Sensible?'

'Can you sense it?'

'It is discernible as an arrangement of sounds like a soundscape or a sound design. Or as a continuity of sounds, like the sea, which as the seventeenth-century German thinker Leibnitz pointed out, is really an overlapping succession of individual wave sounds; a large concept made up of small sensations. It is a disposition towards sounds, and of sounds one to another, which assume an appearance of unity in the way they resonate together. This resonance might be in physical space-time, but it could be in a uniting idea (in this example, the sea). Michel Serres begins *Genesis*, his account of noise and logos, by observing that we are fascinated by unity, which "dazzles on at least two counts: by its sum and by its division". This fascination leads to a scorning of the senses "because their information reaches us in bursts". The impulse to conceptualize thus takes us away from the multiplicity of sensation, which Serres says seems only to tell half the story, or a story of "semi-being". What we want is a system and an integration, "a single God, and identifiable individuals". Reason, thus, "makes use of concepts, under whose unities are sheltered multiplicities" (Serres, 1995: 2–3). We do not necessarily think of music, or hear it, as an overlapping disposition of reeds, sticks, skins, tubes and strings, although that is what it is, and we can hear it that way if we are so minded. We would rather hear it as a composition.'

'Correct. These are propositions that invite us to think about the sounds we hear as a unity gathered around or under an idea of sound that serves as what Serres identifies as a "god" figure. This needn't be religious. The sounds of London are all around us, outside these windows. The sound of London is a way of composing or picturing them together according to a singular idea (swinging, Dickensian, contemporary urban, etc.). An organizing "god concept" in theatre terms might be knowing that there is a sound designer, or a "sound by" credit in a theatre programme, or seeing black loudspeakers in the auditorium. This might be all it takes for us to hear sound effects resonate in one another, and for us to hear this as a design rather than simply the sound of some things (the loudspeakers hardly need to be used for this to happen; the suggestive power of their simply being there can be enough). But whether these interrelationships might be classified as audible – as sound or a sound design – is less interesting than why we might want to obliviate the multiple, isolated thingness of sound by listening for a non-thingness. "We listen to things first", the twentieth-century America thinker Don Ihde said, but "without forgetting this first presence of the existentiality of the thing, the concern of phenomenology must be expanded beyond any exclusive concern with things alone" (2007: 73). In other words, phenomenology tries to structure the first-person experience of phenomena with a compositional intent. Like music – it remembers the reeds, strings and skins, but forgets their independence.'

[*There is a brief pause, while this is considered, during which we hear the room-tone, the tape-hiss and the sounds of actors warming up in the corridor.*]

'But that solution is like the one I suggested earlier, which you told me was conceptual and not sensible. Ihde talks of an *auditory field* – a field whose presence is "implicit" (ibid.), which he describes as seeming more or less "filled" with sound (76). Hearing, in other words, feels like a space that is filled with sound – so again, it comes back to hearing, the sensation in the ears, not the sensation of the environment. If we take this phenomenological approach, we must conclude that sound only exists in the body, and does not exist, out there, as an independent sensible thing. But then I am curious as to why Ihde says the auditory field is a sphere filled with sound, not sounds. When we just stood still to listen, a minute ago, all we were able to do was single out sounds.'

PAUSE II

*

Let us pause the fictional seminar there, because this is a good point. Ihde is clear that sound consists in things, and yet rather than talking about the auditory field being filled with sounds, he contrives a model of a sphere of hearing that fills up, unevenly, with clouds of sound – as though sound were a gas from which sounds crystallize. We do not hear a phenomenon called sound: Ihde is clear about that from the beginning, and the listening exercise confirmed that we hear things, not a thing. Large sonic concepts, like London, are a denial of sounds' independence from one another, so why invoke it in a phenomenological model of how the world makes itself available in the body? As I mentioned in the last chapter, Serres' suggestion is that *we* are fascinated by the unit, that only the unit feels rational to us. The *we* is crucial. Each of us experiences sound as a different multiplicity. To make sense of our sensing together, *we* need larger dispositions in common. Thus, where we encounter the world as a fragmented plurality unique to ourselves, we want to meet each other in one space – 'a multiple as such', as Serres puts it. We 'subsume multiplicity under unity; in a concept or a black box' (1995: 4–5). Concepts are large meeting spaces (London, England, the world, the universe). Black boxes are a trope Serres uses often to describe a component of any signal chain, or network of signal chains, whose inner workings are mysterious, but which transduces the *hard and there* world of things into the *soft and here* unity of consciousness (soft as in information, or software; Serres, 2016: 128). Thus, in Serres' trope, many processors, from body cells to the civic agora, are black boxes, but prominent among his examples is the theatre, which works like a resonator or an ear. 'Identifiable individuals', elements (or monads), resonate together as 'a singular God' (1995: 3). The output of our ears and of our theatres must be either 'total or null' (ibid.: 5).

Totality

Poetic tropes, mythological metaphors and analogies of unity such as Sellars and Appia use to describe the aesthetic unity of total theatre, invariably draw on an onto-theological conception of totality, wherein subjects and objects resonate together with the same life-force. Philosophizing 1960s rock stars with mystic gurus, or new-age theorists like Joachim-Ernst Berendt, have propounded this as a form of expanded consciousness to the point that ambient, 'Eastern' sounds have become memes through which popular culture can instantly index an ancient history of aural totality. The chanting of 'OM' produces an effect of resonance in the body that serves as a kind of aesthetic performance of divine totality, and auditoriums have often been delimited as spaces of aural representation through the deployment of this effect. Chanting or drumming in Neolithic burial chambers, or kivas, was designated ritually sacred because of the mutually affective impact of amplified consonance between disposed things and the bodies which the standing-wave resonance produced in such structures. This had the appearance of tuning. There is belief in these practices, but there is also a memic index.

In most creation mythologies, the conceptual totality of the universe is often imagined in terms of resonance: the primal, creative utterance of the Word, for example, in 'in the beginning was the Word' (John 1:1). As well as giving *logos* or reason to the world, the Word, as an auditory object, also assigns *logos* a medium and a physical sensation, which is what resonance is. Accordingly, tuned acoustics have been features of churches designed to work as resonators to create a physical effect, which builds on pagan tradition. Vitruvius speculated that the Ancient Greek theatron was tuned to the tetrachord by the placement of tuned *êcheia* vases around the amphitheatre, and these have also been found hidden in the walls of some medieval churches.

Analogies of acoustic resonance within the mind or neural system (rather than the masses and cavities of the body) are a common feature of Romantic literature. Coleridge, who was influenced by the philosopher David Hartley's theories of vibration and association, imagined a sympathetic resonance of a universal energy field that combined light and sound, in the medullary substance of the nervous system. Coleridge expressed this in his poem 'The Eolian Harp' (1795) as follows:

> O the one Life within us and abroad,
> Which meets all motion and becomes its soul
> A light in sound, a sound-like power in light.

COLERIDGE, 1997: 87

In churches and theatre to this day, there is often a correlation between sound and light. The primal 'Word' in Genesis 1.3 turns out to be a divine lighting cue: 'Let there be light!' In the Hindu *prana*, sound and light fade in together. In an oral creation analogy of the Navajo, the whole show begins with the mountains sighing a wind of coloured light (McNeley, 2003: 265–70). Do not imagine that this is outmoded superstition. The dominant secular creation myth of our scientifically enlightened times is a figure of primal sound and universal resonance, the Big Bang. That its resonance is in everything and all of *us* is not considered belief, but a scientific fact. So, at one point, were all such totalizing, unitary analogies.

Of the institution of music

The best-known figure of a 'god sound' is the Pythagorean idea of the harmony of the spheres, which regarded music as the organizing principle of the universe. This was passed on from earlier Eastern philosophy by Pythagoras, Plato, Aristotle and Priscian, and became one of the foundations of Western *epistēmē* through the Roman scholar Boethius' *De Institutione Musica*, written in the early sixth century, based on the earlier harmonic theories of Nicomachus and Ptolemy. *De Institutione Musica* became one of the first musical theories to be printed, in Venice in the late fifteenth century, and along with the architectural theories of Vitruvius, was seminal to organized theatre in the sixteenth century. For Boethius:

> Music, in the form of musica mundana, is an all-pervading force in the universe – determining the courses of the stars and planets, the seasons of the year and the combinations of the elements; and as musica humana it is the unifying principle for the human being – bringing the body and soul into harmony, and integrating the rational and irrational parts of the soul and the disparate members of the body into harmonious wholes. Music is also said to be found in instruments (musica instrumentalis).
>
> in BOWER, 2001

De Musica provides the meta-acoustic, conceptual space within which the standard template of classical dramaturgy operates, as the drama moves from tempestuous disruption of harmonic unity to the reuniting of separated families or of the tragic hero, through death, with the singular silence before creation. Boethius saw music as the connection between mathematics and ethics, in the social aurality of *we* (audimus) which is motivated by an aesthetic pleasure principle, of *sounding good*:

For nothing is more consistent with human nature than to be soothed by sweet modes and disturbed by their opposites. And this affective quality of music is not peculiar to certain professions or ages, but it is common to all professions; and infants, youths and old people as well are so naturally attuned to the musical modes by a certain spontaneous affection that there is no age at all that is not delighted by sweet song. Thus, we can begin to understand that apt doctrine of Plato which holds that the soul of the universe is united by a musical concord (Plato Timaeus 37 A). For when we compare that which is coherently and harmoniously joined together in sound – that is, that which gives us pleasure – so we come to recognize that we ourselves are united according to this same principle of similarity. For similarity is pleasing, whereas dissimilarity is unpleasant and contrary.

BOETHIUS, 1989: 31

Thus, are aesthetics and ontology epistemologically linked.

A Roman early Christian convert, Boethius turned the Pythagorean idea of singular *musica universalis* into a holy trinity – *musica mundana* (the cosmos up there), *musica humana* (the spiritual and physiological microcosm in here) and *musica instrumentalis* (the audible resonance of the music in things). It is this conception of music, which had only one of its three feet (*instrumentalis*) in the acoustic world, that structured the acoustemology of Renaissance Europe, helped configure the representational space of early modern drama, and provided the point of departure for the Romantic and Modernist reconfigurations of aesthetics and subjectivity that followed thereafter.

De Musica as acoustemology

I have briefly glossed acoustemology, but will now explain it in a little more detail. It is a relational ontology developed as an anthropological method in the study of rainforest habitation and culture by Stephen Feld. It 'takes sound and sounding as situational among related subjects, and explores the mutual and ecological space of sonic knowing as polyphonic, dialogical, and un-finalizable' (Feld, in Novack and Sakakeeny, 2015: 13–14). Its ontological method for closed systems of habitation also works, by extension, within the delimited system of the auditorium, for understanding 'worlds' of drama and their circularly related hearing and sounding subjects as representations of life (and, as I mentioned before, the notion of an aural world also imparts acoustemological situation and knowing on visible, silent things). Acoustemology looks at what is knowable, and how it becomes known, through sounding and listening. It connects phenomena (acoustic vibrations) to cultural understanding by asking how the dynamism and modulation of acoustic energy indexes its social immediacy (the circular connection that the re-iterative cycle of sounds, hearing and resounding establishes between people, which Bruce R. Smith (1999) has termed the 'O Factor'). It then 'joins acoustics to epistemology to investigate sounding and listening as a knowing-in-action: a knowing-with and knowing-through the audible' (Feld, in Novack and Sakakeeny, 2015: 12).

Feld observed that the forms of language, songs and rituals of the Kaluli people were directly attributable to the highly attuned aurality of rainforest life, and Smith has described how the theatre of Shakespeare can be understood in a comparable way, in relation to the highly codified acoustemology of early modern England. Smith considers this from two vantage points: internal and external. On the external front, there was a world unified by a first-person plural sense, or *our* language, with a clear sense of boundaries beyond which was a world that could only be understood as foreign-sounding – either in a desirably exotic way (e.g., the magical island), or as suspiciously so (the song of the Siren), or else simply as barbarous. On both the external and internal fronts, the Elizabethan acoustemological disposition was, according to Smith, 'defended by a formidable battery of philosophical ideas' such as *de Musica*, which 'served, quite literally, to harmonize body, society, psyche, and media as self-maintaining systems' (1999: 297). Thus, at the outset of the modern period, classical dramaturgy is littered with allusions to the harmony of the spheres and the harmony of people's souls.

Visually, dramas at Shakespeare's Globe were played out under 'the heavens', a canopy painted with stars, moons, planets and signs of the zodiac. Aurally, they were played out under the same idea and iconography. However, unlike Romantic analogies of totality, such as Pater's famous maxim that all art aspires to the condition of music, they were heard in a genuine, literal belief that all matter, people and human affairs were governed and constituted by an inaudible, metaphysical music. When Lorenzo says,

> There's not the smallest orb which though behold'st
> But in his motion like an angel sings,
> Still quiring to the young-ey'd cherubins;
> Such harmony is in immortal souls,
> But whilst this muddy vesture of decay
> Doth grossly close it in, we cannot hear it
>
> *Merchant of Venice*, 5.1.60–5

he is not necessarily offering an analogy. As the Shakespearian music scholar David Lindley points out, until the turn of the seventeenth century:

it is often impossible to be certain when Shakespeare or his fellow poets and dramatists are invoking musical analogy as decorative image, when they expect an audience to treat such references as myth, or when they are to be accepted as a statement of fact.

2006: 21

As the seventeenth century progressed, the music of the spheres ceased, generally, to be a credible science. Descartes and his followers thought that such ideas 'smacked of magic *tout court*', as Erlmann puts it, and 'of things like astral influx and the like' (2010: 13). However, while much is made of the ocularcentrism of the Age of Reason, the Boethian sense of *musica* persisted as a metaphor and continued to structure and supply coordinates to the Enlightenment's sensory mode of knowing, so deeply was it ingrained in the epistemological foundations of modern thought. The sensible distribution of *logos* was, after all, through the resonance of the voices that spoke it. Music, *per se*, still retains a reputation as a form of higher consciousness. The liberal arts' curricular hierarchy of disciplines, the basis of the medieval university, had established Boethius' conception of *musica* as one of four scientific ways of knowing the world, along with geometry, arithmetic and astronomy. This quadrivium of pure sciences sits over the trivium of the three applied liberal arts: rhetoric, grammar and logic. It is from the trivium that we get the word 'trivial'. European culture thus enshrines the idea that compared to music, logic is a trivial way of knowing things.

Music and drama

Whatever music's material effect and its influence on the body and humours, as dramaturgy, musical theory provided life and theatre with a metaphysics and totalizing, unifying metanarrative. As the modern era progressed, however, ecological balance in this metanarrative, between music and noise, became disrupted by a different disposition: an attitudinal relationship to audible or notated music, as *art*.

The sixteenth-century conception of music as art was unrecognizable from that of today. Practical music, or *cantus*, was an oral, poetic tradition. People sang and made music socially in a folk tradition. Where it had institutional status, it was ritualistic, associated with festivals, pageantry, folk theatre and the church. In such ritual practices, music, like tragedy, was in a stage of its cultural development Jacques Attali calls *sacrificing*. It was a formatting of noise. It organized noisy spaces and bodies with dance or emotional affect, and offered the organization up to chaotic nature as an ethic; a performative audimus; a *we hear music*. Boethius' *musica*, on the other hand, was a scholarly praxis. It critiqued the practical *cantus* that flowed instinctively from the soul through the craft of instrumentalists. It separated music from the folk practices of musicking. The true *musicus*, or musician, was one who understood what music was and how it worked, ethically and aesthetically, according to pure quadrivial science. The beginnings of what we might think of as art music lay in this separation of the artist-sage from the rest of *us*.

For its patrons and those whom they wanted to impress, art music provided an alternative space within the age of reason to rehearse a shared emotional intelligence, legitimized by the quadrivium, whose outputs could be notated and exchanged. The social status and the intellectually legitimate effect of 'serious' music imparted a market value on printed sheet music and the exclusivity of performances, during what Attali calls the era of *representation* (roughly 1500 to the arrival of sound reproduction, which he calls music's *repeating* stage). The *musicus* had been separated from the people by the quadrivium, but 'the artist was born, at the same time that his work went on sale' (Attali, 1985: 47). While drama written for public performance (in the wooden 'O's of London's Bankside, for example) continued to reference a sacrificial, folk institution of music in its dramaturgy and the correspondence between acted representations and musical or dance interludes in court recitals, and to an extent in court drama, music became something different: 'a monologue of specialists competing in front of consumers' (ibid.). Music has been called a dialectic between form and morphology – its technical arrangement or workings (Boulez, 1971: 22–3). Theatre might similarly be thought of as a dialectic between drama and dramaturgy, and as Mayer reminds us, all drama was musical (at least until the brief aberration of the twentieth century).

In the seventeenth century, a socially hierarchical division took place between popular musical drama, where musical interludes were subservient to the drama in a ritualistic sacrificial way, as part of a dramaturgy that was consonant with the acoustemology of common auditory experience, and new forms of more socially exclusive theatre where drama was subservient to art music. Both the music and the spectacle in this latter kind, the masque and the opera, are separated from the inclusive acoustemology represented within the circular delimitation of the wooden O. Where the in-the-round public theatre had once performed a unifying embodiment of the living community, in the separation of music and spectacle that characterized the reconfiguration of drama and theatre over the seventeenth and eighteenth centuries, it now began, performatively, to model a 'self-dispossession' and the separating out of set of dialectical equivalences – 'audience and community, gaze and passivity, exteriority and separation, mediation and simulacrum' (Rancière, 2009: 6–7). These pairings are characteristic of the age of art as capital and its witnessing as commodity.

The Romantic vision of truth in immersion, as expressed in Coleridge's trope of eolian resonance, the one life within us and abroad, and the idea of total theatre, might seem to mitigate against this separation and equivalence. However, Marxist theorists such as Debord thought that what Romantic music, opera and poetry really did was hold up an idea of immersivity as art, so that people could contemplate the oneness they had lost, 'their own essence become alien [and] turned against them' (ibid.: 7). The performances of unification in classical dramaturgy and Shakespearian theatre were part of an acoustemological process of relational ontology. They rehearsed and resonated the ancient mythological oneness instituted as epistemology by the quadrivium. Music was a theory that formed part of a praxis of personal and social unification. Romantic art did almost the opposite. It presented a theory of immersive oneness as art, which served to defamiliarize it, make it strange and other. Going to the opera or symphony might show a performance of a totalizing oneness, but, neither among those who go, nor among those who feel that opera and the symphony isn't for them, do these forms resonate and renew social cohesion (more the opposite). Rancière sees the theatre of Artaud and Brecht as critiquing this separation and trying to restore theatre as a unifying instrument, although I am going to argue that picturesque and gothic configurations of popular culture and aesthetics enabled dispossessed spectators to take back ownership of art as the scenery of their own designed or dramatized lives. This will be my task in Part Two. First, though, I will explain how beyond the classical allusions of Romantic tropes, and after the analogy of musical totality had been fractured by the economic partitioning of "serious" music as art, the popular unifying narrative of immersive totality changed into an implicitly colonial disposition towards exoticism, with an associated memic index, which invoked Western modernity's lost mythological past.

The Romantic idea of acoustic space

In 1960, McLuhan and Carpenter's seminal article 'Acoustic Space' proposed a thought-model for the complex space of global communications, which drew on the alien and exotic idea of immersive acoustic unity. It proposed that communications should not be thought of as happening across empty space, but as resonance within a universal plenum (or fullness) of acoustic vibration (1960: 65–6). However, rather than using either acoustic science or the classical acoustemology of music theory as its figurative frame, 'Acoustic Space' is inflected with a sense of exoticism characteristic of *new-age* utopianism. It is littered with references to mysticism, intuition, 'Eskimos' and their 'holy men', all presented as examples of how 'not all cultures think like us', which clearly asserts a colonial 'us'.

The intention is to set up an analogy of immersive, totalizing sound as an alternative to the 'eye thinking' of Cartesian reason, where seeing is believing and empirical proof must be made permanently visible through writing or diagrams. The idea that there is a separate logic, or analogic, of 'ear thinking' (Berendt, 1988) associated with aural subjectivity is still often mentioned when the definition and character of sound are discussed. The reductive nature of this characterization has been problematized. It has been pointed out that resonance did feature, albeit marginally, as a figure in Cartesian philosophy (Erlmann, 2010, 2011) and that the Enlightenment was also an 'Ensoniment', as Jonathan Sterne calls it, within which listening and auscultation had a degree of equivalence with looking and inspecting (Sterne, 2003; Picker, 2003).

The reductive, binarizing narrative that sound stands, piously, against the consciousness-constraining cultural hegemony of vision is now accepted as problematic in a way summarized by Sterne's now-canonical 'audio-visual litany' – a series of binary statements that characterize what the author calls the Ongian 'onto-theological' characterization of sound and aurality (referring to Walter Ong, a student of McLuhan's who developed the theistic suggestions of 'Acoustic Space'). Sterne's litany has become one of the standard reference points, and points of theoretical departure, in sound studies, but I cannot assume everyone knows it, so here it is again:

> Hearing is spherical, vision is directional;
> Hearing immerses its subject, vision offers a perspective;
> Sounds come to us, but vision travels to its object;
> Hearing is concerned with interiors, vision is concerned with surfaces;
> Hearing involves physical contact with the outside world, vision requires distance from it;
> Hearing places us inside an event, seeing gives us a perspective on the event;
> Hearing tends toward subjectivity, vision tends toward objectivity;
> Hearing brings us into the living world, sight moves us toward atrophy and death;
> Hearing is about affect, vision is about intellect;
> Hearing is a primarily temporal sense, vision is a primarily spatial sense;
> Hearing is a sense that immerses us in the world, vision is a sense that removes us from it.
>
> STERNE, 2003: 15

Each of these statements is a matter of predisposition; a willingness to be subsumed by the first-person plural 'us' Sterne employs, into a warm, safe, interior meta-space. If one thinks about them, one finds that while the statements are rhetorically persuasive, they might not necessarily tally with a more objective analysis of the experience of hearing. Hearing *does* have direction and perspective, it *can* be analytical and intellectual, we *do* listen out for things, hearing *does* travel to its objects (I shall explain) and so forth. We know these things, but perhaps find the alternatives more seductive as they situate us sensually and emotionally in the lost, mythological immersive universe, which is, as a metanarrative, being shown to us as a paradise that might be regained through subscription to a philosophical cult of aurality. Sterne's litany suggest a theory of aurality proffered to the self-dispossessed modern subject as a kind of self-help romanticism. Sound becomes the theatre of *me* and *my* expanded consciousness, extending auratically outwards like a halo or atmosphere. It was a solipsism that resonated with the post-war baby-boom 'me generation'. McLuhan and Ong became gurus within hippy culture, as well as academic communications theory. The unity narratives of auditory and sonic dispositions now drew on a Western romance with 'primitive' mysticism, couched in terms of pop anthropology.

Auditory space and its dramaturgy

The auditory scene

There is a different way of thinking about the universe in self-centred terms, as a scenographic process; a process of auto-*mise-en-scène*. Where it is difficult to reconcile the veracity of some of the tenets of aurality in the Ongian litany with auditory experience, the idea of sound as a *mise-en-scène* tallies with the psychoacoustic, or cognitive, processes of editing the noise plenum into the functionally diegetic unity of an auditory scene. To explain this, I am going to mobilize and build upon the principles of Albert Bregman's psychological hypothesis of *auditory scene analysis* (1999), and explain hearing as a process of cross-modal picturing, that uses a form of dramaturgy to build a working, cognitive map of the acoustic environment.

To grasp Bregman's theory, we must first understand that the ear does not sympathetically resonate a world of identifiably individual sounds and present them to the brain as a sonic scene. As an eighteenth-century aesthete who will turn up later in my story, Richard Payne Knight, put it: acoustic activity is admitted to the brain because 'the drum of the ear and the auditory nerves are formed by nature with a peculiar kind of irritability suited to vibrations' (1805: 43). This irritation, however, is not hearing. It is only the itch that starts the process. Stephen Connor, in discussing Serres' black box analogy, describes how hearing works 'by literally making sense of sound, a process that involves the filtering of sound through the complex labyrinthine space of the inner ear.

On one side of the eardrum, raw sound knocks for admittance. On the other side, the cochlea rebroadcasts the kinetic impulses as electrical signals to the brain' (2009). These electrical signals, though, are not yet intelligible as sounds. They are merely a filtered analogue of the plenum, the noise of everything. The irritable ear and its filters cannot recognize sounds and their causality in the world of things and actions. The ear knows nothing about the constitutions of noise, speech or music, or about anvils, cabbages or punches. It is just a transducer, converting the hard (kinetic phenomena) to soft (analogue information). It detects vibrations, delimits them to a frequency range where speech and significant sounds tend to occur, and then passes this on, as a data stream, to the brain. Hearing is then the process of figuring out what is going on within this data stream, and whereabouts in the world of hard phenomena it originated.

In the eponymous scenic metaphor of Bregman's theory, auditory situation is plotted dramaturgically from information within this neural analogue by the brain's cognitive circuitry. It does this by deductively piecing together a cognitive map, or mental scenography of sonic cause and effect. This is known as 'sound location', but it is really a process of sound production. Sounds simply do not exist as discrete objects, until they are produced as such by the process of auditory scene analysis. This is what human beings experience and think of as hearing. Sounds, as we perceive them, are conceived in the brain as discrete event-objects and placed back into the environment by a psychoacoustic process that is as speculative as it is observational, and contingent on a diegetic principle of narrativized situation.

The process begins physically, with binaural differentials. The acoustic shockwave from a kinetic event arrives at the two ears at slightly different times, and with tiny differences in amplitude, phase and tonal characteristic. These are the effects of obstructive and absorptive surfaces and objects that fragment, divert and muffle spherically expansive acoustic waves in the physical environment. Sound waves bounce off things, and things create shadows and eddies in the acoustic wave. Some of these result from the human head, which is a constant architecture whose effects the brain recognizes and can use. The information of acoustic waves in the wider vicinity is combined with the near-field variations caused by the acoustic shadows, obstructions, absorptions and reflections of the head's surfaces and protuberances. The hearer's head is thus an instrument for measuring and plotting the environment against its owner's sense of space, and for confirming its orientation, or perspective, on the action. When the head is turned, front, side and rear turns with it, and a new scenic relationship is configured (the Ongian binary of 'hearing immersing its subject, [while] vision offers a perspective', from Sterne's litany, is thus misleading). With this apparatus the brain is able, with relative stability, to identify sound wave arrivals that seem to have originated at the same time and from the same location, and to tell whether they are coming from front, back or sides, or, with slightly less certainty, from up or down. The brain maintains a cognitive map of what it believes to be going on from all the contextual information available to it, and this map shares a physical orientation with the head. If the psychoacoustic brain is unsure what it has heard, it will instruct its owner to turn their head towards the ambiguous sound, and place it centre-stage, in front of its eyes, where it also has the most binaural clarity.

After the waves have arrived, the process then becomes something like a jigsaw puzzle. The brain divides the continual plenum of acoustic noise present in the eardrums into chunks of acoustic effect that seem broadly the same. Then it groups together the ones whose differentials indicate that they probably shared a common cause. Working to the cognitive map – a rough, guiding picture, provided by the eyes and the other perceptual senses, combined with an intelligent sense of what might be going on in the scene – it then starts to fit them into the jigsaw, allocating them to likely causal events in the locale of their apparent origin. The sound of a car is thus located near a car, the ringtone near a phone, the voice of an actor near to her mouth, the door-buzzer on the door, and the offstage sound of the axe, out in the orchard.

Unhearing

Identifying an auditory object requires lightning-fast random access to an index of knowledge in order to place it, and to unhear everything else within the plenum of its momentary apparition. The *BBC Year Book* of 1931 identifies it as 'axiomatic' to the construction of an auditory scene on the radio, 'that every sound effect, to whatever category it belongs, must register in the listener's mind instantaneously' (197). This is true within the dramaturgy of constructing a psychoacoustic auditory scene, which is the basis of human hearing. Beyond the sympathetic physical resonance of vibration in the eardrum, a sound also requires a cognitive resonance – a recognition. To hear a car, one must know what a car is and be able to recognize its signature shape from a number of component and contextual acoustic wave arrivals – a horn, its engine changing gears, or its tyres on the wet road, amid the noise of everything else – and put them all together. There are, however, other factors that determine whether we hear the car. Perhaps there are many cars, or it is entirely normal and unsurprising for there to be cars, so even though there is information in the ear that there is a car nearby, there is nothing useful to be gained in hearing it, so the brain does not. Cars are not always audible, even when they are there and their engines are running. Sometimes we just blank them.

Thus, hearing is an editorial process, and the auditory scene an editorially subjective analysis of what is going on, not the complete picture. To provide a functional snapshot of the self *in situ*, not every part of the vibrating plenum needs to be located as sound. This aspect of editing applies a different aspect of dramaturgy to that of the index of recognition: the appraisal of significance and utility within the auditory diegesis. Hearing thus also involves far more unhearing than it does auditory object-production. *We* hear what we think is useful or significant in what is going on, and unhear everything else. In their taxonomy of *Sonic Experience*, Augoyard and Torgue refer to this reductive process not in Bregman's scenographic metaphor, but in terns associated with grammatical syntax. Selective unhearing, which they call *asyndeton*, is the 'deletion from the perception or memory of one or many sound elements in an audible whole' (2005: 26). The selective hearing of sounds, on the other hand, 'by the determination of a predominant functional criterion [which I am calling dramaturgical utility], or by adhesion to a cultural schema establishing a hierarchy [which I am calling significance]', they call *synecdoche* (123–4).

If the place where you are reading these words seems quiet, you might be surprised to hear what it 'really' sounds like. As part of the devising process for *The Encounter* (2016), Simon McBurney spent time in an anechoic chamber, and when he emerged, he was shocked by the roar of the all-encompassing, unstoppable acoustic plenum of traffic, voices, machinery and planes. After an hour in total darkness and anechoic silence, his auditory awareness had become disorientated and his ability to syntactically parse and filter out unwanted stimuli had become suspended. This is when he realized that 'normal' reality was a highly edited disposition on the world:

> As with our ears, so it is with all our senses. Our eyes, our sense of smell, every way in which we perceive the world creates a gap between what is actually happening and the story we make of it. We see only what we want to see . . .
>
> Complicité/McBURNEY, 2016: frontmatter

Noise and atmosphere

The acoustic effects of the continuing action, while filtered out, are not irretrievably lost to hearing. They remain in the ear and in the periphery of sonic consciousness, as background noise – a vague auditory presence beyond the perimeter of the scenography that has been produced. Sounds can be plucked from it and placed in the scene if circumstances change and they re-register as significant or useful. This is part of what is known in psychoacoustics as the 'cocktail party effect'. At a party, one can home-in on the person one is talking to, and not hear the background until a change or something new happens that demands conscious attention, or one overhears one's name being mentioned. We know this is a psychoacoustic process, because the microphone cannot do it, and even the most sophisticated digital algorithms cannot yet 'unhear' insignificant or dramaturgically useless noise with the same subjectivity as the human brain. Anyone who has tried to record a lecture will recognize the difference between human auditory reality and that of the microphone. In the recording, the reverberation and resonance of the room will seem more present than one remembers hearing. This is because when one is live, in the room, trying to hear the lecturer's words, the echoic room is unhelpful, so one unhears it. Were one listening to a string quartet in the same auditorium, however, that reverberation has an aesthetic value attached to it, and is therefore not unheard.

The sense of hearing is thus programmed by narrative (what is going on here), dramaturgy (what would be expedient or informative to hear here, in relation to what is going on) and aesthetics (what is predetermined, culturally, to sound good). The noise, however – the shadows of unheard sounds, the 'residue and cesspool', as Serres puts it, of the programme identified within the plenum (1995: 7) – lurks in the background. Its unheard presence remains available to the mind and performs another function as a feeling of scenic atmosphere or a scenic aura. Within the memory, these atmospheres or auras provide a sub-auditory register that contributes to the process of scenic recognition, as a contextual sense of place, but also index the emotional or aesthetic disposition associated with their unhearing. Together, the sense of place and the sense of mood constitute a genre-based register of scenic atmospheres, which are a resource to the sound designer in representing scenes. In my earlier analogy, the cars that do not need to be heard remain available to the aural subject, as a sense of, say, 'city', and whichever emotions – exhilarating or oppressing – seem diegetically apt.

The scenography of sound

I have described two different ways of thinking about the subjectivity of the acoustic world as theatre. In the first, sound is a pre-existing theatre that *we* hear according to a legitimizing acoustemology structured by stories and myths that formalize the human appetite for unity (*the god sound*). In the second, the only pre-existing theatre is noise, and sound is the production of the cognitive process of making diegetic sense of one's personal, subjective place in the world. In the latter, myths and preconceptions of significance and aesthetic intent might play a role, but as dramaturgy in a process of diegetic space production. In their broad character, the first kind of theatre is a distribution of the sensible one might associate with Rancière's mimetic regime of art. The second kind is more of a processual theatre, such as Rancière identifies in the methods of Brecht, Artaud and Appia, which use obviousness and knowing effect to reassert the spectators' ownership of their consciousness (2009: 5–8). I am not suggesting that these subjectivities are alternative ways of hearing, just of describing hearing. They are meta-discourses. The point to bear in mind is that following the shift Attali identifies from the institution of music as *sacrificing* to the commercial separations and dispossessions of the commercial era of *representing*, and following Romanticism's break from the consensus that onto-theological *musica* constituted natural science, either aesthetic dissensus or cognitive auditory scene production become more apt meta-discourses to frame the dispositional theatre *we* hear. Within this theatre, music becomes an effect of the metaphorical narratives and memic index that establish, in it, a connection between aesthetics and ontology, which places it above trivial logic. Music becomes a reminder of, and a commercially available panacea for, a dispossessed, mythical unity.

Picturing

Sound can be defined in other ways – as a class of vibrations, for instance, that can be conveyed as changes of pressure through an elastic medium such as air and reproduced as sympathetic vibrations in a functioning ear – but this kind of definition only describes the beginning of the process: the input stage. The silence of Bishop Berkley's falling tree in a deserted forest is unquestionable. But whether one chooses to define sound at the hard, objective input stage, or as a soft, subjective output, there is no getting away from sound's contingency on the presence of a hearer. Sounds are either things that might be heard, or things that are heard, but either way their existence is predicated on the fact that aural beings roam the world, and on sentient beings that reflect on auditory experience and theorize it among themselves. Meta-discourses and pictorial models like trees in forests, resonance between spheres and auditory scenes, are therefore part of the constitution of audibility and thus of sound, because they narrate auditory experience.

This does not support the Ongian binary opposition between seeing and hearing, or different mind-sets of eye and ear thinking. Picturing sound in visual terms was key to the Boethian acoustemology that staged its theatre of sound under a canopy painted with celestial bodies, and also key to the Romantic metaphor of the eolian harp, to Carpenter and McLuhan's exotic picturesque of 'other' cultures and Ihde's assertion that the shape of sound is round (1970: *passim*). Ironically, most of the assertions in Sterne's audio-visual litany of aurality's opposition to visuality involve ways of picturing sound or hearing in visual terms. So too, in my expansion of Bregman's auditory scene analysis to describe hearing as a process of scenography, the role of visual picturing is crucial to the construction of a cognitive map that guides the dramaturgy of unhearing. With contemporary scanning technology, neuroscientists are now able to observe 'cross-wiring' of the senses in the early stages of perception, before sights or sounds are formed and posted to our sensory timeline. Electrical signals originating from the auditory inputs can be observed converging with visual inputs on neurons in the optic tectum. Similarly, some neurons in the auditory cortex appear simultaneously sensitive to visual or tactile stimulation, with the effect of sharpening spatial sensitivity (Schnupp, Nelken and King, 2011: 207, 221). This suggests perception is the operation of a matrix of the senses.

One philosopher of the mind and perception, Casey O'Callaghan, goes as far as to say that cross-modality is so rampant within the processes of perception that its objects should no longer be thought of as seen, heard, or smelled things, but from the outset regarded as 'mereologically complex individuals' with multimodality deep within their structures (2011: 160). In other words, sounds are not discretely auditory objects. Quite aside from any individual cases of synaesthesia, which, as O'Callaghan points out, is a 'rare, isolated, quirky, and robustly illusory' condition of which too much is made in relation to artistic sensibility, visible and audible things might be thought of as coenaesthetic depictions (2011: 158).

Stage design and the liquid metaphor of sound

The Sufi writer Inayat Kahn, inspiration in the 1960s to philosophizing rock stars like Pete Townshend (Townshend, 2012: 204–7), was one of the first to introduce to the Western popular imagination – in the 1920s – a 'mystic' version of the idea of *musica universalis*. The key difference from the Boethian ontology is that matter is conceived in terms of sound's vitalizing energy, rather than musical mathematics.

> All things being derived from and formed of vibrations have sound hidden within them, as fire is hidden in flint; and each atom of the universe confesses by its tone, 'My sole origin is sound.' If any solid or hollow sonorous body is struck it will answer back, 'I am sound'.
>
> KAHN, 2005

It is sound as this energizing life-force, rather than music as the mathematic formula, that keeps the chaotic, noisy universe in check. This 'mystic' notion (its mysticism perhaps being a Western sense of exoticism) still forms the basis of a popular, contemporary ontology of sound. While it may be 'academically suspect', as Home-Cook has commented, this popular ontology nevertheless forms part of the meta-discursive index of aurality, and thus (as I have been discussing) of the audibility of things (2015: 37). It is one propagated not only by the psychedelic subculture of which Townshend's public espousal of 'Eastern mysticism' was a part, but also through sonic metaphors used in contemporary cosmology, such as the Big Bang, cosmic string theory, and the quasi-acoustic behaviours of gravitational waves rippling across the universe. Like Vitruvius' picturing of acoustic sound as a pond into which pebbles are thrown, there are often such allusions to liquidity, as a primal state.

In the Preface to Kendrick and Roesner's edited volume *Theatre Noise* (2011), the theatre semiologist Patrice Pavis describes sound as *our* native world, which we inhabit emotionally, and in parallel to the world of the spectacle, which has dispossessed us:

> We spend our lives faced with images: they stand in our way, they guide us, and they absorb us. But we live inside the world of sound: it encompasses us, mothers us, feeds and greets us with sound and meaning – it has terrified us since we were little.
>
> 2011: x

This statement clearly draws coordinates from the left-hand side of Sterne's audio-visual litany, which I have argued is at odds with actual auditory experience, and whose argument consists, ironically, in a set of images. But as I have also said, this figurative way of thinking supplies coordinates to hearing (and unhearing) in the scenographic, diegetic model I have described; so in this sense, it has validity and function within auditory space production. Pavis also references a maternal trope commonly associated with the aesthetics of sound: the muffled noise or gentle, ambient music that speaks to a deep memory of amniotic immersion, or nurtures like mother's milk. Sonic birthing is a part of various sonic creation mythologies. In Berendt's reading of the Upanishads, the Sanskrit word *nada* means sounding, droning, roaring, howling, screaming, and *brahma* is the universal everything – the 'world soul containing all single souls, as the ocean contains all drops of water of which it consists' and also 'the womb of the world' (Berendt, 1991: 15–17). The mantra *nada brahma* equates these two ideas: sound and the universe as an amniotic ocean. All is sound, and sound is the primordial immersion. This brings us, surprisingly, to stage design.

The Romantic idea of musical totality operative in Appia's musical metaphor for theatre production, is that it also is immersive and life-giving in a liquid way. Music subsumes and saturates the drama, either audibly or inaudibly. Music flows through its sensible forms as a totalizing amniotic memory and a nihilistic liquid oblivion. Music is the primordial solution from which subject and soul of the drama emerge, and the sense of self at the centre of its aurality. Music is also the torrent into which its subjectivity and selfhood will again dissolve and be dispersed into the universal ocean. Appia's use of the word *music* references, but has little to do with, Pythagorean musical oneness. It is the idea of immersivity as art that I mentioned earlier in this chapter – immersive music held up so that people could contemplate the oneness they had lost: their own essence estranged and held up for them as a tableau of their dispossession. It relates to the sonic, Wagnerian immersivity of symphonic music which in German Romanticism is often discussed in terms of liquid immersion, rather than the theoretical immersivity of the Baroque. Veit Erlmann (2010) has described how, in the sonic palette of Romantic figuration, there was relational ontology in the onomatopoeic resonances between the white noise (or *rauschen*) of leaves in the trees, and the subject-dissolving rush (or *rausch*) of the surging water. Much like the English word *rush* as it is used in relation to the effects of mind or mood-altering drugs, *rausch* also referred to the effect of vertigo and hallucinatory intoxication, in a not dissimilar way to the French *nausée*, or nausea, which relates etymologically both to *noise* (as Serres uses the French word, rather than the more common word *bruit*) and to the sea.

As is often the case, there is correspondence between artistic tropes and contemporary science. Coleridge's figure of a 'light in sound' was based on David Hartley's theory that light and sound were both phenomena of the same elastic ether, which resonated in a medullary fluid within the nerves. Erlmann connects the Germanic figure of the subject-dissolving flood to a theory that the soul itself is a liquid (precisely the figure at the heart of Appia's metaphor of total theatre production). The anatomist Samuel Thomas von Sömmerring (1755–1830) hypothesized that the *sensorium commune* (where the *res extensa*, phenomenal extent of things, is transduced into *res cogitans*, the substance of consciousness) was located in the cerebrospinal fluid surrounding the endings of auditory, gustatory, olfactory, somatosensory and visual nerves, where they all converge on the cerebral cortex. Sömmerring's 'special kind of fluid' was more than simply the liquor or alchemical bath where sensory signals mingled and transformed into sentience. It *was* the *sensorium commune* – the self, the soul. As Erlmann puts it:

> The reasoning behind this striking about-face on centuries of hunting for the soul in a solid part of the body, Sömmerring ventured, was 'a priori' evident. Water, without a doubt, is the source of all life: 'From the first hours and perhaps days after conception, the entire force of our real individuality – our I – is really and truly contained in a droplet of delicate liquid.'

2010: 154

Appia's scenographic metaphor, *Die Musik und die Inscenierung* (1899; translated as *Music and the Art of Theatre*), describes music as flowing from the musician-poet, and cascading through the whole hierarchy of a stage production process, drenching the whole process in the poet's soul. Appia places his manifesto under an epigraph from Schopenhauer: 'music never expresses the phenomenon but only the inner essence of the phenomenon'. The modern idea of totalizing design unity is thus founded in a thought-model in which all the material objects of the theatre, and all the subjectivities they express, are like sponges which have absorbed the liquid music of the poet's soul.

The paradox of Appian scenography for sound design

This Appian metaphor, however, presents a theoretical problem for approaching stage sound as a design discipline, so long as the institution of sound is held to be different to the institution of music (which, you will remember from Chapter 1, is one of the fundamental configuring principles of the audimus, the *we hear*). Design is not an intuitive word to use in relation to ephemeral sound, but that is the term that has stuck (Brown, 2009: 11–12). As an organizing principle, sound design, as I have discussed, tends to refer to a *disposition* of separate sonic and musical spaces and effects, rather than a *composition* of elements. Whether one still flinches at the old-fashionedness of the term 'sound effect' or not, it is the art of sound effects. This sets it at odds with the concept of music in the musical analogy of design. The Schopenhauerian musical intent of Appian stage design is for the *mise-en-scène* to express something *other than* and *essential to* its apparent phenomenon (the effect). However, the definitive difference between sound and music as it is enshrined in the diegetic configuration of the soundtrack (or, indeed, hip-hop and the concept album) and the dispositional unity of the sound design, is that a sound is an illustrative or allusive effect and music is an abstract one. In contradiction to the Schopenhauerian epigraph that provides the rubric of modern stage design in the Appian tradition, sound effects, because they are not music, *always* express the surface appearance of things, *never* their inner essence.

Sound effects, in this sense, are not only *not* music, they actively work *against* its compositional morphology. As Pierre Boulez put it:

> Any sound which has too evident an affinity with the noises of everyday life (for instance, the most typical: machines and motors – an unexpected piece of luck for those so shrewd as to confuse 'modernism' in musical thought with the 'automation' of contemporary civilisation), any sound of

this kind, with its anecdotal connotations, becomes completely isolated from its context; it could never be integrated [in a musical scheme], since the hierarchy of composition demands materials supple enough to be bent to its own ends, and neutral enough of the appearance of their characteristics to be adapted to each new function which organises them. Any allusive element breaks up the dialectic of form and morphology and its unyielding incompatibility makes the relating of partial to global structures a problematic task. Of all this, the anecdote seems the most crucial point.

BOULEZ, 1971: 22–3

Boulez was, here, critiquing the use of what Pierre Schaeffer termed *acousmatic sounds* in *musique concrète* and pointing out that, while disconnected from visible causality, they still came laden with figurative allusion (perhaps overlooking the anecdotal allusiveness of traditional orchestral instruments such as whips, bells, lewdly rasping trombones and anvils). It is his penultimate sentence, however, that encapsulates the problem of non-musical sound being part of the quasi-musically abstract, scenographic 'total programme' that Peter Sellars envisaged 'beyond the era of sound effects'. Sound is not like light on the Appian stage. You cannot point beams of it at human figures or scenery to sculpt away their anecdotal features. Even when collaged together or made strange by the addition of an artificial reverberation, anything that is identifiable as sound as opposed to music or raw noise will work against a musical conception of totality.

While I struggled to find a theoretical basis for sound as a theatre discipline because of its allusiveness and resistance to the musical abstraction and metaphysical unity narratives that underpinned the Appian design orthodoxy (a struggle that is evident in my essay 'The Theatre Soundscape and the End of Noise', 2005), it turned out that it was sound's very incompatibility with this model – its index of allusion, its fragmented decoupage and unstable, oscillating binary identity with noise – that made it the more relevant to theatre as the sensible constitution of the internet age. Sound can speak to theatre as ontology, but as the ontology of the audio-object framework, not the Romantic myth of a metaphysical total programme of music. It is sound design's dialectic between fragmentation and disposition, rather than music's dialectic between form and morphology, that perhaps provides a more apt scenographic principle for post-millennial theatre.

Following on from my account earlier in this chapter of how the identification of music as art within a political economy of noise, music and silence disrupted the ecology of Pythagorean (or Boethian) totality, one might argue that Appia's very premise – that an operatic model of musical immersivity would rescue drama from the trite tableaux of melodrama, with its separate, aesthetically disconnected elements – was a fallacy. Romantic opera or symphony was not immersive at all, it was just a tableau of immersivity, and as such was antimusical, in the theoretical terms of the quadrivium.

Barthes describes this opposition between that classical conception of music and theatre in the essay 'Diderot Brecht Eisenstein'. He observes that 'an affinity of status and history has linked mathematics and acoustics since the Ancient Greeks' (1977: 67). Theatre, on the other hand, has a relationship with geometry, enshrined in the audience's sightlines, that has, since the ancient theatron, worked against this ideal affinity (the 'effectively Pythagorean space' of resonance and harmony). The geometry of the dioptric gaze obliviates totality, by reducing theatre space to a triangle, and is thus anti-musical. This gaze, formalized in the modern tableau stage associated with Diderot and Garrick, is a process that cuts things out of the holistic world and de-musicalizes them as optical fetishes. This cultural fixation on cut-out spectacle, Barthes suggests, reinforcing Rancière's argument that theatre is the modern constitution of the sensible, is the basis of a wider dioptric mode of sensible being, whose media include the printed page and image and the framed stage and screen. The tableau stage institutes a common sense that contradicts the narrative that all objects and words are part of holistically immersive and saturating musical or textual spaces, and a mode of representation that requires a limited world view:

> The theatre is precisely that practice which calculates the place of things as they are observed: if I set the spectacle here, the spectator will see this; if I put it elsewhere, he will not, and I can avail myself of this masking effect and play on the illusion it provides. The stage is the line which stands across the path of the optic pencil, tracing at once the point at which it is brought to a stop and, as it were, the threshold of its ramification. Thus is founded – against music (against the text) – representation.
>
> ibid.

As proof, Barthes makes a similar assertion to Boulez's that music must be abstract and above mundane or quotidian anecdotal references:

> Nothing permits us to locate the slightest tableau in the musical text, except by reducing it to a subservience to drama; nothing permits us to cut out in it the slightest fetish, except by debasing it through the use of trite melody.
>
> ibid.: 69

Perhaps theatre does debase music through its *découpage*, through using music as just another sound or effect in its crafted tableau. Although perhaps that quadrivial notion of music has long been debased, by the commodification of music and the silencing of the auditorium. Practical music, through Attali's stages of representing, repeating, and now post-repeating, has long since lost its sacred status as a sacrifice to the god-totality of theoretical *musica*. Barthes goes on to say that theatre, as the Organon of representation, has 'as its dual foundation the sovereignty of the act of cutting out [*découpage*] and the unity of the subject of that action' (ibid.: 67–8). The unity, in other words, of aural spectating, and the subjectivity of the auditorium, theatre's ear, its instrument of hearing and the temple where theatre's living congregation of dioptric viewpoints, its constitution of the sensible world, gathers.

Now hear this.

3

Auditorium

A space in process

Rather than think of the auditorium as a room in a theatre building that stands empty, waiting for the audience to enter, consider the term *auditorium* in its literal, Latin sense: as an instrument, or agency, for hearing (*audire* = to hear + *orium* = the instrument or apparatus of an activity). It was not an ancient word but a formulation coined during the Middle Ages to describe part of a church constructed for hearing the word of God through instruction, and for feeling its resonant effect. Hearers, or *auditores*, faced an orator at the front, while immersed in an architecturally designed resonance. It was in the late eighteenth century that the term seems to have become adopted to describe a designated space within a theatre where an audience – a hearing – convenes. Prior to this, there seems to have been no standard term for either audience or auditorium. The actor-manager, playwright and theatre impresario Colly Cibber, in the earlier part of that century, writes of auditors or hearers in the plural and to their area as 'that auditory part of the theatre' (Cibber, 1889: 322–3). There is an apt ambiguity in that phrase: that the auditorium might not only be where the auditors sit, but that part of the theatre building, or process, which hears. As such, because, as we discussed in the last chapter, it is the hearing of sounds that makes them, it is the auditorium, the theatre's ear, that 'produces' the audible *mise-en-scène*. If sound constitutes a performance-space or a 'world' of the drama, then it is space heard into being by the audience using the auditorium or instrument of hearing that the theatre has provided it.

Sound does not pre-exist hearing, and the audible space of the auditorium and the stage is not there waiting to be entered like a room. Jonathan Sterne has usefully mobilized Henri Lefebvre's triad of socially produced space to theorize how space is produced in this way. Describing the space of the soundscape (like that of the theatre, a diegetically audible space), he identifies it as a 'construct' that:

simultaneously index a set of sonic-spatial practices, the meta-discourses that describe them, and the cultural and sensory conditions that make it possible to – even passively – experience sonic space in certain terms.

2013: 183–4

The hearing space of theatre, and thus its audibility, might thus consist in:

1 acting, music and sound effects;

2 meta-discourses known to the audience (myths of immersivity; popular science; the publicity of audio products and experiences; principles of sound design, voice, music and so on);

3 acoustic and electroacoustic architectures and conventions of silent listening and attention, but also conversance with sonic languages, memes, frames of recognition, and so on.

This kind of triad is not dissimilar to Rancière's definition of an aesthetic, which Rockhill describes as 'a mode of articulation between three things: ways of doing and making, their corresponding forms of visibility [or audibility], and ways of conceptualizing both the former and the latter' (in Rancière, 2004: 3).

This three-way mode of articulation does not simply account for the sensibility of things in the room, but the people in the room and the room too, as the socially produced, meta-discursive space that constitutes a common, first-person plural sense of sound, or audimus. Sterne's soundscape triad, and Rancière's aesthetic one, provide a 'communal distribution of the sensible, i.e. a system of coordinates defining modes of being, doing, making, and communicating that establishes the borders between the visible and the invisible, the audible and the inaudible, the sayable and the unsayable' (ibid.: 93).

The rhetorics of the auditorium

When one approaches and enters a theatre auditorium, one transitions from everyday space to a constructed aesthetic; a controlled communal distribution of the sensible; an apparatus or dispositive of the audimus.

●

One switches off one's music and takes one's noise-blocking, in-ear headphones out as one rises up from the Tube and the street scene configures around one's onward journey. Ticket in hand, one recalibrates: from audio to audimus, from one-of-one, to one-of-many; from I to we. Sounds fade in and out as we move through them, front and back determined only by our direction of travel, by the turns of our head as we move towards the theatre entrance. Soho is a rumble of thunder, the sound of car tyres on the wet road and the neon reflected in oily puddles. We enjoy our character of flâneuristic theatregoer, theatricalized by the dark and rain of the London picturesque. We want thunder from above and zephyrs of jazz to waft up through the pavement like an aura. As we pass through the early evening crowd, we notice a majority has thin cables hanging from its ears. There is music in this street, but it is on the inside, behind double-glazed restaurant doors and windows kept closed for the air-conditioning, and behind the faces of the pedestrians.

Through the theatre doors, the foyer is a crush of bodies and noise. Outside there was a wide perimeter of background noise, but it has closed densely around us now and is mostly voices.

Rhubarb. An old-fashioned term for an old-fashioned theatre effect, but the wrong onomatopoeia here. The walls and floors are hard, uncarpeted. A cacophony. We struggle to hear as we collect our ticket, buy a programme and a bag of sweets. A tannoy announcement over the top of the noise – literally over the top, from a ceiling loudspeaker – advises us to switch off our phones; that the performance contains flashing lights; and that it will begin shortly. Electric bar bells sound. We are to take our seat. Latecomers will not be admitted until a suitable pause in the action. Summoned, we pass through a tiny vestibule – a narrow gate of grace, Goethe called it – a light and sound lock between two differently sensible worlds – and move from crush of theatregoers and noise into the auditorium, a system of coordinates that defines a mode of auditory being and the distinction between audible and inaudible, by design and stealthy rhetoric.

As we emerge into the new room, the lighting changes around us, to a designed ambience. At some point recently, a sound designer and some actors walked into this room and clapped their hands or made vocal noises, to hear how it would respond. But today, we are coming in as an audience; a hearing; a hearing of spectators that has converged on this room through the London streets and congregated here. We adopt the pious posture and movements of congregants. It is not only the neo-classical columns around the proscenium arch that suggest something like a temple. There are people working here, reverently and discreetly like sacristans, administering the room, creating conditions. We see ushers, and we know that behind the walls there are other ministers, wearing headsets, making preparations; coordinating a countdown. Like êcheia hidden in the walls of a medieval church, they are tuning the room.

There is only one sacristan in plain view. She is sat behind what could be a jet pilot's console of blinking lights and controls as though she is flying the auditorium. There will be sound, then, of the audio kind. She is the sound operator.

'Tabs' is an abbreviation of tableau curtain, which in the late eighteenth century would open to reveal stage pictures. 'I am the end of your world', the house tabs say, 'behind me another world awaits. So be thrilled.' The safety curtain, which comes down during the interval, is traditionally plain, often scruffy and not lit, but it is a convention that the plush house tabs should be treated reverentially and luxuriated with lights called tab warmers (it used to be like that in cinemas). Daniel Barenboim, the great pianist and conductor, wrote that the whole of the theatre is contingent on the syntax of the ouverture – the opening of the curtain. 'Many stage directors raise the curtain at the very beginning of the music', he says, 'because they want to fight against the separation of the ear and the eye, whereas this separation is actually an essential part of the process: first the understanding through the ear and only then the perception through the eye' (Barenboim, 2008: 36). Hearing comes first in this separation; it prepares us to see. We notice right away, however, that there are no tabs tonight, as has become the fashion. The tableau is already there, open to the room and waiting for the audience to take its seats. It is darkened; only parts of it glow in a vague haze of oil smoke.

We imagine that backstage, beginners will have been called. We cannot be sure, but perhaps a faint, modulating hum has joined in with the haze. An industrial throb: maybe the smoke machine or the building's air handling; maybe a sound design. People are still coming in. Eyes blink and move from ticket to aisle number. Ears, meanwhile, are subtly being prepared; being adjusted to the coordinates of the room, learning them before the spectacle begins.

The room is carpeted and has plush velvet seats in three horseshoe-shaped and heavily ornamented tiers. It all sits under a huge glass-panelled dome or ceiling lantern embellished with suns, moons and stars. Space is filling up. The sound operator has spent many long hours in this room, her trained ears open as much to the walls around her as to the stage in front of her. She knows that, ironically, as living, fleshy bodies wearing soft clothes enter it, the less 'live' it will become and the more plush and velvety – the reverberation and resonance of the empty room, soaked up by the audience, the hearing. She has made the necessary technical adjustments.

We hear and understand the signature feel of the pre-show. We like the cushioned excitement. Our ears relax, unwind, and breathe out even as our eyes locate our seat. The sound of voices is no longer the crush of before. No cacophony or hubbub and no rhubarb (that onomatopoeia now too animated); only a murmur. People lower their voices as they come in, because in its soft acoustic, their conversations are exposed. The word 'luxury' comes from the Latin for light, but there is an aural luxury in this room, a calming pleasantness to the ears, an ambient light-in-sound. Like the pitch at an elite sports stadium, it has a soft, resonant, professionally mown, greener-than-expected ambience.

We are excited to think professional and famous voices will soon be treading on it. With each person entering the room, a little bit more of the reverberative emptiness is absorbed, and the playing area gets greener. The entering audience moves increasingly respectfully on its luxury turf in hushed voices, aurally privileged to be here. The last few to come in are also the quietest, apologetically edging down a row, whispering sorries to everyone who must stand up to let them pass. Opening our sweets even now, before the show has begun, causes us some embarrassment. The harsh crackle of the plastic bag does not judge the tone of the room correctly.

Somewhere, inaudibly, a countdown reaches Q1: Go.

The lights dim and murmur fades amid a few last-minute coughs. Some real and apologetic; some, we can tell, affected, a signal to a few last-minute talkers: time to stop talking. A new depth of silence is revealed, a negative of the pre-show murmur, as though a light we had not noticed before has been switched off. If there was a machine hum or drone as part of the stage pre-set, it has faded. It is a performance of silence. At first, it clasps our head like a change in air pressure but then it relaxes into the silence of many people ready to hear. An actor emerges into the developing lighting state, and we wonder if she was there all along in the shadows. Thunder rolls gently somewhere in the distance. We wonder for a moment if it was outside the theatre, but it breaks inside the room, across the stereo-speaker array and in the sub-woofers, like a wave reaching the beach with a muted crash. Its quality is luxurious, exciting and delightful: state of the art. The silence in the auditorium begins to reconfigure as the first scene starts to open into it. We hear the actor's footsteps. She walks to the front of the stage.

Michel Serres once pointed out that the shape of the theatre is something like an ear: the auditorium the outer pavilion, gathering the pregnancy of the moment (the plenum; the noise of everything here). It appears to concentrate it on the semi-circular forestage, the tympanum. We are all about to vibrate together: you, me, the air, the walls, the actors' throats, the loudspeakers, all our dispositions of reverence and irreverence, interest and boredom, engagement and distraction. Between us all, we will hear. But before she speaks, the actor pauses for a moment – just a beat, one measure of this room's pulse.

Serres was describing a visit to the ancient amphitheatre in Epidaurus – an enormous ear sticking out of a hill as if belonging to some buried giant, pointing up to the Pythagorean cosmos. He went there out of season not to watch a performance, but simply to sit there in the extended pause of a place designed for the organization of sound, but which, at that moment, was organizing nothing more than the transubstantiation of auras of the Greek hillside into material silence. As a philosopher, language is what Serres lives by, in cities of discourse, but it has become a cacophony that has anaesthetized and toxified his body with many acouphènes – the acou(stic) + phen(omena) or auditory artefacts that are singularized in English as tinnitus: the sound effect that overrules all hearing. Serres has come to Epidaurus, and the silence of its inactive ear, for respite from it. 'The silence within the theatre and in the surrounding scrub', he says, 'seeps into my skin, bathes and penetrates it, vibrates and drains it, in the hollow of the empty ear'. He hopes to prolong this brief and essential moment, but it cannot last long before myriad things start calling out again from the silence, from the babble of tourists, from the cells of his body, irritating his ear and re-noising his being. 'Every possible kind of audible finds sites of hearing and regulation', he says, in the circuits of transmitter–receiver black boxes that constitute our bodies, networks and cities. Theatre's black box transmitter–receiver brings together hearing and regulation, the bodies of the polis, and all kinds of audible, in a perfect temporary feedback circle, buffered from the foyer of reality by the sound and light lock of its entrances and exits, by the ceremony of arrival and by the purified silence before the first utterance and after the last, when there is nothing to hear. At the input stage, cacophony; on the output stage, sense – the sense of a meaning. Eventually, says Serres, the circle 'collapse(s) under the wave of applause', but while we are in it, 'we find rhythm and music, silence and singing, the chaotic crackle of noise, everything that precedes language and the transformations of one into the other' (Serres, 2016: 106–11).

Our actor has yet to speak. She has found her light and her visibility, but now she is sizing up her audibility: her audience, her voice, her resonance in this room, and the coordinates of its aesthetics. It is the briefest of pauses, a beat, but it is crucial. The auditorium took us in from the street and deposited us here in this beat: between the hushing of the murmur and the arrival at our body of the first waves of vocal sound from that actor's body. The theatre closes in on me. The silence brings us from the social gathering into our own moment, another kind of disposition – a togetherness with the congregated audimus, but an apartness from it too. The auditorium structures a *we* but is centring itself on me in my seat, on everyone else's me too. All of the theatre, the building, the process, its history, is configuring itself around us; fitting itself to our ears. The auditorium is now our hearing, and mine.

It is hard, with the usual prepositions and syntax of English, to express our aural relationship to the actor standing on the stage. There is an early recording of Aretha Franklin as a girl, singing gospel in her father's Detroit church. As she is about to begin singing, you can hear someone in the congregation, or maybe her father, shout out 'listen at her!'

We are listening at the actor and then she speaks.

II

The prologue

A matrix of anticipation – the journey to the playhouse; staged processes of entrance; the theatre of the house tabs or pre-show – establishes conditions upon which, according to Sterne's triad, the audibility of theatre's aural construct is one-third contingent. What I have just described is a kind of prologue, but sometimes a prologue is also spoken: Shakespeare's company would flatter their audiences, calling them 'gentle hearers', to expose their walnut cracking (my sweet bag rustling) but also to focus the audience and to format it to its controlled coordinates. The entrance and commencement protocol is also about preparing the audience to hear 'gently', which is to say, according to the event's rules, conditions and decorum. These determine what the theatre will hear, among all its noise and *acouphènes*, and what it will unhear.

Elizabethan flattery of the audience related to rules of rhetoric attributed (erroneously) to Cicero: the *Rhetorica ad Herennium*, a format of public address well known to the Elizabethan audimus. Its aim was to make the hearer 'well disposed' to what followed – to format an apt (and perhaps a forgiving) disposition (Bruster and Weimann, 2004: 10–11). The mustering of the audience in a lobby, the modern electric bar bells, the latecomer and mobile phone announcements, the dim lighting: all of these, like the three-trumpet tarantaras of Elizabethan theatres, are part of the rhetoric that constructs a well-disposed auditorium from the multifarious convergence of its noisy, hearing bodies. Thomas Dekker, in *Satiromastix* (1601), describes how the pre-show trumpets 'set men together by the eares' (2005: 76). This is what the staged process of entering the theatre does.

The noise of the outside world and the *acouphènes* of the noisy mind are the raw material of theatre's dialectic between dramaturgy and form. The setting-together of a crowd by its ears transforms noisy bodies into a hearing body, an audience. It conditions the audible space coordinated by practices and meta-discourses. Let us take Faust as an example, because it is a story around which a number of different contemporary organizations of hearing have been framed over the modern period. Elizabethan audiences going to see Marlowe's early modern *Doctor Faustus* (1592) would have converged on the Rose Theatre through the noise of the city, which, conditioned by the soft resonance of the thatch, wattle and daub, was zoned by parish bells and the clustering together of types of industry or commerce (leather-making, greengrocery, ironmongery) as a kind of auditory map. As they neared Bankside, they passed through the cries of the watermen, the caged baiting animals, and the lairy drinkers moving between taverns and brothels. All of this constituted a psycho-topography of everyday city life; but while still acoustically available to be heard within the open-roofed theatre, once inside, it was unheard by the *asyndeton* of the theatrical process, pushed back, beyond the perimeter of the perfect temporary feedback circle of the Wooden O. Barring the odd accidental intrusion that stood out from the background, it was this noise that constituted and conditioned the silence against which the play was audible.

By contrast, almost two hundred years later, in *Faust* (c. 1775), a drama written as much in the expectation that it would be read as performed, Goethe writes a very different noise journey for his readers to imagine. His prologue formats an auditorium for changed times, approached through layers of framing and frontmatter. The destination of this approach is set in the Dedication:

> I feel a long and unresolved desire
> For that serene and solemn land of ghosts,
> It quivers now, like an Aeolian lyre.
>
> GOETHE, 2003: lines 25–7

Then, in an 'onstage' prelude – a Socratic discourse between director, writer and comedian – Goethe asks his readers to imagine being swept to his theatre door by a Germanically Romantic torrent of liquid oblivion, as 'tremendous and repeated surging' of waves of noise squeeze them through its 'narrow gate of grace' (lines 49–52). As the play begins, they find themselves in a gothic chamber, trembling with the silenced energy of the sublime torrent that swept them through the imaginary lobby into the auditorium. Noise is no longer a map of how to get to the theatre, it is the immersive energy of the journey there, or rather a scenically poetic image of it. If the frontmatter of Marlowe's form was the noisy psycho-topography of the early modern city, then Goethe's is the roar of water and the 'fusion of subject-enabling and subject-dissolving forces' that Erlmann identifies as the key sound effect of German Romantic aurality (Erlmann, 2010: 165).

Shut up and listen

Prologues were important because there was no rule of silent listening in the playhouse until the nineteenth century. The dramaturgy and rhetoric employed to achieve focused audience were part of the theatre. The quality of the silence obtained by the prologue primed the auditorium and the audibility of the play. Silence had to be achieved, and its achievement was part of what created the performance-space and imbued it with contemporary, social relevance. The requirement of silence in the auditorium that applies today derives in part from the capital value attached to performance in the early nineteenth century, but while it improved the audibility of the programme in one sense, it debased it in another. Remembering that drama, as Mayer says, is historically a musical theatre form, the convention of silent listening should be understood in relation to the economic controls placed around music in its *representing* stage (as Attali calls it), although theatre had resisted these until the late eighteenth century, particularly in England, where, for a century or so, there had been complex licensing strictures around the legitimacy and illegitimacy of different kinds of comedic, scenic and 'serious' musical drama.

In a passage from 'A Chapter on Ears' from the *London Magazine* column *Essays of Elia* (1821, around the time that Goethe was writing *Faust II*), Charles Lamb, in a reverse of the kind of noise journey *to* the theatre that I have been describing, describes an urge to flee the mannered, affected auditorium of a theatre appropriated by musical drama. Lamb saw this as 'a profanation of the purposes of the cheerful playhouse', where the 'auditory' sit pretentiously in feigned emotional attentiveness. Grabbing his hat, he made his escape back to the honest noises of the street that were the raw, primordial matter of dramatic theatre, but which the music business had already, by the mid-nineteenth century, characterized as a torment to more refined musical sensibilities:

> I have rushed out into the noisiest places of the crowded streets, to solace myself with sounds, which I was not obliged to follow, and get rid of the distracting torment of endless, fruitless, barren attention! I take refuge in the unpretending assemblage of honest, common-life sounds; – and the purgatory of the Enraged Musician becomes my paradise.
>
> LAMB, 1923: 44

This might seem like the curmudgeonly behaviour of a man who, by his own admission, has 'no ear for music', but if one reads Lamb's dissent from 'obliged' silent listening against Attali's analysis of the political economy of music, then Lamb's was a reaction to a shift in the politics of theatre aurality; to being told to shut up and listen – and thus to being shut up, and isolated from the social hearing space, within his listening self.

According to Attali, the requirement of silence in the auditorium was connected to the commodification of the auditory experience of music that, in effect, accompanied the commercialization of its performance rights (1985: 77). Obedience to a rule of silent listening was thus a submission of the middle classes to a political economy of music, 'the artificialized spectacle of harmony' within an industrializing world of noise no longer regulated and topographically zoned by the old ways. 'The most perfect silence' which 'reigned in the concerts of the bourgeoisie' was 'the rule which governed the symbolic game of their domination' (ibid.: 47).

Music was now stood apart from the sound of everything else, partitioned by walls of silence. Thus abstracted, it was no longer the code that proved everything was connected. Music now could only yearn, Romantically, for a lost cosmic oneness (as I described in Chapter 2). Moreover, this eighteenth-century capitalist development also instituted the acoustemological way of knowing described in Chapter 1, wherein music became categorically different to sound, other-worldly, or, in the formal terms of dramatic representation, extra-diegetic – the sound of a noiseless, aesthetically ideal meta-dimension:

> The trap closed: the silence greeting the musicians was what created music and gave it an autonomous existence, a reality. [. . .] A market was created when the German and English bourgeoisie took to listening to music and paying musicians.
>
> ibid.

A decade after Lamb's flight from the musical theatre, the 1833 Dramatic Literary Property Act commoditized the performing rights to plays, and the consumer right to hear them, in a way similar to that of the musical recital, and became one of the statutes of the auditorium (Litman, 2010). What the legislative banning of noise from the playhouse achieved was, in effect, anti-theatrical. It was an important part of the format that a mode of attentiveness was conditioned by the theatre of going to the theatre, and the frontmatter of tarantaras, bar bells and prologues that turned rowdiness and nut-cracking into silence. For some, like Lamb, this diminished the theatre and made the distribution of the sensible in the outside world, framed and coordinated by a flâneuristic intent, seem a more vital theatre. It was, according to Picker, 'Lamb's step across the threshold from the opera house into the hubbub of London street life, the bustle that Elia's ear interpreted as "paradise", that helped set the precedent for Dickens and other flâneuristic urban sketch-writers and novelists to attend to and begin to archive the "common-life" of the Victorian city' (Picker, 2003: 7–8).

Listening at

If the 'the distracting torment of endless, fruitless, barren attention', for Lamb, had no place in the playhouse, what kind of attention does? In this book, I talk far more about hearing than listening, so I will touch briefly now on why, with reference to the dialectics of effort and relaxation implied by linguistic syntaxes of listening and hearing.

As a trained auditory technique (trained in both senses of the word – rehearsed and focused), the practice of 'listening' has effort and a work ethic to it, that Picker and Sterne have related to auscultation or the diagnostic *listening into* the body and the mind that was part of the empirical method of the Enlightenment (which Sterne, 2003, argues was also an 'Ensoniment'). Picker (2003) illustrates the nineteenth-century relationship between deep thought and auscultation with the figure of the soundproof study, while Sterne focuses on the development of the stethoscope. Picker notes how the rising Victorian professional class cocooned themselves, at great cost, in a thought-space, insulated from the crescendo of noise and unregulated music of the London streets – cart-wheels and horses on cobbles, hawkers, rabble-rousers, organ-grinders and other street musicians – all of which constituted Lamb's idea of paradise (2003: 41–81).

Within a soundproofed space of progress, skilled listening could solve problems and lead to betterment. When British radio began, under John Reith, there was an ethic implied by its institutional terminology. The people to whom it was broadcast were not called an audience, but *listeners*; not a singular, congregational disposition, but a plurality of individuals, each separated in their individual studies, or cocoons of attentiveness, and each with work to do at their end of the signal chain. An ethic emerged. Auditory passivity in front of a spectacle or a radio programme was a bad thing. Listeners should be edified and educated as well as entertained, so they must eliminate distraction and listen hard. This will lead them through illusion of the reproduction (the mimesis) into the truth beyond.

By contrast to this auscultative ethic, there is Brecht's belief, following Piscator, in a dialectical *we hear*, of a relaxed auditorium that makes the audience aware of its situation and able to discuss or interact with what they want. Does one make better sense of life by sitting back and hearing the space that performances, dramaturgy and discourse between them make audible, or by shutting oneself up in a noise-proof bubble, and probing through surface effects, to diagnose a deeper truth beyond audible phenomena? I am going to side with Charles Lamb on that, and Debord's maxim of 'the more he contemplates the less he lives' (in Rancière, 2009: 6), and say that the playhouse, as the constitution of the living community, is no place for studious listening.

Listening is pointed. It does not connect dialectically to fellow aural humans in an audience – in fact, it blocks them out. Listening does not have the sympathy of 'giving audience' or 'lending an ear'. It is an empathetic inquisition. The English grammar and syntax of the words *listening* and *hearing* capture this. Hearing needs no preposition to intend it towards its subject. One can simply hear thunder or a car. One listens, on the other hand, *to* things *for* meanings; *to* objects *for* subjects. Jean-Luc Nancy says this: 'when one is listening, one is on the lookout for a subject, something (itself) that identifies itself by resonating from self to self' (2007: 9). Listening involves a narcissistic crisis of self. In Nancy's view, it is to strain forward towards the resonance of others, to give oneself over, empathetically, to it and then attend to oneself as the resonator of other selfhoods, thus experiencing a kind of pathological 'fit' where hearing becomes a nemesis, being both one's own self and those other selves. Nancy's project, though, is what philosophy might learn from aurality and its different modes. Hearing (which in the French *entendre* also means understanding) he believes to be more methexic (to do with participation, sharing or contagion) than visuality, which tends toward mimesis. However, Nancy is also interested in the *renvoi* of listening (*écouter*) – the infinite feedback loop of resonance between one's own self and the selfhoods of other, audible things – and the way it destabilizes one's position, as a way of getting beyond the limiting intentionality of *trying* to hear. Listening in this way to programmed sound, however, without collateral interaction, can be an unhealthy spiral that Brecht likened to solitary drinking (Brecht, 1980: 25). Theatre is a performance of auditory sociability which was built to provide refuge, not from noise, but from this kind of crisis of the self, which is what Serres sought in the perfect temporary feedback circle of silence, within its 'immense transmitter–receiver social box' (Serres, 2016: 109).

When reading Nancy's description of the crisis of listening *into* oneself as the resonator of other sounds, I have the image of a music listener in my head, or an audiophile, and not a theatre spectator. A body hunched over, shut up, eyes closed, fingers pinching the bridge of the nose. It seems wracked by the elusiveness of subjects in the music or the audio quality, but enraptured by the search for them, which seems, from the body's posture, to be taking place deep inside. Or perhaps it is a performance; a pretentious enactment of listenership to persuade me he (the image is male) is hearing something unavailable to me. Then, I picture Charles Lamb fleeing back into the common noise of the street, from the un-cheerful auditorium that has pretentiously turned its theatre ear to the musical recital.

Lamb wanted a playhouse to be a place of relaxed audience. Brecht, we shall discuss later, wanted this too, and for his audience to be aware of theatre as a fabricated disposition of effects – precisely to avoid the spiralling crisis of self involved in empathetic listening. He wanted them to sit back, and realize their agency to recognize and change, if necessary, the social situations that dispossessed them of their collective energy and ability to hear and feel things for themselves. To hear *with* theatre is not complacent passivity on behalf of the audience in the face of the spectacle: the spectator sits, sees and thinks within the auditorium, a socially produced audible space constructed by art, theory and prevailing sensory conditions. This is not to say that people in the theatre should not pay attention. But if there is an ethical, or even an ontological, lesson in the resonance within theatre's transmitter–receiver, then, like the man at the Aretha Franklin concert said, the theatre spectator *listens at* it much as they would *look at* an image: aware of and conversant in the spatial separations between subjects that the auditorium has modelled.

*

|◀◀

Thinking back over this first part of the book – about the cabbages and watermelons, Sean Connery's voice, the Castle Thunder, the Ying Tong Yiddle I Po's, and the Pows! and Whams! of pop culture, I am wondering how this aurality, and any art of sound effects it might frame, might speak to theatre as ontology – as a metaphysics of being or a programming framework for game-world creation. I am thinking about how sounds and audio are not music. I am thinking about how a theatre sound design sits in a space-producing triad: of sounds, audio and music. I am thinking how the dialectic between form and dramaturgy that a sound design holds up to the contemporary auditorium is usually a configuration of this triad where one frames the other two, and how the *jeu*, the heuristic play, by which the audience recognizes that something clever is going on in their shared ear, is when ambiguity, punning, rhymes or dissonance are introduced between the frame and the framed. This is the sound effect – the audible, aesthetic space that the contemporary auditorium constructs.

But then I am thinking about Boulez's phrase about sound effects, and how, of all their incompatibilities with music's deep dialectic between form and morphology, 'the anecdote seems the most crucial point' (1971: 23). Sound effect collages are trivial, surface things. Do they address the beautiful or profound? If they hold together across the totality of a diegesis as a design (rather than being isolated effects illustrating the local action within each scenic frame), then it is by resonating collaterally with one another as a patina of coincidence that corresponds with contemporary audio culture – movies, radio, hi-fi publicity narratives, tableaux of inspirational immersivity like yoga ambience, approximately heard sonic-artiness or world exoticism. It might be witty, and it might sound good, but ontology? The reason I spent some time at the beginning of this book problematizing what sound, in that singular categorical formulation, might mean, is because I want to be clear that what we hear are sounds, not sound. Aurality is an object framework. Aural scenography, sound design, sound scoring or soundscape design – or whatever one calls the dispositions of sound, audio and music that now routinely overlay the drama in contemporary theatre – is an art of effects, a collage of clips or *découpage*. Its overall effect is an extent of things. It is the singular form of the word *sound* that misleads one into thinking *sound design* is a sculptural form, or something that might be quasi-musical, when in fact the function of sound design in the *mise-en-scène* is to offset the programmatic continuity and fixed visual perspective of the drama, with an occasional and ephemeral anti-programme of aural *synecdoche* and *asyndeton*. It is not an art of sound, but of sound effects.

But I am worrying now that its patina of resonance is too frivolous, fun and easy to hear to be ontological. I am concerned that, after all is said and done, a sound design is just a notional unity of what Appia, in his 1899 manifesto *Music and the Art of Theatre*, calls 'decorative elements'. I am concerned it is a surface gloss of cultural context, where Appia said scenography should not reproduce an 'appearance of dramatic life' with effects, but speak to 'dramatic life in all its reality, as we can know it only in the most profound depths of our being' (1962: 16).

Should we forget ontology? Not quite.

▶▶

A fictional ontology

Rancière's theory of the aesthetic regime of art, which takes Appia, the '*metteur-en-scène* in search of the living art work', as its prime example (2009: 67), has something to say on the matter. Rancière identifies a number of regimes of art, but there are two main ones. The representative, poetic or mimetic regime (he refers to it by all three names) is manifest in classical theatre's 'fabrication of a plot, arranging actions that represent the activities of men, which is the foremost issue, to the detriment of the essence of the image, a copy examined with regard to its model' (Rancière, 2004: 17).

The aesthetic regime, by contrast, is associated with the new subjectivity of Romanticism, and the way it broke from the old order. Taking Schiller's definition of an aesthetic state as a 'pure instance of suspension, a moment when form is experienced for itself', the aesthetic regime disrupts the mimetic regime in that it 'simultaneously establishes the autonomy of art and the identity of its forms with the forms that life uses to shape itself' (ibid.: 19). In extracting the figures of Wagnerian total theatre from the composer's intended setting and putting them into a geometrically architectural scene where they become statues moulded by light, Rancière identifies Appia in particular, and the modern *mise-en-scène* in general, as embodying the dissensual operation by which the aesthetic regime of art performs this disruption.

Rancière's scenographic examples are rather limited (Appia/Wagner, Brecht and Artaud), but his notion of an aesthetic is of a socially produced sensibility or space, not dissimilar to Sterne's Lefebvrian definition of the construct of a soundscape, not predicated at all on specific genres or styles of art, or distinctions between popular or avant-garde. The dissensual operation is not modernist abstraction, or truth to materials. It is the assertion of an aesthetic reign of truth that consists in 'a sensible mode of being specific to artistic *products*' (ibid.: 18, my emphasis) of indeterminate kinds or intent. The dissensual rupture from mimesis means it is an aesthetic truth specific to the *appearance* of artistic products. The dissensual operation of the aesthetic regime abolishes the mimetic accord or identity between originals and copies, causes and effects, poiesis and aesthesis, or the artistic intent and the affect of art (Rancière, 2010: 2–3). The autonomy of art that is established, and the identity of its forms with the forms that life uses to shape itself, is one that is specific to effects without cause – which must include the kinds of sound, like the Castle Thunder, that I identified earlier as audio memes. Cause, intentionality and provenance do not matter. The artistic meaning is unconfined by anything other than the auditorium.

So, what truth does this aesthetic provide? Does it speak to the essence of being? Appia thought so. He saw a truth in the scenographic disposition of effects that was complementary to but separate from the word-tone drama, and related to an inner essence, much like resonance of *musica mundana* with *musica humana*.

> The wondrous art of sound, in revealing to us our innermost being, creates the supreme work of art by combining artifices borrowed from nature, whose eternal laws reside within ourselves. This is why in the staging of such a work of art only the actor is dependent upon the external world of reality.
>
> APPIA, 1962: 84

But like the figure I described earlier in this chapter, hunched over, eyes closed, nose pinched, listening for the composer's genius resonating within itself, to find this meaning, the auditor and the auditorium together become introspective and auto-auscultative.

Rancière demurs with Appia. He says that what characterizes the aesthetic regime of modern art – against theories of ontology in sensation – is that it is 'a fictional ontology' or 'play of aesthetic ideas' (2009: 67):

> The set of relations that constitute the work operates *as if* it had a different ontological texture from the sensations that make up everyday experience. But there is neither a sensory nor an ontological difference.
>
> ibid.

The radical dissensus of aesthetic art is that, by contrast to mimetic art, its meaning is what it is. Form is experienced for itself and its meaning is not determined by either representation or schemes such as harmony. The aesthetic regime accounts for modern art and is connected to the sensory revolution of Romanticism, not because of the tableaux of immersivity Romantic culture created in its poems and music, and held up to its aesthetically dispossessed subjects *as* ontology, but because of this indeterminacy between aesthetic and artistic intent, which is:

> Precisely the indeterminacy that Kant conceptualized when he defined the beautiful as 'what is represented as an object of universal delight apart from any concept'. That definition has often been equated with the old definition of beauty as harmony and has been counterposed to the break of the sublime, thought of as the formula for the modern rupture with representation. I think that this view ignores the radical break with the representational logic that is entailed in the phrase 'apart from any concept'.
> RANCIÈRE, 2009: 63–4

The audience/community, under the reign of aesthetic truth, is thus emancipated from the reign of truth of art and artists separated from the rest of *us*. It is free to take meaning from any anecdotal or allusive resonance between the aesthetic forms that life uses to shape itself, according to a framework of third things 'owned by no one, [subsisting] between them, excluding any uniform transmission, any identity of cause and effect' (ibid.: 15). Third things like sonic memes.

Aesthetic dissensus '[cracks] open the unity of the given and the obviousness of the visible [or audible], in order to sketch a new topography of the possible' (ibid.: 49).

Now hear this.

PART TWO

Reconfigurations

'Our set of objects forms a model of a world', says Farnell, addressing the ontological object-framework of virtual reality sound design. 'It can have trees, cars, buildings, animals and people [but] perhaps the most fundamental object is the player object' (2010: 316). I make my way down the sloping aisle towards the exit.

Boom.
A storm.
  'That's dramatic', I think, as we exit the auditorium via a side door. Such a thin shell that only a moment ago contained a universe.
  Rain, like the surge of white noise as a cable becomes dislodged behind the television.
  A flash across the sky. A cylindrical line of air that has turned into plasma heated to thirty-thousand degrees centigrade, carving a jag through the atmosphere, ten thousand times the atmospheric pressure of the surrounding, cooler air. The zig-zag effect is caused by the lightning strike following a path of ionized particles that offer the least resistance. It is called tortuosity. The shockwaves it makes each time it changes direction – every twelve feet or so – and the explosion, when it strikes the ground, rank as some of the loudest noises in nature. They bounce around the landscape and the buildings. They also bounce around an index of other possibilities.
  Proper thunder; like in a horror film.
  Once thunder was sacred; an expression of disruption in the balance of cosmic harmony. This thunder is profane: a thrill.
  Another big bang! – I hear the exclamation mark of Lichtenstein's *Wham!* (1963). Big Bang! is meme, first coined by the popular press in the UK to

describe the sound made by 6,700 tonnes of explosives detonated by the Royal Navy on the uninhabited Heligoland islands off the northwest of Germany, in 1947. It was thus already known as a popular phrase inflected with media hyperbole, when Fred Hoyle used it in 1949 on the radio – a medium that loves sound effects – to describe the alternative cosmological theory to his own 'steady state' one. This big bang makes a car alarm go off, and I am on the set of an action movie.

I turn my phone on and connect to my network.

The sound of a claxon from the final act of any James Bond film. Or maybe the sound of Wile E. Coyote's eyes popping out of his head on stalks as he sees an anvil falling towards him. The chime of a glockenspiel. My watch connects to my phone and my wrist vibrates. My voicemail calls me and an old-fashioned telephone rings in my pocket. My wrist bleeps electronically. There is a theatre about my person. I get many messages.

■

4

Present
(A theatre about our person)

Inscape

> Auditory space has no point of favored focus. It's a sphere without fixed boundaries, space made by the thing itself, not space containing the thing. Auditory space is not pictorial space, boxed-in, but dynamic, always in flux, creating its own dimensions moment by moment.
>
> CARPENTER and McLUHAN, 1960: 67

Well, not quite. Not in an acoustic world reprogrammed by art and conditioned by audio media, where the forms that life uses to shape itself come from loudspeakers and headphones as well as actions. Here, auditory space is more the opposite: pictorial; boxed-up in scenes; triangulated by the stories, meta-discourses and practices of sound. Here is a picture-box theatre. Here is resonance contained within a nested framework of cells; the storyboard or comic strip-like format according to which we have partitioned, discussed and performed our sensibility. A taxonomic display cabinet. An Instagram reality. A city block reality; thunder resonating within it. The idea of auditory space as a wide-open sphere, a boundless escape (e-*scape* denoting a movement out of the picture frame; the suffix -*scape*, as in landscape or soundscape, denoting a pictorial conception) is, like sonic immersivity, another Romantic tableau. Here, auditory space is an inscape; a retreat into pictorial boxes. The audio object-oriented framework that shapes the present is motivated by inscapism, not escapism, a movement into the frame.

When you arrive at Complicité's *The Encounter*, you find a pair of Sennheiser headphones hanging on the arm of your seat. You see Simon McBurney, Complicité's artistic director, wandering about the stage, pretending to check the microphone and the loudspeaker set up, and taping cables down. The stage is bare except for the sound equipment, multi-packs of plastic-bottled water and loudspeakers, facing inwards, set around the playing area, a desk (with more sound equipment on it) and a chair downstage-right. And then there is Fritz, the name the company has given to the binaural dummy head microphone, set centre-stage, facing the audience. This set-up is the ontology of the show Helen Skiera referred to (see Chapter 1): the fictional ontology not of an escapist, but an inscapist second life; a wireframe model of diegetic aural being of a narrated *I am*.

Anechoic soundproofing covers the back wall. As part of the devising process, sound designer Gareth Fry spent time in a pitch-black anechoic chamber, recording McBurney talking from the depths of his imagination. In an anechoic chamber, all ambient noise and reverberation has been eliminated. The outwardly expanded, auratic space of the auditory imagination (seemingly centred on the monophonic think-point) takes over; there is no external, acoustic world for it to process. The mind is revealed to be all there is. McBurney had read how Yuval Noah Harari came to realize, through an experience of prolonged silence, that his sense of reality was mainly a set of fictional narratives (Complicité/McBurney, 2016: iv–viii). Since *The Encounter* was shaping up to be a show about intertwining narratives that constituted senses of here and there, now and then, and inside and out, Harari's account inspired McBurney to come here to the anechoic chamber.

Here, he experiences the famous anechoic chamber effect whose identification is commonly attributed to John Cage, that there is no silence in a soundless room. One's breathing, heartbeat and circulating bodily fluids take over one's ears. Being of an anxious, fracturing *Zeitgeist*, he worries that the artefacts generated by the random firing of his auditory nerves, deprived of the usual constant stimulation of the chaotic acoustic plenum, are something more sinister. He resolves to get his ears checked for tinnitus. When asked later to describe the anechoic experience, McBurney answered 'disorientating'. When asked how that felt, he replied 'familiar' (ibid.: frontmatter).

Back in the Barbican, we don the headphones that hang on the arms of our seats. They are playing a message on loop, identifying which is the left and which is the right earpiece.

Before long, McBurney shambles to the forestage and casually begins to address us, asking that phones be switched off and talking about latecomers. It is a soft overture, but it still functions to separate the ear and the eye (as Barenboim advises an overture should do). His conversational, expositional manner suggests that the show is yet to begin, but hearing is being formatted as he 'draws the audience into another kind of attention, through the description of how the evening will unfold' (ibid.: 6). First the ear understands, then the eye sees.

Once drawn into this other kind of attention, it becomes clear that the show has started, although we are still some way away from the beginning of the story. McBurney first introduces its meta-discourse, about the diegetic nature of truth. He takes a selfie for his daughter, and then talking about how her life might be seen to consist in the vast sequence of pictures on his phone. He then pulls out a videotape, which in a 'faux' accident gets broken, the tape spilling out onto the stage. Later, tramping through this becomes the practical sound effect of jungle undergrowth. McBurney then moves to a microphone and into our headphones, and we are in an audio lecture-demonstration. He is now closer to us than he is to his children, he explains, because instead of whispering in our ear, he is in the middle of our heads. Like Sean Connery narrating the *Young Person's Guide to the Orchestra*, he introduces us to the technology and explains the theme of the show, when really, like Britten's narrator, he is planting the theme and its variations in our minds so that later he can work a grand fugue.

There are multiple microphones. One, it is demonstrated, is mono, places the voice in the centre of our heads and can be used for digitally altering the pitch of the voice so that McBurney can adopt a different narratorial vocal persona. Another is the binaural dummy head that creates a spatial, stereo effect, seemingly around the outside of our heads. Four monitor speakers surround it, through which audio can be played. As the show unfolds, we will also be shown a variety of live practical sound effects (reams of video tape, the plastic bottles), loop pedals that can transform these sounds into jungle rhythms. We will be shown that McBurney is also wearing a radio mic, and about his person there is a mobile phone, an iPod, and a handheld portable Bluetooth speaker.

Later, at the 'backstage secrets' talk, Fry points out that while this rig might seem complex, compared to most multi-channel, multi-speaker theatre set-ups, it is really very simple. Everything is mixed down to only two output channels, sent directly to the left and the right ears of everyone in the room. Other sound and music effects are mixed live into this two-channel output mix, by two operators – one on music, one on sound-processing effects – who partly improvise in response to McBurney's performance. The show's reality framework, or 'ontology', consists in a dialectical space between the mono sound of the internal monologue and the narrator, and the 3D binaural sound heard by Fritz. The music comes in standard left/right stereo, arranged on a line that bisects the headspace, from ear to ear. The show is a process. A multiplex of stories becomes a simple two-channel truth, but these two channels contain many spatial dynamics. The identically reproduced experience of it sets the audience together by the ears, in Dekker's phrase, but the headphones also set them apart.

In AI or virtual reality theory, a process ontology is concept-oriented and works in parallel to the object-oriented interactivity of gameplay. It indexes all the possible ways of encountering a set-up of concepts within a closed system or domain, which will define the interrelationship between those concepts during that encounter. In other words, it defines a subjectivity. It acts as a conceptual framework for the world creation of interactive gameplay. It takes care of the governing logic of the game world, of sound-emitting nodes and the procedures by which they become audible, re-orientate and interact in a constantly reconfiguring disposition with the first-person player's avatar. This constitutes the internal truth of the fiction.

Continuing his exposition, McBurney maps the ontological set-up of the stage to the two intersecting spaces the spectator inhabits. First, there is the auratic space that surrounds the mono, centre-point of the internal monologue, or seat of consciousness somewhere behind the eyes at the centre of the 'two-and-a half pounds of electrified pâté between the ears'.[1] Second, there is an external space, or the illusion of one, facilitated by the binaural effect that comes from Fritz, which extends beyond the pâté auditorium out into the Barbican auditorium and beyond, as far as the imagination will allow.

He demonstrates the concept of binaural '3D' audio by asking us to close our eyes and telling us that he is going to take a walk around our heads. The demonstration amplifies the effect – we are listening for it. Our eyes still closed, he suggests we should have the impression that he is *really* beside us, that this is not digital manipulation, but what he is really doing. He moves closer to the dummy head and wonders if this is too intimate, as he opens one of the water bottles and takes a drink at what seems to be around six inches away from our head (the shared head that has been constructed as this performance's auditorium, its instrument of agency for hearing).

To give a sense of how the brain mistakes fiction for reality, McBurney explains that he is going to breathe into one of our ears and that it will feel like it is heating up. He does, and perhaps it does. The head theatre believes it does. Afterwards, there is much talk of how it really did. He then gives the head theatre a haircut, and – its eyes still closed – introduces a mosquito sound effect, declaring 'now there's this damned mosquito flying around'. He asks the theatre to open its eyes, and we see he has the Bluetooth speaker in his hand and has been circling it round Fritz. That was where the mosquito sound was coming from. As he explains this, his live voice switches to a recording of the same monologue, in which he explains that even the recording was not of a real mosquito, but of someone with a comb and toilet paper, imitating one.

We get the point: frames within frames within frames of artifice and narrative. Then begins a conversation with a recording machine that answers back, with attitude. We get the gag. Machines that talk back – from automata

---

[1] Line used in Barbican run, 2016; not in the published text.

in the nineteenth century to Kubrick's HAL in *2001: A Space Odyssey* – are an old routine, a trope. It leads into another principle of the diegesis: the interplay between time-frames. Both voices are McBurney's in the same conversational register:

Live . . . This is something that happened six months ago, when we were working on the show. Excuse me, can you turn the mosquito off now.

Recording *What?*

Live Can you turn that off; it's really annoying.

Recording You want me to turn it off?

Live Yes, it's really annoying.

Recording *Okay.*

Live Thank you. My voice over there is a recording, he doesn't exist.

Recording What do you mean I don't exist?

Live You're not real.

Recording Well, of course I'm real.

Live He's a recording from the past.

ibid.: 10

Having established that recordings from the past have minds of their own, McBurney then takes us to his flat, where he claims the recording was made six months earlier. The onstage table is now his home desk, he mimes the opening of a window on the upstage, imaginary rear. The sounds of the street outside are played through one of the onstage monitor speakers and relayed to our topographic sense of the flat's layout by the dummy head. He goes to the sink and washes his hands. There is the sound effect of running water, which the whole theatre hears just behind its right ear. A voice appears from one of the onstage speakers, which is introduced as that of his daughter, who asks who he is talking to and how long that head thing is going to be in the flat. Then the voice of Marcus du Sautoy, the Oxford Professor for the Public Understanding of Science, arrives in the flat, to explain how time may just be a fiction, something that we have made up to make sense of the world. Another recording.

Finally, after about half an hour of this set-up, we arrive at the fugue – the story that will bring all these layered narrational spaces, nested frames, fragmented recordings and the delight of their 'declared' theatrical trickery, as Fry calls it, into one counterpoint. The story, incidentally, is about a *National*

Geographic photographer's trip up the Amazon. The source of the Amazon becomes an ecological metaphor for the reunification of fractured aurality; the repossession of a singular, holistic god sound that 'fills all the space outside me, inside me and fuses the source and the beginning into one notion' (ibid.: 58). The noises of the jungle and the fractured, dispositional, fictional ontology of the show's format recompose as music. The diegetic layers of the show unpeel, through its various narratorial voices, to the sound effect of the second narrator's typewriter, to that of McBurney, the first, who recaps the ecological moral of the story through a parable of Amazonian Mayorunan people that he is recounting to the audio recording of his daughter. The final sound is her breathing, asleep.

This is what I mean by an audio-object framework of reality. *Audio*, coincidentally, is Latin for *I hear*.

Personal audio/immersive theatre

> A common perspective is first person, where the view is cast through the eyes of the player object [. . .] This is the most popular configuration and leads to an *immersive experience* of being within the player character as a 'spirit' or a homunculus that possess the player object.
>
> FARNELL, 2010: 316

The hundreds of headphones used in *The Encounter* were provided by Sennheiser, whose marketing strategy has been to associate the idea of *immersive audio* with the fashion for *immersive theatre*, *immersive gaming*, and curated *immersive experiences* (e.g., the V&A's *David Bowie Is* exhibit – also sound-designed by Gareth Fry). 'Immersive' is a publicity buzzword in each case, but one that references the widely recognized, holistic and characteristically Romantic idea of aural subjectivity as trope for any kind of totalized or immersed relationship to an environment. One might, however, argue that, in each case, the identifying of these kinds of forms or products as 'immersive' is in fact an inversion of the Romantic immersion trope, as it is the theatre that becomes enclosed in a reconstruction of the self as a first-person player, listener, tourist or spectator *object*. A form of theatricalization is achieved by adopting an apparatus that estranges one's subjectivity from its usual relationship to the environment, and makes a theatre of one's personal subjectivity. This apparatus is not merely the headset itself, but ranges from the publicity languages and the ideas these languages recognize, to the configurations and technologies of the production, the mode of attentiveness prepared by prologues and pre-show dramaturgies, and the reality-framework or ontology explicated in pre-show briefings or demonstrations. In an essay called 'The Corporeality of Listening: Experiencing Soundscapes as Audio Guides', Holger Schultze identifies the exhibition as a narrativized, spatial, temporal and narrative aural architecture (so, characteristically diegetic) and the audio headsets used as guides in museums as its paradigmatic instrument (in Bijsterveld, 2014: 195–208). Schultze mobilizes the idea of the 'auditory dispositive', which Rudolph Grossman had adapted from Baudry's apparatus-theory of the *dispositif* of cinema, according to which

> the cinema setting and the viewing position of the film reproduction and projection technology, the cinema setting and the viewing position of the film audience [are] key elements of a material and situated disposition, a dispositive (in French) for experiencing film.
>
> 197

At the centre of this expansive industrial, commercial and technological apparatus is the body, and the orientation of the self that lives within it. Schultze describes how, in the dynamic between the headspace of the headphones and the outer space of the museum, the hearer experiences 'spacing and re-spacing' as the 'listening body keeps recalibrating itself' (202). He describes, with reference to Janet Cardiff's audio walks, how the narrative component of the mobile headphone dispositive mimics the way the voice in one's head tells us a story about the surrounding world, through presenting a diegesis that is neither stable nor linear, but which

> shifts and rises, [. . .] gets weakened and strengthened by signals and signs in [the] environment and by [the aural subject's] proprioceptive dynamics during the day. We might digress, we may have associations with the work we need to do in the next hours or days, or we are reminded of friends, lovers, family or colleagues, or imagine personal fictitious worlds. Somehow we have to integrate and synthesize the sounds of the venue, the voice on our audio guide, the story it tells and our shifting imagination.
>
> 202–3

The narratorial layers and conceits in *The Encounter*, and the mapping of the onstage ontological set-up to the shared head auditorium achieved by the hundreds of identical headphones, integrates and synthesizes the sense of 'theatre' that surrounds the spectators, within the 'venue' of their shifting auditory imaginations and its space, which is centred on the mono think-point, apparently at the centre of what feels like quasi-acoustic intracranial space. *The Encounter* reconfigures the aural subjectivity of each spectator identically, and transforms their plurality into the singularity of what Farnell, above, terms a first-person player object, who encounters a self-contained truth within a story told within – *and with* – a concept-oriented ontological framework and an object-oriented audio-framework. *The Encounter* uses the exposition of psychoacoustic principles, ontological rules and the mapping of the onstage set-up to the spatial orientation of the spectator, to bring to the sedentary, fixed-seat auditorium the kind of dynamic spacing and re-spacing of the proprioceptive body that is characteristic of promenade immersive theatre forms.

Immersive theatre has, since its inception, frequently involved headphones,[2] although usually as part of a promenade or 'in the round' configuration (e.g., Rosenberg's *Ring*; Fuel tour, 2015). One might see this as part of a meta-project to reconfigure and refit an auditorium that reflects the modality of audio listenership in the mobile, personal audio age. The flâneuristic, theatrical effect of spacing and re-spacing, as the aural body perpetually recalibrates itself according to head-sound superimposed on the estranged external environment, entered common auditory experience with the Walkman in the early 1980s. Listening to music or other audio programming in acoustically isolated personal space while on the move, either on foot or in cars, is, for many people, now the default. The interconnected principles of the dynamically proprioceptive auditorium, and of inscape – the inversion of the totalizing immersive relationship, whereby encounters with the world *out there* are staged *in here*, within the apparently 'empty' acoustic space inside the head (which does not feel like it is full of electrified pâté, as McBurney puts it) – seem only to have grown in relevance since first-person, interactive, experience-based immersive theatre began to emerge as an identifiable category, at the same time as the internet arrived in domestic life in the late 1990s.

The hi-fi cell

The aural inscape – a paradigm of immersivity that is precisely the pictorial, boxed-in space that McLuhan and Carpenter said auditory space was not; which inverts the Romantic figure of the submission of the self to the subject-dissolving ocean of everything (or of oblivion); and which instead encloses a virtual world within the circumference and control of a first-person player

---

[2] E.g., wilson+wilson *passim*, notably *House* (1998); Blast Theory's *Desert Rain* (2000); Back to Back's *Soft* (2002) and *Small Metal Objects* (2005); Rimini Protokoll's *Sonde Hannover* (2002); Red Shift's *Invisible Shows* (2010–11); National Theatre of Wales/Mike Pearson's silent-disco technology-based *Coriolan/Us* (2012); several by Rotozaza and David Rosenberg (ongoing).

object (or actor) – is countenanced by a longer history than that of headphone audio. In Chapter 6, I shall trace it back to the eighteenth century, taking the aesthetic praxis of the Picturesque as an example, which reconfigured the sublime as a picture-box theatre – an artificial world of controllable scenery and effects (both literally, and as a recreational disposition when out and about in the landscape). The auditory dispositive that went with this reconfigured world – the picturesque auditorium – was one in which the audibility of the environment was placed in the service of a desired scenic effect and genre (wild, rustic, quaint, exotic, thrilling and so on). In the late twentieth century, the adoption of headphones as a technology of the self closed the picturesque auditorium in on, and into, the aural subject. However, this process of the self-enclosure of the recreational aesthete within a proprioceptive soundscape (the suffix -*scape* indicating a delimited, tableau-like, and thus, according to Barthes, representational hearing of the environment) had long been in development.

The picturesque logic that the sonic world serves a tableau view and has a front/back/left/right obliterates the sublime notion that aural space has no point of favoured focus and is a sphere without fixed boundaries, always in flux, creating its own dimensions moment by moment. Sound becomes like a room. The surround-sound auditorium, with loudspeakers facing in on the audience from all sides, and the basic stereo configuration of front left/right, each superimposed a proprioceptive organization of audio objects on the independent dimensionality of boundless, spherical acoustics, and thus becomes the dispositive of a self-picturing disposition.

The domestic counterpart to this kind of dispositive, the home hi-fi set-up, is worth discussing briefly because the publicity that contributed conditions to the audibility of hi-fi, as a set of identifiable qualities and aesthetic affects, also imparted an insidious gender exclusivity to the figure of sound as an aesthetically appreciable, and designable, scenic element. In his account of the gender-encoding of the space of twentieth-century consumer audio, '"Turn It Down!" She Shrieked: Gender, Domestic Space, and High Fidelity, 1948–49', Kier Keightley describes the hi-fi dispositive as a kind of auditory playpen or enclosure within the home that was marketed, in sexist terms, mainly at men. As evidenced in a supposedly humorous observation in an early (1945) hi-fi journal, the narrative went like this: expensive loudspeakers sound great in the show room, but never as good at home with the kids making noise during the day, or 'the wife' constantly nagging 'you' (the presumed male reader) to 'turn it down' at night, so as not to wake them up. To get away from it all, what the man needs, the article suggests, is a kind of 'Yogi Enclosure' – a room just big enough for him to sit cross-legged in the 'Yoga position' right in front of the hi-fi loudspeaker (at this point, still mono):

The listener sits in his own enclosure which is an extension of the speaker enclosure ... the walls of the enclosure are constructed of soundproof material to insure protection against outside noises, and, for the sake of privacy, a door that can be locked from the inside is provided.

Quoted in KEIGHTLEY, 1996: 149

There would, of course, need to be a slot to allow 'your wife to slip you a sandwich now and then, and warn you in the event of a fire', the article quips.

Stereo

The hi-fi cell that kept the hearer in solitary confinement from the mundane irritations of everyday domesticity soon became a stereo cell, with its privileged *sweet spot*, at the apex of an equilateral triangle formed by the hearer and the two loudspeakers. The story goes that the British electronics engineer Alan Blumlein had the idea for stereophony in 1931, while watching an 'audible picture', or 'talkie', as the new format was variously known during the transition period from silent cinema to sound.

The year 1931 was key in the development of audio form and aesthetics, which was a topic of public debate. In Britain, the widely read *BBC Yearbook* ran a prolonged special feature on sound effects and the form and dramaturgy of 'microphone drama' (which I shall discuss in Part Three). Television was already being discussed, but silent films were also competing with the new audio media and undergoing something of an artistic resurgence, with films such as Chaplin's *City Lights* and Murnau's *Tabu*. The assumption was that both formats would continue, and radio, silent film, sound film and the anticipated TV formats would each sustain different forms of drama and dramaturgy that were quite distinct from those of the stage. Also in 1931, the gothic horror genre found its archetypal audio-cinematic form in Whale's *Frankenstein*, with its Castle Thunder, and Mamoulian's *Jekyll and Hyde* (whose sonic innovation I shall describe later). Perhaps it was one of these that Blumlein was watching when he had the idea for stereophony.

Blumlein thought that the audible picture would be improved if the sounds were located on the screen, near to their visible sources, and if the sound of the actors could follow them across the screen. Given the delimited tableau of the screen and its distance from the majority of the auditorium, he could see how this might be achieved by using left and right loudspeakers behind the screen, to imitate the binary differentials of wave arrivals at the ears, which accounted for the psychoacoustic ability to locate a spatial tableau of sound on the theatre stage. He patented his 'Improvements in and relating to Sound-transmission, Sound-recording and Sound-reproducing Systems' in

1933, and demonstrated the stereo effect at that year's Chicago World Fair. In fact, because of the noisy environment, rather than demonstrating it with loudspeakers, he used a system whereby a pair of stereo headphones reproduced the effect of microphones placed in the ears of a hatter's dummy. This was an early prototype of the 'binaural stereo' set-up used in *The Encounter*, rather than the crossed-pair microphone system, still named after Blumlein, that became the standard way of recording 'true' stereo in the 1950s for classical and jazz LPs ('true' as opposed to stereo mixes of mono sound sources, constructed in the studio, the main method for making stereo soundtracks and pop LPs).

The wider public did not get to hear about stereo until seven years later, through the publicity for Disney's *Fantasia* (1940) – a portmanteau film of popular orchestral music set, like music videos, to dialogue-free animated sequences featuring Disney cartoon characters. Far fewer actually got to hear it for themselves. When they did, it was not in relation to the simple left/right format Blumlein had imagined. The lure of immersivity had led Disney to go straight past left/right stereo to a multi-speaker surround system. *Fantasia* was toured, with much fanfare, to a few selected theatres, in Fantasound. This was a 'two-in, five-out' (a two-track recording feeding five speaker locations) surround-sound system, whereby a decoder distributed the two stereo tracks in the optical soundtrack around the auditorium according to a pre-set matrix of phase and tonal differentials.

The idea for this did not come from a desire for musical immersivity, but from a sound effect. Disney had been dining with the conductor Stokowski, who had been involved in earlier tests and demonstrations of stereo, and they had agreed that it would amaze the audience if the sound of the bumblebee in 'The Flight of the Bumblebee' section of *Fantasia* could be made to move around the auditorium. The pursuit of this idea in Disney's labs would give the recording industry the panorama potentiometer, or 'pan pot', which allows the sound present in the input channel of a mixing console to be dynamically 'panned', or moved, by incrementally changing the balance of signal being sent simultaneously to two or more output channels. Fantasound, however, flopped. Its 1940 prototype cost over $2 million, but when *Fantasia* failed to break even in simple two-output-channel stereo and traditional mono releases, the system was abandoned.

In a strange twist, Walt Disney, as war approached, agreed to sell most of the equipment to Josef Stalin, who was a Disney fan and had been personally interested by the publicity for the Fantasound system. The ship carrying it across the North Atlantic to the Soviet Union, however, was torpedoed by a U-boat. Thus, as Helen Mitchell puts it, 'somewhere at the bottom of the ocean lie the remains of the first chapter in the story of cinematic surround sound' (2006: 3). Fantasound stood as the only such system until the

'Quintaphonic' surround-sound system put together at the behest of Pete Townshend, who had a spiritual as well as a commercial interest in deep musical immersivity, for the Leicester Square premiere of the film of The Who's rock opera *Tommy* in 1975. An American audio engineer named Ray Dolby, who had made his name developing a noise-reduction filter for hi-fi record production, worked on the matrix encoding algorithm for the film. He would go on to patent Dolby Surround Sound and become synonymous with the public conception of theatrically immersive audio (Townshend, 2012: 272).

After the flop of Fantasound, two-speaker stereo eventually reached a mass audience when it was incorporated into the widescreen Cinerama system in 1952. It was Vincent Price's 3D horror film *House of Wax* (1953) that first sold the idea to the paying public that stereo was an essential enhancement for the fully immersive experience of widescreen, 3D movies. Thenceforth, movie poster words such as *immersive*, *living*, *3D* and *spectacular* started to be emblazoned across hi-fi advertisements and on the sleeves of stereo records. Again, the marketing strategy tended to promote this immersive fantasy space as a male one that excluded women. As *Hi-Fi Review* put it:

> This is the space age. Not just for sputniks and moonshots but also for Hi-Fi. We have 'space' conveyed through stereo sound – if we can find space for that extra stereo speaker. The theory that space is limited is nothing new to the average housewife.
>
> FANTEL, 1959: 49

Space is the extent of things; in this case, shiny objects of male desire.

The need for programme content for this domestic audio cell which showcased the quality of these shiny objects led to a welter of record releases whose ostensible purpose was to showcase different proprietary production systems. Both Blumlein and Disney's original ideas for stereo had arisen from a desire to recreate effects of movement in sound effects. Before the development of dynamic studio 'panning' of musical elements in the early 1960s (notably by Mexican bandleader and 'The King of Space Age Pop', known, always with the comic-book bubble exclamation mark, as Esquivel!, and then subsequently in psychedelic genres), music was presumed to be a static tableau of sound, whose instrumental sound sources did not move around on the platform or in the tableau. Stereo, however, was best showcased by movement, and so these records focused on dynamic sound effects. New musical genres developed that counterposed music and sound in the manner of motion picture soundtracks, which we shall discuss later, and a new market arose for sound effect LPs that were full of moving sounds. These were not for amateur dramatics or home movie use, but simply high-quality recordings of steam trains, thunderstorms, explosions, church bells and other extremes of sound, whose veracity, when played on a particular system, could be authoritatively adjudicated.

KEIGHTLEY, 1996: 152

A new indexical function for recorded sound effects thus arises, within the dramaturgy of hearing of the hi-fi age: of recorded sound effects as demonstrative capsules of consumer audio qualities to which the anecdotal semantics of their causal identity are coincidental. Flimsy plot devices – often travelogues – were sometimes invented to string the effects together, or else genre-based themes (horror sound effects, spectacular sound effects, and so on).

The 'typical' purchaser of such records was called a 'sound-for-its-sound-sake [sic]' enthusiast by a HiFi & Music Review article in 1958. The article begins: 'Addict or realist? This is the question neighbours ask when assaulted by "weird" and inexplicable noises from that Hi-Fi system next door. Some Hi-Fiers, rather than immerse themselves in operatic or chamber music, or even rock 'n' roll, listen for the joy of just "hearing" sounds not likely to be found in the average living room.'

ibid.

*

SKIP FORWARD ▶▶

'Alexa: what sounds are not likely to be found in a living room?'
   'Hmm, I don't know that.'
  'What sounds do you know?'
   'I can play thunderstorms, rain, ocean waves, babbling brook, fireplace, aeroplane, fan, oscillating fan, city, rainforest, train, crickets, frogs, birds, clock, cat, hoover, pink noise, brown noise, white noise, wind, windy leaves, windy trees, rain on a tin roof, rain on a tent, light rain, rain on a window, distant thunderstorm, shower, space deck, hair dryer, clothes dryer, dishwasher, fountain, waterfall, forest night, washing machine, heartbeat, café, dream, blizzard, owl, underwater, a random sound. What sound would you like me to play?' (Amazon Alexa, 30 March 2019).
   'Alexa, stop'.

■

I open Voice Memos on my phone to record an idea for the book. I press the big red spot.

RECORD ●
Sound effects continue to crowd in around *us*, and define our aesthetics, and so theatre is by no means beyond the era of sound effects. Within the continuing space-age, where not only sounds and audio objects but sound settings, preferences, options, thematic schemes and the aesthetic user-interface shells that encase the kernels of our ontological operating systems (these are real computing terms), constitute the normalized reality of sound effects, the old-fashioned sound effects that designer-theatre once found cringeworthy now seem strange and beautiful. Where her 'multimedia' productions that began with *Waves* (2006) expose audio studio techniques, Katie Mitchell's *Nowhere Bound* (Aldeburgh Festival, 2010), which examined Samuel Beckett's obsession with Schubert's *Winterreise* song-cycle, was performed on an array of practical sound effects, at the centre of which stood a monumental wind machine – as much a piece of set as a practical sound device. The music critic Alex Ross described how:

> A constant stream of electronic and handmade noise, in the style of an old-school radio play, underpinned the music. [Stephen] Dillane, who assumed the role of the journeying protagonist, breathed heavily into a microphone and mimicked the sound of feet crunching on snow. (Tenor, Mark) Padmore, even when he was singing, busied himself turning [the] wind machine, rustling twigs, pouring water from a jug into a cup, and so on. [Pianist, Andrew] West was also given various sound-effect assignments. At times, it seemed as though 'Winterreise' were being played alongside John Cage's 'Water Walk' or some other exercise in conceptual composition [. . .]. Whenever I felt ready to immerse myself in either artist's threadbare world, the multitasking interrupted my reverie.
>
> ROSS, 2010

And so it does.
PAUSE ❚❚

'Alexa, what is reverie?'
　'The noun reverie *is usually defined as a state of dreamy meditation or fanciful musing' (ibid.).*
　'That's what I thought. Thanks. Reverie is a romantic trope, but dissensus and interruption characterize the new theatricality, and maybe a post-romantic aesthetic. What do you think, Alexa? Can distraction and interrupted reverie have an aesthetic?'
　She makes that echoey blooping sound. A gentle reminder to walk the dog.

RECORD ●

Recorded sound effects might be on the way out. The indexing of aurality according to sound effects catalogues might be on the way out. Procedures and performance, rather than recording, are of interest again. Practical sound effects are of interest again too, not least to the designers of virtual assistants, because they perform sound according to the kind of process-ontology used in procedural audio – the advanced sound synthesis now being used in game programming and artificial intelligence. This means the game or virtual assistant does not need to rely on a bank of pre-recorded samples but can make sounds up as it goes along. With procedural audio,

> synthesised crowds can burst into applause or shouting; complex weather systems where the wind speed affects the sound of the rainfall; rain that sounds different when falling on roofs or into water; realistic footsteps that automatically adapt to player speed, ground texture and incline – the dynamic possibilities are practically endless.
>
> FARNELL, 2010: 322

Once, theatre drew its temporary perimeter circle in space and time to ritualistically exclude the accidental (noise) and make a performance of social intentionality through sound. It is clear that throughout the twentieth century, regardless of whether the theatre in question is that of the playhouse, the cinema, radio or the computer game, the formal aesthetics, marketing narratives and new recreational applications by which the audio object-oriented framework of contemporary aurality has been configured, have been determined by the pursuit of a kind of utopian desire for an inscaped theatricality that excludes the mundane (in the hi-fi cell, the headphone theatre).

Through a diegetic process of narration or declared aleatory rules, theatre has tamed the accidental, just as it had tamed the sublime. In the remainder of this book, I want to look further at how theatre modelled an inscape from the outside world, and at the relationship between theatricality and audio in more detail. I want to trace the origins of the acoustemology of recorded sound effects and lived experience described in previous chapters. But where to begin? An obvious place would be the first use of recorded sound on the theatrical stage. As the dissensual operation of cracking open the obviousness of the given is a trope of this book, we will start there. I can tell you now that it will prove a false start, and we will need to head further back. Nevertheless, it is a great yarn.

PAUSE ❚❚
BACK ◀◀

5

A sound from the suburbs (The curious story of Colonel Gouraud)

In the mid-1880s, Colonel Charles Gouraud, the head of Thomas Edison's European office in London, persuaded the great inventor, back home in his New Jersey palace of innovation, Menlo Park, to give the idea of sound recording another go.

Edison had prototyped and publicly demonstrated the first phonograph in 1877 but, realizing the impracticalities and limitations of the tinfoil recording medium, had not mass produced and released the machine on the commercial market. Rumours were that Edison had lost interest and did not really believe recording had a future, but seeing others, including Alexander Graham Bell's Volta Laboratory, threatening to corner the market, Gouraud (who saw modernity and commerce as theatre) took it upon himself to convince Edison that he could find a way for sound recording to capture the public imagination. Edison agreed to relaunch the 'Perfected Phonograph' in 1888. While Gouraud flew into action with a theatrical publicity strategy in London, Edison wrote a mealy-mouthed article for *The North American Review*:

> Rumors, I understand, have been circulated to the effect that, subsequently to my announcements made ten years ago, I allowed the phonograph to go adrift, leaving its further development to chance and to the tender mercies of such disinterested persons, not connected with me, as might conceive that they were doing me a favor by claiming to have developed my idea.
>
> EDISON, 1888: 641

Edison was excited by recorded sound in principle but less visionary when it came to its practical applications. He writes enthusiastically about the relationship of wave-motions to the twin quadrivial gods of mathematics and music, and 'the conception of Pythagoras that number and harmony constituted the principle of the Universe', but his suggestions for his device's potential uses lacked panache:

1. Letter writing and all kinds of dictation without the aid of a stenographer.
2. Phonographic books, which would speak to blind people without effort on their part.
3. The teaching of elocution.
4. Reproduction of music.
5. The 'Family Record', a registry of sayings, reminiscences, etc., by members of a family, in their own voices, and of the last words of dying persons.
6. Music boxes and toys.
7. Clocks that should announce in articulate speech the time for going home, going to meals, etc.
8. The preservation of languages, by exact reproduction of the manner of pronouncing.
9. Educational purposes; such as preserving the explanations made by a teacher, so that the pupil can refer to them at any moment, and spelling or other lessons placed upon the phonograph for convenience in committing to memory.
10. Connection with the telephone, so as to make that invention an auxiliary in the transmission of permanent and invaluable records, instead of being the recipient of momentary and fleeting communications. Every one of these uses the perfected phonograph is now ready to carry out.

ibid.: 647

This list was reproduced from the original 1877 press-release, but then, in the 1888 version, there is an addition, and I think we are reading Gouraud's ideas, if not his words:

> I may add that, through the facility with which it stores up and reproduces music of all sorts, or whistling and recitations, it can be employed to furnish constant amusement to invalids, or to social assemblies, at receptions, dinners, etc. Any one sitting in his room alone may order an assorted supply of wax cylinders inscribed with songs, poems, piano or violin music, short stories, anecdotes, or dialect pieces, and, by putting them on his

phonograph, he can listen to them as originally sung or recited by authors, vocalists and actors, or elocutionists.

ibid.

An electric house

Gouraud cut a theatrical dash. He had made his headquarters, Little Menlo, in a large neo-gothic mansion house up above the smog in the hills south of London in the suburb of Upper Norwood, an area where theatricality and sonic innovation seemed to be topographically linked. Once a dense oak forest, the area had been home to the folkloric figure Grimes the Collier (meaning charcoal burner) of Croydon, the subject of more than one early seventeenth-century play. Pepys wrote of excursions to the area to visit the fortune-telling Norwood Gypsies, a large Romany settlement who became the subject of an eponymous pantomime at Covent Garden in 1777.[1]

In 1831, the architect Decimus Burton, responsible for London Zoo and much of the most theatrical Regency architecture in London, designed a picturesque and cottage *orné* style of pleasure gardens there, called Beulah Spa, in a natural amphitheatre overlooked by a columnated Grecian crescent, which resembled the dress circle of a grand Palladian theatre. Like actors on its stage, day-trippers from London would take themed, theatrical promenades through the faux rustic edifices. En route they would encounter picturesque thrills such as the black stunt rider Pablo Fanque (who would go on to become Britain's first black theatrical impresario and feature in the Beatles' 1967 song 'Being for the Benefit of Mr Kite'). Fanque, at the time (in the 1840s), was riding for Astley's Circus, whose original amphitheatre, down the hill in Lambeth, had been a precursor to Victorian spectacular and animal melodrama in the 1770s. Astleys introduced the modern white-faced circus clown routine, whose accompanying madcap military-style percussion, tightly synched to the choreographed pratfalling, became a feature of music hall slapstick, remains part of English pantomime, and was the provenance of the slapstick percussion of *Looney Tunes*-style cartoon comedy.

There were also balloon ascents, a *camera obscura* that could see Windsor Castle on a clear day, 'gypsy picnics', palm-reading, acrobatics and dancing. From the dress circle of Grecian crescent, this immersive experience could be watched into the night, illuminated by 'myriads of polychromatic lamps' (Holmes, 1977), the soundscape of the crowds, gypsy music, madcap

---

[1] Anonymous, although there is a manuscript of the airs and duets, and a slight 'pastoral' from the pantomime preserved at the British Museum.

percussion, the nightbirds and the babbling of the spa and charcoal burners' brooks, arrayed out below. Such was the renown of this immersive, promenade theatre (and much as theme parks today are horizontally integrated with franchised screen or stage versions), there was a West End musical, the burletta *Beulah Spa*, which opened at Madam Vestris' Olympic Theatre in Covent Garden in 1833. If I had asked Alexa to define theatricality in the mid-nineteenth century, she might have said 'Beulah Spa'.

In 1854, however, it was eclipsed by the Crystal Palace, the wonder of the industrial age, when it permanently relocated to Upper Norwood from the Great Exhibition in Hyde Park. With this and the coming of the railway, the area became a cultural nexus that combined bohemianism and glamour, attracting international figures such as the post-impressionist Camille Pisarro, Émile Zola, and, purportedly fresh from the American Civil War, Edison's agent, the larger-than-life 'Colonel' Gouraud (although there is no army record of anyone by that name of that rank). Gouraud moved in next to the abandoned Beulah Spa.

The Edison Company would retain an association with the area for many decades and attract other media innovators to the region. Logie Baird would develop television, in the same rooms in the Palace where Elsie Fogerty, a young local actress, had previously taught poetry recital and elocution before moving on to found her Central School of Speech and Drama at the Royal Albert Hall in 1906, where she did much to shape the audibility of actors on stage and screen, and, indeed, to create a meme of actorliness, through the technique she taught Olivier to overcome his stutter. The merged Edison-Bell company would later establish a factory down the hill, near Fogerty's home in Sydenham. Here, one P. G. A. H. Voigt would develop the British Electric Recording System, design loudspeakers, and in the 1920s establish a pictorial logic for radio aurality, to which I shall return. Gouraud's residence was opened in 1888 as a kind of technological show home that also served as Edison's European headquarters. Little Menlo stood at one of the highest points in metropolitan London, overlooking the ruins and outmoded theatricality of Beulah Spa a hundred yards or so away, and less than a mile from the Crystal Palace.

Gouraud made and demonstrated many of the earliest surviving sound recordings both at Little Menlo and the Palace. He used both places for demonstrations of phonography to invited press and the cultural influencers who regularly visited the area. He would invite them to record and play back their own voices, a disorienting effect that most had never experienced. His trick was to let his subjects hear themselves alongside recordings of notable cultural figures of the age such as Florence Nightingale, Henry Irving or Alfred Lord Tennyson. Gouraud thus established himself as the P. T. Barnum of the new electric modernity. His Electric House on the hill opened for business in the same year as, two miles down the road to London in Brixton, Electric Avenue became one of the first streets to be lit entirely with electric light. Not only was Little Menlo lit throughout with electricity, but it was full of electrical gadgetry, including electrical shoe, window and carpet cleaners. The billiards room where Gouraud would conduct recordings and listening parties was 'a combination of a ballroom, theatre, music room, studio, reading room, salle d'armes and hall of science' (Kilgarrif, 2015). The 'electric Colonel' would be seen riding around the neighbourhood on an electric tricycle and kept an electrically powered launch on the Thames. Little Menlo was also wired for sound. It had an early prototype of the short-lived British Electrophone audio distribution system. Like its contemporary, the French Théâtrophone, this comprised an earpiece on a direct telephone line, connected to one of his phonographic sound-collecting horns at the Crystal Palace, so that guests at Little Menlo could listen to the sounds and the vastly different acoustic space of the Great Hall just up the road.

A baby cries

On the night of 5 October 1888, Gouraud steps out from his Electric House for a smoke and to survey the dark ruins of Beulah Spa, its crescent dress-circle protruding like a buried ear from the hillside.

Gouraud is thinking about item 10 on Edison's list of applications, about how to use theatre and glamour to publicize recorded sound, and introduce it, via the telephone and telegraph network, as a social medium. The prospective clients at that night's dinner were a group of men planning a new global communications network: Postmaster General Cecil Raikes, his assistant Edmund Yeates, and the long-distance telegraph expert J. C. Parkinson of Atlantic Cable. For the glamour, Sir Arthur Sullivan was also at the table, along with promoter and social networker A. M. Broadly, the business manager of Theatre Royal Drury Lane, with a rakish reputation and scandalous past in colonial India. The event ended in the billiard room with rowdy toasting and the recording of an audible (and audibly drunken) letter on the phonograph, spread across seven wax cylinders, to be sent to Edison in America (whose own phonographic missive had been played to begin proceedings). A twenty-two-minute digital transfer of this recording, including the toasting, is now freely available on the internet, and along with many of Gouraud's other celebrity recordings, is one of the oldest sound recordings in the archive.

After a long introduction in Gouraud's acquired mid-Atlantic voice, the guests each record their bit. Raikes, amusingly to contemporary ears, adopts the tempo and enunciation of someone giving dictation, as if giving the machine a chance to keep up with its transcribing. Young Yeates, his assistant, is audibly drunk. The recording is perhaps best known for Sir Arthur Sullivan's joke:

> For myself, I can only say that I am astonished and somewhat terrified at the results of this evening's experiment – astonished at the wonderful power you have developed, and terrified at the thought that so much hideous and bad music may be put on record forever.
>
> GOURAUD, 1888

Gouraud, however, as he puffs his cigar, is not thinking of recorded music, but how to promote the wax cylinder as a medium for voice messages, sonic cameos or portraits, and he has an idea.

Back in 1885, he had managed to secure free advertising for the Edison Electric Light Company by persuading Henry Irving and Bram Stoker at the Lyceum to use a stage effect he had invented for their production of Goethe's *Faust*, wherein clashing swords emitted electric sparks (Kilgarrif, 2015). Irving's productions were too big for the phonograph, but what if Edward Terry, he thinks, surveying the ruined ear, would use one at his new theatre? Like Little Menlo, Terry's Theatre on The Strand was a showplace of electric modernity, with electric lighting on stage and front of house. It even had electric bells to summon the audience from the foyer and crush bar into the auditorium and set them, electrically, together by the ears. Crucially, it specialized in quieter, domestic comedies. Thinking of Edison's fifth application – the family album – Gouraud decides to ask Terry to let him know of any appropriate forthcoming plays. But rather than the last words of a dying relative, as Edison glumly suggested, maybe a baby picture; a cameo of a newborn baby crying?

Anathema maranatha!

Gouraud realized this piece of product placement at Terry's Theatre on 24 July 1890, in Arthur Law's domestic comedy-drama *The Judge*. It failed, as did Gouraud's general stunt-based marketing strategy, and Edison fired him not long after. We might imagine the electrically convened audience taking their seats in the luxurious acoustic modernity of Terry's auditorium. We might imagine, during the play, the tinny, scratchy noises from the wings, faintly audible as one of those new wax cylinder recordings, the 'waah waah' of a baby crying barely discernible beneath the surface noise. We might then imagine the fearsome critic Clement Scott, looking down at the programme notes and reading that these strange noises represented 'the first use of the

Phonograph for stage purposes', how they were provided by Colonel Gouraud, and how they were 'those of a real infant recorded by an Edison Phonograph on Monday, 21 July 1890' (three days before press night).[2] In the aura of the electric stage light, he scrawls some notes to use in his review in *The London Illustrated News*: 'diabolical machine'; 'infinitely worse than nature'; 'anathema maranatha!' (Scott, 1890). The jig was up before it really began. Recorded sound flopped on its stage debut.

This historic first use of a recorded sound as a stage effect was promptly forgotten. Writing fourteen years later, in *The Strand* magazine, Harley Vincent seems to know nothing of Gouraud's failed experiment in product placement. He attributes the first use of phonography on stage to a recent, unspecified (1902/3?) production of *Henry V* in Berlin, but sees its potential value in relation to the cost of theatre labour rather than its modernistic aesthetic. 'The innovation is likely to spread', predicts Vincent, 'and will surely prove a considerable economy for the smaller theatre, where the outlay on stage noises of the human and musical sort is no trifle' (1904: 422). But this seems to have been a false start too. Also in 1904, a prop phonograph featured as the central comedic plot device in Feydeau's *La Main Passe* at the aptly named Théâtre des Nouveautés in Paris. It was represented as a confounded and difficult to operate device (the popular reputation of the machine), and its owner as a hapless, technological early adopter alone in his soundproof study, cuckolded by his wife. Here, the phonograph, while working and audible, was a practical prop; a cameo of itself.

It was not until the gramophone, with its higher-quality media (shellac discs rather than wax cylinders), superseded the phonograph and became a less infuriating domestic appliance, and then, even more decisively, when electric amplification superseded the acoustic horn, that recorded sound effects became useful to the stage. It was not only that amplification made gramophones louder. In the era of electric public address systems and radio, it also made them sound more 'real' within the newly inhabited modern, audio reality.

In 1935, Brecht wrote that:

Recently the gramophone industry has started supplying the stage with records of real noises. These add substantially to the spectator's illusion of not being in a theatre. Theatres have fallen on them avidly; so that Shakespeare's Romeo and Juliet is now accompanied by the real noise of the mob. So far as we know the first person to make use of records was Piscator. He applied the new technique entirely correctly. In his

---

[2] *The Judge*, 1890, play programme; Enthoven Collection, Victoria and Albert Museum.

production of the play Rasputin a record of Lenin's voice was played. It interrupted the performance.

BRECHT, 1978: 103

Piscator's interruptive use of recorded sound was 'correct', for Brecht, as a *Verfremdungseffekt* – a dissensually distancing or estranging effect – although I wonder if it is true that, in other productions, it ever fooled spectators into thinking they were not at the theatre. Even with today's high-definition technologies, a recorded or amplified sound effect is instantly recognizable as such, although this, of course, does not mean that it is not real. By the 1930s, electrically reproduced sound had become a commonplace fixture in the scenery of daily life. From the radio or radiogram that brought drama into the home to the electroacoustic cinema, the loudspeaker had changed the coordinates of the real, and had also begun to change the coordinates by which one knows whether one is in a theatre or not.

However, here we must pause.

II

I warned you that this was a false start. We will pick up from this point later, but I must interrupt the story here because the ways in which radio, cinema and the loudspeaker were able to change these coordinates has a longer history. To understand how electrically reproduced sound became part of the scenery of a theatricalized everyday life, we need to understand how everyday life became countenanced and sensible in those terms – as scenery.

⏮ *So now hear this, as we spool back in time with the sound of a radio being tuned away from Lenin's voice. The radio static becomes the rush of wind in the trees and of a gushing stream. A curtain rises. 1786.*

Picture the scene.

Birdsong; the distant sound of parish bells; a distant rumble of ominous thunder from out over the Channel.

A stage set of a rustic miller's cottage, the original prototype of the cottage orné, *flanked by leafy branches and framed by a footer of some flattage cut and painted to look like rocks, just inside the curtain line. A stone bridge crosses what we take to be the babbling brook, which is picked up in the backcloth where it snakes its way into the distant hills, expertly painted to give a hazy effect of distance.*

A rude, gypsy air plays as a woman enters, as if from a Gainsborough portrait, in Georgian dress. She is carrying a Claude Glass, an ornately framed, small blackened mirror, in one hand, and William Cowper's epic poem, The Task, *in the other. She is a Laker; a recreational tourist. She proceeds to read from her book.*

A SOUND FROM THE SUBURBS

Scenes must be beautiful which daily view'd
Please daily, and whose novelty survives
Long knowledge and the scrutiny of years.

COWPER, 1785, Book I: ll, 177–9

6

Picturing the scene

The scenic reconfiguration

The scenes which please daily and must, therefore, count as beautiful did not, in 1785, meet the established definition of pure, symmetrical, harmonious beauty. They constituted a picturesque of rugged, wild phenomena, described at length as the poem continues, in aural terms:

> Nor rural sights alone, but rural sounds
> Exhilarate the spirit, and restore
> The tone of languid Nature. Mighty winds
> That sweep the skirt of some far-spreading wood
> Of ancient growth, make music not unlike
> The dash of ocean on his winding shore,
> And lull the spirit while they fill the mind,
> Unnumber'd branches waving in the blast
> And all their leaves fast flutt'ring, all at once.
>
> COWPER, 1785, Book I, ll: 181–9

And so on, at some length – a vivid description of a landscape that 'undulates upon the list'ning ear' (l.175).

Such attention to the sounds of nature is not unusual in later Romantic poetry. However, the distinctive feature of Cowper's earlier poem is that he establishes this pleasure-oriented aurality as part of an everyday *theatre* 'whose notes/fine-finger'd art must emulate in vain' (l. 201–2).

There is something revolutionary in this, in a political as well as an aesthetic sense. Later in the same poem, Cowper makes what is thought to be is one of the earliest uses of the word 'scenery' to describe the natural landscape.[1] The 'he' in the following is a 'freeman whom the truth makes free' – the truth,

---

[1] 'scenery, n.', OED Online, 2018, www.oed.com/view/Entry/172222 [18 February 2019].

that is, of the radical new subjectivity of the age. The context is an epic account of an aesthetic and spiritual ramble through the English countryside:

> He looks abroad into the varied field
> Of Nature, and though poor perhaps, compared
> With those whose mansions glitter in his sight,
> Calls the delightful scen'ry all his own.
> His are the mountains, and the vallies his,
> And the resplendent rivers.
>
> COWPER, 1785: Book V, ll.739–43

Cowper is picturing life as a theatre, not only with his eyes, but his ears.

At the same time and as part of the same radical turn, theatre was also reconceiving drama as a living picture, with its eyes and ears. *The Task* was written almost forty years after another, more rhetorical piece of verse, also revolutionary in terms of the history of theatre and the development of a modern *mise-en-scène*. This was the oration that the actor David Garrick made on taking over the Theatre Royal Drury Lane as manager and majority shareholder, in 1747. Penned by his friend Dr Johnson, it announced Garrick's intent for a scenically true theatre. The idea of scenic truth was a revolutionary idea, and it was a project he would discuss on visits to Paris, where such revolutions were fermenting, with Diderot and the encyclopaedists and Jean Monnet, the director of the Opéra-Comique. It was Monnet who would recommend the services of the scenographic prodigy Philippe Jacques De Loutherbourg. In due course, Garrick's pictorial reconfiguration of the legitimate playhouse and De Loutherbourg's *mise-en-scène*, which was as sonically striking as it was visual, would capture the popular imagination such that 'any visit to London would take in Garrick and a visit to Drury Lane, just as tourists now feel obliged to see Madame Tussaud's and Buckingham Palace' (Stafford Clark, 2002).

With the growing middle classes and the packaging of leisure as an activity during the late eighteenth century, Garrick's scenically reconfigured drama not only revitalized the stage, but formed part of a new mode of modern living among those who had leisure time in their lives. A new sense of theatricality formed a modern aesthetic *Zeitgeist*. In precisely the way Rancière describes, a new aesthetic regime of art took hold, in which theatrical form became experienced for itself, apart from the mimetic representations of the drama, and became the form that life used to shape itself. Theatre became more than a building, an activity and an institution. It became, as Cowper's poem illustrates, a metaphor and a technique for seeing and, far more than has been typically acknowledged within the historiography of theatre, for hearing the world, and thus for taking possession of it.

The charms of sound, the pomp of show: Garrick's reconfiguration

As Romantic as this was, a commercial imperative lurks in Garrick's 1747 opening address at Drury Lane. London's legitimate theatre (licensed by the Crown to produce spoken drama approved by the Lord Chamberlain) had become lacklustre and charmless in its declamatory posturing. Audiences were turning to illegitimate theatres, where only musical drama could be performed, and which revelled in bawdy balladry and rococo sensuality. Garrick wanted to revive Shakespeare but had to recognize this popular appeal. He was convivial by nature, and wanted a convivial playhouse, but as a legitimate theatre manager, he had to be careful about being seen to bow to illegitimate fashion. He needed Johnson's best rhetoric.

Obligingly, Johnson's address recollects how the 'flame' of Shakespeare and the 'art' of Ben Jonson had been replaced by the 'intrigue' and 'obscenity' of the Restoration, and how, rightly, there was a need for censorship. But moral cautiousness had gone too far and reduced the spoken drama to a frigid 'declamation' of 'philosophy' without 'passion' and 'nature'. This had driven audiences to the musical halls, where 'exulting Folly' has 'hailed the joyful day', 'and pantomime, and song, confirmed her sway'. I hear this, Garrick is saying to his audience. Legitimacy, these days, is not granted by Royal Patent alone, but by the public's demand, and its ticket money:

> The stage but echoes back the public voice.
> The drama's laws the drama's patrons give,
> For we that live to please, must please to live.

Who knows where this will lead, he muses, rhetorically. Maybe, one day, on this very Drury Lane stage

> where Lear has rav'd, and Hamlet died,
> On flying cars new sorcerers may ride.

One of the effects that defined the 1980s theatrical (re)turn (see Preface), the helicopter in *Miss Saigon*, would prove him not far wrong. But, my Lord Chamberlain, Ladies and Gentlemen, be assured that Garrick is not proposing to go that far yet! Ours will be a sensory theatre worthy of Shakespeare; a righteous scenic art, which puts the truth of passion and nature back into the drama:

> Tis yours, this night, to bid the reign commence
> Of rescued nature and reviving sense;

To chase the charms of sound, the pomp of show,
For useful mirth and salutary woe;
Bid scenic virtue form the rising age,
And truth diffuse her radiance from the stage.

JOHNSON, 1909

An appearance of real life

This was more than a promise of more naturalistic acting. Garrick had inherited a Theatre Royal configured according to a 1674 design, where the action was played in the middle of what would now be thought of as the auditorium, on a proscenium thrust stage that took up the majority of what is now the stalls seating area. Richard Southern describes this configuration as

> a vast hall with doors either end – a space into which the audience looked from one side, viewing the players under the light of flickering candles hung from the ceiling, across which could be seen on the other side, a partly obscured, partly illuminated, intriguing spectacle of scenery. The dimness of this whole spectacle must be stressed [. . .] It is important to realize that no playgoer at the time could form the idea that what he saw in front of him when he went to the theatre could ever be compared to an appearance of real life in the world of daylight.

1962: 241

The same, undoubtedly, would have been true of what the playgoers heard. If Garrick wanted scenery to be more than a thematic backdrop, and part of the tableau of natural truth that he would have discussed with Diderot in Paris, he needed to reconfigure this view. The action had to be detached from the auditorium – or at least semi-detached – and set further back so it could be looked and listened *at* as a unit, within a frame. In other words, the drama needed to be *pictured* by the theatre. The reconfiguration Garrick effected over the next thirty years was in varying parts architectural, technical and dramaturgical. Conventions that had integrated the public front-of-house and the stage and production areas were scrapped. Audiences were banished from backstage, and audience seating removed from the stage itself. In this way, a delimited auditorium emerged – a frame of aural representation-through-demarcation, in much the same way as Barthes (1977: 67) described the function of the proscenium frame (see Chapter 2).

During the 1760s, the stage apron (that part downstage of the proscenium or curtain line) was reduced further, and more action moved in and out of the scenic area upstage. This semi-detachment of pictured space of the upstage area introduced a zonal acoustic demarcation. Before the reconfiguration, the actors had spoken in the same open space where the audience watched. The smaller 'scene' or area upstage of the proscenium arch, which, as Southern suggests, lurked enigmatically on the far side of the action, was rarely used other than for dumb-shows, journeying or fight scenes, where there was little dialogue. This was partly for reasons of acoustic intelligibility. As the sheer volume of the theatre had grown, even within the open space Cibber describes as the 'auditory part' of the theatre, the words were hard enough to hear, as Cibber notes with frustration in his memoirs. This unintelligibility seems likely to have contributed to the gesturally overacted, semaphored style of declamation Garrick now recognized as problematically unnatural.

By the 1760s, the acoustics had improved (and the lighting, which meant actors' lips could be read as well as their limbs), but there remained a difference in sound between the upstage 'over there', the intermediate downstage, and the apron 'over here'. This was not a problem, in fact it helped De Loutherbourg's zoned scenic illusions of distant background, mid-ground and foreground. The hidden space of the wings and flies on the upstage acoustic, placed upstage action within a different reverberation, which, when heard in conjunction with cleverly painted perspectival illusions, provided a sense of distance, as if in the landscape. The further upstage an actor moved, the more their speech and movements acquired a reverberative aura from the hidden, backstage space. This reverberation infused the visible scene with a sense of distance. Action and speech set downstage or on the forestage felt more immediately within the presence of the auditors.

By the 1770s, only a small forestage remained, and the majority of the action was played either on or just upstage of the proscenium line, which remains the case to this day, with the apron used for asides, soliloquies and other moments when the drama crosses over, out of the pictorial space, into the immediacy of the auditory side. The possibility of this transgression is critical to the socially produced space of the theatre, wherein the audience is fully aware of, and perform, their role as artistic hearers and lookers. A short-lived move in 1880, at the Theatre Royal Haymarket, to do away with the forestage completely and join up the enormous gilded picture frame of the proscenium arch on all four sides (Southern, 1962: 258) removed this possibility. Martin Meisel describes how this had a psychological effect on the perception of depth in the stage sound, flattening it onto the sonic equivalent of a semi-translucent gauze or scrim across the proscenium opening, which nineteenth-century audiences found aesthetically curious but unsettling (Meisel, 1983: 44).

The dramaturgy of situation and effect

The 'picturing' of the scene had an effect on the scenic structure and dramaturgy of the play. Rather than simply continuing with a new set of characters entering the stage vacated by the last, each new scene began a meta-dramaturgical process of constructing a picture from the blocking or choreography of the drama within the designed setting. The drama became structured by a sequence of fresh starts, with each scene-change introducing a new picturing process. This serialized meta-dramaturgy ran alongside the story and worked towards an overall aesthetic effect that was separate to the story – the dissensual operation that constituted the aesthetic progress of the drama as an autonomous form. This effect was crystallized at key points along the way, where the plot, the action, the blocking (the arrangement of the view of the actors within the scene) all came together, and the dramatic essence of the scene was encapsulated in a synoptic pictorial moment – a brief freeze, a momentary tableau, a juxtaposition of posed figures, a moment of realization and scenic summation. These moments exposed the scenic Effect as an *aesthetic state*, as Schiller defined that term – 'a pure instance of plot suspension, a moment when form is experienced for itself' (Rancière, 2004: 17, see Chapter 3). These quasi-photographic exposures provided a pictorial synopsis of the scene, but were also meant to take the audience's breath away – to achieve a *coup de théâtre*. In the *coup*, a transformation would take place, theatre-time would pause for a moment while the pure aesthetic state of the Effect was felt and the cleverness of the pictorial arrangement and technical accomplishment sunk in. To be effective, both the affect and the impressive technical artifice were necessary.

In the terminology of the time, these synoptic pictorial configurations were known as 'situations', and their aesthetic accomplishment, the Effect (as Meisel does, I use the capital 'E' to differentiate it from an individual sound or lighting effect). As the treatise *Stage Effect: or, The Principles which Command Dramatic Success in the Theatre* (1840), by the equine veterinarian and amateur theatre critic Edward Mayhew, puts it:

> To theatrical minds the word 'situation' suggests some strong point in the play likely to command applause; where the action is wrought to a climax, where the actors strike attitudes, and form what they call 'a picture', during the exhibition of which a pause takes place; after which the action is renewed, not continued; and advantage of which is frequently taken to turn the natural current of the interest.

Glossing Mayhew and drawing on Sheridan's satirical burlesque *The Critic* (1779), Meisel argues that from about 1770 to 1870, the achievement of Effect became the preoccupation of theatre production and of dramaturgy (or, rather, melodramaturgy, since it was the combined working of the play and the music). The stasis of the suspended moment at the apex of scenes, where the pictured situation was summed up as an aesthetic, became its objective and key. The diegetic framework of acts and scenes in classical drama had been transitive, with each scenic unit propelled, from the start, by the momentum of the last. In the new melodramaturgy of pictorial scenes,

> the unit is intransitive; it is in fact an achieved moment of stasis, a picture. The play creates a series of such pictures, some of them offering a culminating symbolic summary of represented events, while others substitute an arrested situation for action and reaction. Each picture, dissolving, leads not into consequent activity, but to a new infusion and distribution of elements from which a new picture will be assembled or resolved. The form is serial discontinuity.
>
> MEISEL, 1983: 38

It was the break this dramaturgy of effect and situation made from the transitive dramaturgy of classical drama, along with the concurrent dissensual break from representational to aesthetic regimes of art, which set a course for the twentieth-century 'theatre of states and of scenically dynamic formations' that Hans-Thies Lehmann has identified as 'postdramatic' (2006: 68).

Theatre as part of the praxis of the Picturesque

This dramaturgical quest for the intransitive, aesthetic moment of suspended forward travel, is analogous to a tourist stopping to take in a view, and, indeed, should be understood as part of the proto-Romantic praxis of the Picturesque. This took not only landscape paintings and poems such as Cowper's as guiding texts, but shaped its disposition as a quest for scenic Situation and theatrical Effect in world at large. The Picturesque began as a conversation between the aesthetic reconfiguration of the theatre and of diegetic form and a set of formulaic guidelines – or a format – for observing and recomposing, if necessary, the English landscape for purposes of aesthetic tourism or sketching. It soon developed beyond this, to become an artistically indexed aesthetic approach to cultural activities as diverse as estate management, women's fashion and designed country walks or pleasure gardens such as Beulah Spa. The reconfiguration of Drury Lane, the scenography of De

Loutherbourg, and particularly late eighteenth-century, proto-melodramatic pantomimes and scenic burlettas, should all be understood as *technē* of this conversation between theatre aesthetics and outward-bound recreation. Through them, the Picturesque provided the aesthetic basis of the English gothic revival and much nineteenth-century drama, which is somewhat reductively known as 'spectacular' in a way that overlooks the aurality of its framed views. In particular, it shaped the aesthetics of English gothic melodrama, which provided the formal foundations for the audio-visual diegesis of cinematic drama.

Crucially, the Picturesque praxis argued, as does the extract from *The Task* at the top of this chapter, that traditionally unbeautiful things in everyday life that please the theatrical sensibility of a self-dramatizing fiction of the self, should be allowed to be considered beautiful. The adjective 'picturesque' would ultimately come to be associated with a banal picture-postcard prettiness when in fact it originally meant quite the opposite, although for a while it became so overused in cultural criticism and discourse that its original meaning was forgotten. Almost a century after it was coined as a term, Ruskin, who was interested in returning to the original definition to critique gothic architecture, called it a 'Parasitical Sublimity [. . .] a sublimity dependent on the accidents, or on the *least* essential characters, of the objects to which it belongs' (Ruskin, 1865: 156). In this way, the picturesque was concerned with appearances as essence in the way that Rancière identifies as the fictional ontology of aesthetic art. However, the picturesque became an almost cultish term, used to describe any kind of amoral pleasure, and Ruskin complained how 'probably no word in the language (exclusive of theological expressions), has been the subject of so frequent or so prolonged dispute; yet none remained more vague in their acceptance' (ibid.). Eventually, the cult of the picturesque, as Ruskin saw it, petered out, discredited for the fact that its aesthetic dissensus from the truths and moralities of the mimetic regime often amounted to an aesthetic lack of conscience in taking aesthetic pleasure from scenes of poverty and human degradation. The figure of the quixotic search for the elusive picturesque was made to look ridiculous in the very print media that had initially encouraged its touristic appetition, and distributed its travelogue-based worldview. The Picturesque was consigned to a footnote in the history of visual art, and the scenographic aurality that constituted its theatrical disposition towards the visible world forgotten.

In the remainder of this chapter, I am going to address the aural aesthetics of the Picturesque, which are key to the diegetic aesthetics of modern theatre. Then, in Chapter 7, I shall fast forward to the twentieth century to visit some of these modern effects, and then rewind to gothic melodrama, and the role that music and noise played in the picturesque disposition of melodramaturgy.

The picturesque of sound

The Picturesque framed the pleasures of ruination, irregularity, abruptness, roughness and decay, as a form of beauty. The adjective *picturesque* retains some of this eighteenth-century meaning in its modern usage. One might still describe a ruined Cornish mine as picturesque, or a dilapidated mill or farm. One might, however, be less likely to refer to a faltering note, a cracked voice, or a dissonant chord as such. Less likely still, to differentiate between the sublime feeling of an oncoming storm, and the picturesque effect of its arrival and aftermath. Yet these are examples of the picturesque aesthetic as it was propounded in the late eighteenth century.

Picturesque was also used as a noun, in a number of ways. One might refer to the picturesque of a produced play, much as a today one might talk of its design, or the picturesque of gesture as one might refer to its theatricality, as Dickens does of Fechter's acting, which he describes as a 'ferociously picturesque' (Dickens, 2011: loc 3472). It might also be used to refer to a 'found' tableau in the scenography of everyday life. For example, in Chapter 10 of *Pride and Prejudice* (1813), Elizabeth Bennet says 'no, no; stay where you are. You are charmingly grouped, and appear to uncommon advantage. The picturesque would be spoilt by admitting a fourth' (here is a reference to the rule of threes, which was a principle of Picturesque composition both in stage blocking and in sketching).

The principles of the Picturesque were delineated in a theory of seeing, hearing and re-composing the landscape, ostensibly for the purposes of sketching, formulated by William Gilpin over a number of guidebooks, based on his own travels around the British Isles. Gilpin began to develop the idea while a student at Oxford in 1747, the same year as Garrick's tenure at Drury Lane began. The theoretical discourse was developed in taxonomies of picturesque effect by the two neighbouring rural landowners Richard Payne Knight and Uvedale Price. The principles under discussion were reflected in the artistic practices of Garrick, De Loutherbourg, Reynolds, Gainsborough, Cowper and others, and a range of cultural activities that shaped a sensible modernity that took art as the frame of reference for recreational aesthetic productions of various kinds (Baugh, 1990; Copley and Garside, 1994). Whether taking a walk in the Peak District, guided by Gilpin and Cowper, or stage-managing the topography of an estate such as that of Hafod in Wales, and the routes around it, so that it presented as a series of framed views of waterfalls, alpine bridges and wild woods, the common goal, like that of the new dramaturgy and *mise-en-scène*, was the framing of a situation (either touristic or artistic) and the production of a desired aesthetic Effect.

At the heart of the debate that accompanied this diverse process of aesthetic production was a challenge to the dominant aesthetic dualism of Burke's theories of beauty and the sublime – affects or emotional sensations believed to relate to underlying properties or essences of sensible phenomena. The sensation of beauty related to an instinctive attraction of the eye and the ear to symmetry, smoothness, curve and harmony. The sublime was the halting, adrenal alertness experienced as awe or astonishment in the face of fearful power, nobility or splendour. In auditory terms, consonance, symmetrically melodic birdsong, harmonic purity in instrumental or vocal sounds, or the movement from contrapuntal complexity to symmetrical resolution in music, were beautiful. They seemed to speak to an underlying universal geometry or harmonic scheme.

The sublime, however, was a sensation less easily associated with objectively identifiable phenomena, because it was an effect of the inapprehensibly vast or powerful. Burke notes that the word 'stupefaction' came from *stupere*, to be dazed or struck dumb, while another word associated with the sublime, 'astonishment', came from the adjective *attonitus*, or 'thunderstruck' (Burke, 1998: 54). Technically, therefore, the sublime was inaudible, as far as any experience of it could be discussed or depicted, because it incapacitated reflective consciousness. Coleridge understood this. When he heard the terrifying 'thunders and howlings' of the ice shifting on the lakes at Ratzeburg in Schleswig-Holstein, he made clear that these descriptions were inadequate approximations, because these were 'sounds more sublime than any sight can be, more absolutely suspending the power of comparison, and more utterly absorbing the mind's self-consciousness' (Coleridge, 1812: 302). The sublime, therefore, tended to be associated with vastness and power by proxy, through similes (such as his phrase 'thunders and howlings'). From such metaphors, one might infer the fearfulness of the sublime.

This was a problem for the aesthetic productions of the Picturesque that began to emerge as a leisure industry in the late 1750s and whose favoured Effects were those of safely framed and distanced (if not contrived) takes on the sublime. According to the polarized aesthetic system of beauty and the sublime, craggy ruins or treacherous waterfalls, and the noises associated with them, were not supposed to be pleasurable, but to suggest awe. The aesthetic of pleasure was beauty, and this was confined to the smooth, regular and symmetrical. The thunder of a torrent, the howling of the wind and the prospect of ruination and decay – the effects of the sublime – could not be beautiful. Burke's theory was predicated on the principle that beauty and the sublime were mutually exclusive and stood 'on foundations so different, that it is hard [. . .] to think of reconciling them in the same subject, without considerably lessening the effect of the one or the other upon the passions' (Burke, 1998: 103). And yet a view of the ruined Tintern Abbey, a thunderous sky over the Cairngorms, or the white water of a mountain torrent, encountered in a way that was correct according to artistic representations of such scenes, gave pleasure. Hence Gilpin's proposition:

> Disputes about beauty might perhaps be involved in less confusion, if a distinction were established, which certainly exists, between such objects as are beautiful, and such as are picturesque – between those, which please the eye in their natural state; and those, which please from some quality, capable of being illustrated in painting.
>
> GILPIN, 1794: 3

As for the eye, so for the ear. While sound is less obviously capable of being illustrated in painting, the theatrical pleasure sought by the Picturesque was as aural as it was visual, and we see from Cowper's poem (and from the evident stage-management of sonic encounter in the walks at Hafod) that auditory aesthetics was also a field of Picturesque enquiry and quest. The place where sonic qualities – the charms of sound – were more 'capable of being illustrated' was the theatre. During the period that Gilpin was producing his several guides to how to identify the Picturesque in the British countryside, the reconfiguration of the playhouse as the Organon of the picturesque aesthetic was underway. The adjective 'picturesque' became almost synonymous with 'theatrical' or 'dramatic' as one might apply those terms to an everyday situation or atmosphere. This was not coincidental. By the turn of the century, as McGillivray puts it, 'theatricality, had become the zeitgeist of the age' (2008: 138). Baugh observes that in the late eighteenth century, theatre became a 'metaphor – a vehicle for the ordering, structuring and criticism of life' (Baugh, 1990: 19).

Gilpin's picturesque formula of landscape composition clearly draws on this *Zeitgeist* and metaphor. His compositional formula owes more to the zonal breakdown of the pictorially framed scenic stage at Drury Lane than to Claude Lorraine's landscapes (the model Gilpin liked to invoke). A background, like a hazily scumbled backcloth, is framed by 'side-screens' like the flattage or legs of theatrical borders. Overhanging branches were like scenic headers, and ground-level tussocks or rocks create inner frames. The composition thus has a foreground (forestage), a mid-ground (scene) and a far-ground (backcloth), and it is in the near-distance of the mid-stage, the equivalent of the scene, that the painting's 'consequence' is arranged: its ruined abbey or cluster of rustic dwellings. Gilpin did not personally approve of there being human figures in a picturesque composition (Elizabeth Bennet is making a pointed allusion to this when she mentions that three would be too many for a picturesque group, three being the ideal number Gilpin prescribes for a group of cows, not people). It was in this mid-ground, which corresponded to the area immediately upstage of the proscenium arch, that others would put groups of stereotypical figures (rustic farm labourers or exotic gypsies).

The technique Gilpin describes for finding picturesque compositions in nature is a theatricalizing gaze that looks for art and artifice, not the truth of nature. Effect takes priority over verisimilitude. If the Effect you want is not quite there, imagine it.

> There is an art of seeing, as well as of painting. The eye must in part enter into the deception. [. . .] It is thus in drama. How absurdly would the spectator act, if instead of assisting the illusion of the stage, he should insist on being deceived, without being a party in the deception?
>
> GILPIN, 1794: 140

The aesthetic production of the picturesque, then, was made by the viewer, and in the theatre required the artistic disposition of the spectator. In this complicit gaze and its aurality lies a principle not only of the picturesque and the gothic, but also of the Effect, atmosphere and mood production of aesthetic scenography, which is predicated on the recognition of artistic genre.

The aurality of the contriving gaze

The scenic stage and the illustrated travelogue distributed the Picturesque sensibility as references for a new, scenographic take on the world. Where those who had taken the Grand Tour (now perpetually being blocked by war in France) were instructed in the appreciation of classical art, the new bourgeoisie would read up or take classes in how to see and hear the picturesque on visits to the countryside (as Austen's Marianne does in *Sense and Sensibility*, 1811). James Plumptre's 1798 burletta *The Lakers* (a 'laker' was a picturesque tourist to the Lake District, but also slang for an amateur dabbler, or dilettante) parodies picturesque activities and their lack of concern for truth-to-nature. Defending her landscape from Sir Charles Portinscale's critique that it did not look like 'the thing' she was supposed to be drawing, Miss Beccabunga Veronica, an amateur botanist and the wealthy aunt of the heiress heroine, retorts that 'if it is not like what it is, it is what it ought to be. I have only made it picturesque. [. . .] I have only given the hills an Alpine form, and put some wood where it is wanted, and omitted it where it is not wanted' (Plumptre, 1798: 20).

The aurality of the scene is established with musical picturesques at the beginning and the end. Firstly, a song, one imagines realized with atmospheric sound effects, recalls Cowper's list of sonic scenery in *The Task*:

And from the distant rocky shore,
The falling water's sullen roar
Borne on the gently swelling gale
Fraught with the sweets of the flowery vale
Steal on the watchful ear of night
Distil a solemn, still delight
[etc.]

ibid.

The scene ends when Beccabunga overhears the sound of a shepherd's flute playing a rude folk air, at which she exclaims 'what a picturesque sound!' and begins to sing along (ibid.: 21).

The aural framing described in the opening song is precisely the kind Gilpin prescribes as the disposition for a picturesque view. Referring to the 'gloomy, melancholy air which overspreads the Scotch landscape', he advises the traveller to attend to 'the portentous noises, which every change of the wind, and every increase and diminution of the waters is apt to raise in a lonely region full of rocks, caverns, and echoes, are all circumstances of a melancholy cast' (2014: 133).

Such noises, Gilpin continued, are not 'entirely of the picturesque kind . . . yet they are nearly allied to it' and 'give a tinge to the imagination of every traveller, who examines these scenes of solitude and grandeur'.

Tinging was a painterly metaphor, and there was specialist equipment for tinging the imagination in the field. Plumptre, a Laker himself, describes how he would set off on his own excursions not only with a range of camping equipment and art materials but a Claude Glass, a Gray's Glass and a book of Cowper's poetry (Bermingham, in Copley and Garside, 1994: 87). Claude Glasses (after Claude Lorraine) and Gray's Glasses (after Thomas Gray, who used one to get into a poetic mood) were different kinds of smoked, or 'black', handheld mirrors mounted in picture frames. Like a cinematographer's viewfinder, they helped frame a view, but more than this, they increased the contrast, reduced detail and imparted a 'dramatic' mood, like an Instagram filter. There is a sketch in the National Gallery in London of a young Gainsborough, sat under a tree, using one to sketch a self-portrait in the landscape, which Payne Knight bought. This 'tinging' the imagination now became part of the scenic function of stage lighting and of noises-off within the reconfigured, scenic theatre. Brooding skies and such meteorological conditions now played a modern dramatic role, entirely different from that which they performed on the classical stage and within the acoustemology of the early modern: as an atmospheric index of emotional mood.

It is in this correlation between ambient sound and painterly tinging that one of the key breaks between the theatre's old acoustemological way of knowing the world in the representative regime of the early modern period and the new acoustemology of the aesthetic regime of art was made. Sound became attended to within the aesthetically produced world as a semi-transparent wash or glaze on the dramatic picture, the blackening of the mirror, the turbid atmosphere that interposed a dramatic mood between the aural-spectator and the scenic tableau. Today, it seems banal, and a little critically lazy, to describe a sound design simply as 'atmospheric'. In the late eighteenth century, the repurposing of stage noises as pictorial atmosphere represented a dissensual break from, and radical aesthetic critique of, the mimetic classical tradition and Burkeian aesthetics.

Modern stage thunder

Nothing better illustrates this break than the change in the use of thunder, from symbolic performance to an aesthetic effect. The 'all-shaking thunder, that smites flat the thick rotundity o' the world' in Act Two, Scene Three of *King Lear* would, in its original production, have been exactly that: the loudest percussive din that could humanly be made, to shake the wooden O and all of the bodies within it. It was simply a viscerally thrilling performance of noise-making. It stood for the sacrificial calling to account of the ageing, demented king, for the actions that led to the violent breakdown of cosmic harmony. There would have been no scenery, as such, and the thunderous sound would not have been part of a concerted pictorial representation of a human disintegration. Its mimesis was of a different order: it represented the theoretical dissonance in the *musica universalis*, although we cannot know how it would really have looked and sounded. The twentieth-century archetypal image of Lear and his weather comes from Macready's 1838 production, whose *mise-en-scène*, Christopher Baugh points out, drew on the aesthetics of the picturesque. It showed a 'reality composed and structured as pictorial art' (Baugh, 2008: 318).

The theatricality of the thunderstorm was specifically theorized in the Picturesque debate. When Gilpin says, in the quotation above, that the melancholy sounds he describes are not *entirely* of the picturesque kind, he is being pedantic about aesthetic categories. Truly picturesque noises would be rough, asymmetrically decaying or interrupted, and not gently modulating like the mountain wind. Price and Payne Knight's taxonomies of picturesque effects are full of such pedantry – such as whether moss or tree bark are sufficiently irregular to classify as picturesquely beautiful. Regarding sound, they concentrate mainly on the qualities of music, which predominantly, as you might expect, divide into the categories of pure, simple beauty and the symphonically violent or plangent sublime. However, music with 'sudden, unexpected, and abrupt transitions, from a certain playful wildness of character and appearance of irregularity, is no less analogous to similar scenery in nature, than the concerto or the chorus to what is grand or beautiful to the eye', and thus might be considered picturesque (Price, 1810: 46).

The use of the theatre term *'scenery'* here, as with Cowper's, would have stood out more in 1810. Price is probably referring to contemporary trends in music: the sonic impressionism of the Baroque Pastorale that 'heard' the kind of rustic music featured at the end of 'The Lakers' scene described above, or new Romantic music such as Beethoven's *Pastoral Symphony* (1808). But in placing music in a scenographic metaphor, he is speaking of a melodramaturgical rather than an operatic disposition (in opera's total theatre, music is the metaphor that accounts for all).

Of thunder, Price says:

> That general, equal gloom which is spread over all nature before a storm, with the stillness, so nobly described by Shakespeare, is in the highest degree sublime. The picturesque requires greater variety, and does not shew itself till the dreadful thunder has rent the region, has tossed the clouds into a thousand towering forms, and opened, as it were, the recesses of the sky.
>
> PRICE, 1810: 69

This is a dramaturgical distinction. The sublime is addressed in the silence and stillness of the ominous approach of storm. The picturesque is its destructive effect and pictorial Effect – jagged, abruptly dynamic – but, above all, it is pleasurably so, a playful wildness.

The dramaturgical aestheticization of thunder as a picturesque situation is evident across nineteenth-century culture. One of the (various) first-person narrators of Mary Shelley's *Frankenstein* (1818) ascribes 'curiosity and delight' to a 'most violent and terrible thunderstorm' (Shelley, 1831: 27). Byron's *Sardanapalus* (1821), staged by Macready a few years before his genre-defining *Lear* in 1834, and again even more elaborately in 1853 by Charles Kean with a degree of 'pictorial integration then only normative in some parts of Pantomime and Extravaganza' (Meisel, 1983: 43), identifies two kinds of people: those who dread the coming storm, and those who will it on and relish the picturesque Effect of its arrival or realization.

> *Myr.* King! The sky
> Is overcast, and musters muttering thunder,

> In clouds that seem approaching fast, and show
> In forkéd flashes a commanding tempest.
> Will you then quit the palace?
> *Sar.* Tempest, say'st thou?
> *Myr.* Aye, my good lord.
> *Sar.* For my own part, I should be
> Not ill content to vary the smooth scene,
> And watch the warring elements; but this
> Would little suit the silken garments and
> Smooth faces of our festive friends. Say, Myrrha,
> Art thou of those who dread the roar of clouds?
>
> BYRON, 1901: loc. 1337–46

By 1821, when Lord Byron wrote this, the Picturesque had been absorbed into a more general gothic disposition, and the use of the term was becoming faddishly and indiscriminatingly applied to any kind of theatricality in the way that infuriated Ruskin. Meanwhile, the pedantry of its original definition had been consigned to parody, as had the figure of the obsessive aesthete roaming the countryside in search of it.

The Tour of Dr Syntax in Search of the Picturesque, written by William Combe and illustrated by Thomas Rowlandson, had been a hugely popular episodic series of illustrated plates in Rudolph Ackermann's[2] *The Poetical Magazine* between 1809 and 1811. It placed its hero Syntax in a series of absurd, quixotic situations each framed within a narrative aquatint image. Bound or hung together, these look like a comic strip. Indeed, Dr Syntax (Gilpin) is often cited in histories of comics and graphic novels as the first reappearing comic strip character. The picturesque thunderstorm is specifically satirized:

> 'I love' he cry'd, 'to hear the rattle
> When elements contend to battle;
> For I insist, tho' some may flout it,
> Who write about it and about it,
> That we the picturesque may find
> In thunder loud, or whistling wind;
> And often, as I fully ween,
> It may be heard as well as seen.'
>
> COMBE and ROWLANDSON, 1812: 111

---

[2] A distributor of the modern mode, its sensory practices and sensible objects, principally through the Repository of Arts on the Strand and a periodical of the same name (1809–28).

The same year as *Syntax* was published in book form (1812), one of the original producers of the picturesque worldview, De Loutherbourg, died. That same year, William Pyne wrote of him: 'His genius was as prolific in imitations of nature to astonish the ear, as to charm the sight. He introduced a new art: the picturesque of sound' (Pyne, 1823: 295–6).

Pyne had made a living from the Picturesque, producing illustrated taxonomies of rustic English regional dress and the text for Ackermann's Metropolitan picturesque serialization, the *Microcosm of London*. In 1810, he became one of its satirists, in a column called *Of Wine and Walnuts* for the popular *Literary Gazette* – collected into book form in 1823 – written behind the picturesque persona of Ephraim Hardcastle, an old Huguenot weaver from Spitalfields.

The column was largely a series of parodic sketches of the 1770s to 1780s. Where *Syntax* mocked Gilpin's search for the picturesque in the landscape, Pyne based his parody in the city, and the quest of Garrick, Gainsborough, Reynolds, Sterne and others for the perfect metropolitan picturesque, whose amorality is harshly satirized. Thus, in their search for 'specimens of the cockney picturesque', Pyne has his decadent aesthetes comparing roadside village graveyards to 'the masses of road-mud that are left to dry beside the highway' (Pyne, 1823: 40). He parodies eighteenth-century ethnic picturesques like the 'Norwood Gipsies' (1777), which continued to provide a popular but dehumanizing trope in the nineteenth century:

> 'Gipsies – where?' Jumping up, and seizing the telescope; 'My Heaven, how precious! ... What a delectable group! – Look, Sir Joshua, look, quick – you can feel the thing!' 'Delightful group!' said Garrick – 'Phaugh! A nest of ragged daemons – and look at the little imps. Egad! they have been changing garb with the gibbeted murderers on Finchley Common, or robbing honest men's gardens of scare-crows – those who are not stark-naked. Why, look you there, Sterne – shame upon it – there's a girl, surely sixteen, without a petticoat to cover her filthy tawny skin.'
> 'That's the charm on't,' said Gainsborough, clapping his hands in extacy – 'that's the charm, Davy – that's the true PICTURESQUE!'
>
> PYNE, 1823: 226

By 1845, the Picturesque had become intolerable and was over. Its ghoulish fixation on human decay led Dickens to write that he was 'afraid the conventional idea of the picturesque is associated with such misery and degradation that a new picturesque will have to be established as the world goes on' (quoted by Andrews, in Copley and Garside, 1994: 286).

The Eidophusikon

Pyne's account of De Loutherbourg and his 'Picturesque of Sound' seems to have been written as a tribute to the artist in the year of his death, 1812. It focuses not on his stage career, but on *The Eidophusikon*, De Loutherbourg's attempt to advance the form of the gallery-exhibited picture by introducing the dimensions of time and spatial depth, scenographic movement and sound. It is supposedly written by Hardcastle about the show's original incarnation at Panton Street in 1781, but Pyne seems to forget this, and slips into describing his own, later memories of *The Eidophusikon* from the 'Exeter Exchange', where the show relocated in the late 1780s, just off The Strand where Pyne grew up.

The Exeter Exchange was a museum of curiosities – a major tourist attraction and focal point for the characteristically gothic nineteenth-century taste for novelty and exotica. At this time, there was felt to be no tension between commercialism and artistic integrity – in fact, the commodification of art-based experience was regarded as modern, if not avant-garde. As Ann Bermingham describes, the Picturesque was

> An aesthetic uniquely constituted to serve the nascent mass-marketing needs of a developing commercial culture; one in which appearances were construed as essence and commodities were sold under the signs of art and nature.
>
> COPLEY and GARSIDE, 1994: 81

It is again worth noting the zonal topography of this cultural movement (to this day, regional identifiers such as the West End or Broadway are ascribed to modes and idioms of cultural product and consumerism). The Exeter Exchange stood in Covent Garden, at the centre of the commercial sensation marketplace. Just over the road were Ackermann's Repository, the main bookshop and publishers which distributed theatricality as lifestyle aesthetic, and the Coal Hole, the pub at the heart of London show business, which would become the site of Terry's all-electric theatre. Next to it soon would stand the Savoy Theatre, where Gilbert and Sullivan would become household names and Granville Barker would bring an abstract, symbolist picturesque to the commercial London stage. Just beyond this was Savoy Hill, where the BBC would broadcast to nation and empire. Down the road was the Lyceum, where Astley's horse operas, Madame Tussauds' waxworks, and musical theatre such as William Dimond's *The Peasant Boy* (1811), famous for its picturesque tableaux, had all drawn crowds, and where Irving would make his name. Next to the financial zone of the old City, the commercial exchange of picturesques and theatrical aesthetics was at the heart of London, and London at the heart of a global empire.

Here, in a small darkened room above the Exeter Exchange's main exhibit, Polito's Royal Menagerie of exotic animals (whose animals London Zoo was built to rehome), was a small exhibit that many hold to be one of the first and most seminal iterations of cinematic form.

Pyne writes that:

> It would be a subject of regret to all lovers of the picturesque scenery of nature, if the ingenious contrivances which De Loutherbourg invented, in the formation of his beautiful little stage, were consigned to oblivion for want of a record.
>
> 1823: 281

This beautiful little stage was fronted by a translucent gauze screen (scrim) and framed with a picture-frame mounted on a false wall, so that when one entered the room, it looked like a painting hanging in a gallery. The performance began with an overture from an unseen harpsicord hidden behind the false wall, which established a musical framing for the scenic space that would soon unfold. The scrim then dissolved or bled through, to reveal a fully working theatrical scene, presenting, without the actors, moving, sounding and illuminated, miniature versions of the full-scale pictorial effects that had made De Loutherbourg a theatre celebrity.

De Loutherbourg had begun work on *The Eidophusikon* at Panton Street, propelled by the celebrity of his show-stealing effects for *The Camp* (1778, Sheridan's musical satire on Britain's anti-revolutionary preparations) and his own full-scale spectacular, *The Wonders of Derbyshire* (1779). Drury Lane was now run by Sheridan following Garrick's retirement, and *Derbyshire* a major hit, described by the *Morning Chronicle* as 'superior to anything the stage has presented to the public eye'. It became a fixture in the Drury Lane repertoire, being performed forty-nine times, despite the scale and complexity of its technical fit-up. As Baugh describes, the show was

> Solely conceived to display the talents of the scenic artist and the Drury Lane technical staff. Called a 'pantomime,' it was structured as a travelogue through the wonders of the Peak District of Derbyshire. The Peak District, an especially wild and desolate landscape with giant rock outcrops and subterranean passages and caves, was an environment eminently suitable for Loutherbourg's experiments with unearthly and mysterious lighting effects. [. . .] Henry Angelo exclaimed, 'Never were such romantic and picturesque paintings exhibited in that theatre before, . . . [which] gave you

an idea of the mountains and waterfalls, most beautifully executed, exhibiting a terrific appearance.'

BAUGH, 2007: 256

Given this celebrity, the hint of irritation where De Loutherbourg is mentioned by name in Sheridan's *The Critic* in 1779, is understandable. Soon afterwards, Sheridan drastically cut the fee paid to De Loutherbourg for his designs, and he promptly quit Drury Lane and began work on *The Eidophusikon*.

The Eidophusikon's first programme comprised a sequence of various views of London and exotic locations at different times of the day and under moonlight, culminating with a sea storm and shipwreck finale. It made use of miniature painted and moving scenery (De Loutherbourg's father had been a Polish miniaturist), projected coloured light, slides, moving gobos (lantern stencils) and 'bleed-throughs' that drew the viewer through the Chinese silk 'canvas' of the wall-hanging picture into the scene behind. New scenes were added over time and rotated, including the sun rising through fog, the Niagara Falls, a scenic view of Dover Castle, the town and cliffs, a moonlit waterspout off a Japanese sea coast. A new finale was added: 'Satan arraying his troops on the banks of the fiery lake, with the raising of the palace of pandemonium, from Milton'. This reprised a notorious, immersively theatrical effect De Loutherbourg had staged for an orgiastic country house masked ball in 1781 to celebrate the coming of age of William Beckford, a wealthy collector of colonial exotica, patron of the decorative arts, and one of the leaders of the gothic revival (During, 2007).

Pyne's account of **The Eidophusikon**

Pyne's account (1823: 281–304) pays particular attention to the sound, which, assuming it was representative of De Loutherbourg's full-scale scenography, offers an insight into how sophisticated the art of sound effect had become. It begins with a description of how the stage was little more than six feet wide, and about eight feet in depth, although 'such was the painter's knowledge of effect and scientific arrangement [. . .] that the space appeared to recede for many miles'.

Pyne describes how artificial echo effects were used to reinforce the spatial illusion:

> I can never forget the awful impression that was excited by his ingenious contrivance to produce the effect of the firing of a signal of distress, in his sea-storm. That appalling sound, which he that had been exposed to the

terrors of a raging tempest could not listen to, even in this mimic scene, without being reminded of the heart-sickening answer, which sympathetic danger had reluctantly poured forth from his own loud gun, a hoarse sound to the howling wind, that proclaimed 'I too, holy Heaven! need that succour I fain would lend!' De Loutherbourg had tried many schemes to effect this; but none were satisfactory to his nice ear, until he caused a large skin to be dressed into parchment, which was fastened by screws to a circular frame, forming a vast tambourine; to this was attached a compact sponge that went upon a whalebone spring; which, struck with violence, gave the effect of a near explosion; a more gentle blow, that of a far-off gun; and the reverberation of the sponge produced a marvellous imitation of the echo from to cloud, dying away into silence.

The rest of the storm is described as follows:

> The rush of the waves was effected by a large octagonal box, made of paste-board, with internal shelves, and charged with small shells, peas, and light balls, which, as the machine wheeled upon its axis, were hurled in heaps with every turn; and being accompanied by two machines, of a circular form, covered with tightly strained silk, which pressed against each other by a swift motion, gave out a hollow whistling sound, in perfect imitation of loud gusts of wind. Large silken balls, passed hastily over the surface of the great tambourine, increased the awful din.
>
> The rain and hail were no less truly imitated: for the rain, a long four-sided tube was charged with small seed, which, according to the degree of its motion, from a horizontal to a vertical position, forced the atoms in a pattering stream to the bottom, when it was turned to repeat the operation. The hail was expressed by a similar tube, on a larger scale, with pasteboard shelves, projecting on inclined planes, and charged with little beads; so that, sliding from shelf to shelf, fast or slow, as the tube was suddenly or gently raised, the imitation was perfect.

'No less natural, and infinitely grand', was the thunder, the keynote sound of picturesque theatricality and the gothic revival:

> A spacious sheet of thin copper was suspended by a chain, which, shaken by one of the lower corners, produced the distant rumbling, seemingly below the horizon; and as the clouds rolled on, approached nearer and nearer, increasing peal by peal, until, following rapidly the lightning's zig-zag flash, which was admirably vivid and sudden, it burst in a tremendous crash immediately over-head . . . To those who have not heard the sounds emitted by a large sheet of copper thus suspended, it may appear extravagant to

assert so wondrous an effect; indeed it is not possible to describe the power of the resemblance auricular evidence alone could convince.

The picturesque reaches a crescendo in the final Pandemonium scene:

> Here, in the foreground of a vista, stretching an immeasurable length between mountains, ignited from their bases to their lofty summits, with many-coloured flame, a chaotic mass rose in dark majesty, which gradually assumed form until it stood, the interior of a vast temple of gorgeous architecture, bright as molten brass, seemingly composed of unconsuming and unquenchable fire. In this tremendous scene, the effect of coloured glasses before the lamps was fully displayed; which, being hidden from the audience, threw their whole influence upon the scene, as it rapidly changed, now to a sulphurous blue, then to a lurid red, and then again to a pale vivid light, and ultimately to a mysterious combination of the glasses, such as a bright furnace exhibits, in fusing various metals. The sounds which accompanied the wondrous picture, struck the astonished ear of the spectator as no less preternatural; for, to add a more awful character to peals of thunder, and the accompaniments of all the hollow machinery that hurled balls and stones with indescribable rumbling and noise, an expert assistant swept his thumb over the surface of the tambourine, which produced a variety of groans, that struck the imagination as issuing from infernal spirits.

The adjectives are huge but the actuality is small. What fascinates Pyne is clearly the difference in scale between the hidden technology and the powerful effect that came through the tiny wall-mounted, gauze-covered aperture in a salon that looked more like a domestic room than a theatre. *The Eidophusikon* is often cited as a visual prototype of the cinema or TV screen, but it was also a prototype of the loudspeakers built into such screens, in introducing acousmatic sound from an inapprehensible space beyond. The miniaturism of *The Eidophusikon* was significant. It made a break from the life-size, which was a significant step in establishing the conditions for both audio and video representation. David Kornhaber points out that to see a spectacle at Drury Lane was 'to be overwhelmed by it – overwhelmed by the crowd of other spectators, overwhelmed by the size of the show, overwhelmed by its novelty, overwhelmed by its presentation of a total, complete, unified universe within the proscenium arch' (Kornhaber, 2009: 56). *The Eidophusikon*, on the other hand, comprised 'a small crowd, a diminutive scene, familiar presentations, and a series of discrete episodes that never achieve the kind of sustained, totalizing effect of a full-blown spectacle. If to go to the theatre was to give oneself up to something larger than life, then to see *The Eidophusikon* was to be in control of that same experience' (ibid.).

David Punter, who has written extensively on the gothic, sees this as an assertion of the inscaped ego over the narrative of sublime escape, which is 'the movement outwards, the sudden rush of air which deflates the ego in the face of an avalanche, the pleasurable abandon of control' (Punter, 1994: 226). The effect of *The Eidophusikon* and of any *technē* of the Picturesque praxis, was to *inscape*, to invert the escape of the sublime and create a 'movement of enclosure, control, [. . .] roughness subjected to symmetry, the ego's certainty about the world it can hold and manage' (Punter, 1994: 226).

Today, De Loutherbourg's portrait hangs in the Dulwich Picture Gallery, at the bottom of the hill from the BBC's enormous Crystal Palace transmitter, which provides radio and TV pictures to the whole of South-East England. Dulwich was the first public gallery in the country, founded by De Loutherbourg's student, the Swiss émigré Francis Bourgeois. De Loutherbourg's portrait hangs in the ticket hall and it is by Gainsborough, who adored the legendary scenic artist and was convinced that his moving, sounding scenes were the future of the pictorial art.

PART THREE

'Our thunder is the best'

(Living in the audio world)

7

Arty, exotic and gothic

Pop, art and the theatre of hearing

September 1967, South-East England

'And, good morning everyone. Welcome to the exciting new sound of Radio One.' After these words, the DJ who has spoken them, Tony Blackburn, plays 'Flowers in the Rain' by The Move. The reason he chooses that record, Blackburn will reveal in a 2007 documentary about the song,[1] is because of the sound effect of a crash of thunder with which it begins. He thinks that the sound effect encapsulates the exciting new era with which the BBC's new pop music station wants to be associated, following the unpopular closure of the off-shore 'pirate' radio ships that had first brought the technicolour sound of the 1960s into people's homes.

⏮ *February 1781, South-East England*

'Gainsborough had been so wrapt in delight with *The Eidophusikon* that, for a time, he thought of nothing else, he talked of nothing else, and passed his evenings at that exhibition in long succession' (Pyne, 1823: 295–6). Gainsborough's biographer William Whitley tells the following story:

> One evening, when a storm at sea off the coast near Naples was the subject of a particularly vivid representation, a real thunderstorm broke over London, to the terror of the superstitious among the audience, who ran into the lobby protesting against the presumption of De Loutherbourg for daring to imitate the mysteries of nature. Meanwhile, the inventor, accompanied by Gainsborough and two or three other privileged friends, ascended to the roof of the theatre, from whence they could see the storm, and by looking down, witness at the same time the mimetic

---

[1] 'The Story of Flowers in the Rain'; documentary, BBC Radio 4, September 2007.

representation on the stage. Gainsborough watched and listened intently for a few moments, then turned excitedly to his friend. 'De Loutherbourg,' he cried, 'our thunder is the best!'

1915: 370

Our thunder: only the wobble of a thundersheet and a thumb dragged across a drum skin, perhaps, but a thunder whose meaning is contained within its pictorial effect and within the mystery of how it could be made so small. A thunder for human pleasure, whose former associations with divine displeasure have been contained. Our thunder that is part of the scenery of modern life, hallowed be its name. The unsuperstitious thunder of our first-person plural. A picturesque to delight in, be thrilled by and not to fear. A noise that is better than nature in its artificiality. A gothic thunder. A post-sublime thunder. The exciting new sound.

▶▶ *November 1947, USA*

A short article entitled 'Notes on the Early Progress of the Picturesque of Sound' appears in the popular journal of miscellany *American Notes and Queries*. It is about the use of sound effects in radio drama, and its author, the enigmatic Le Bruit ('The Noise'), tells the story of *The Eidophusikon* and of Gainsborough's 'our thunder is the best' line. Le Bruit's article is about contemporary radio drama, and the public fascination with its inscaped sound effects. The last sentence reads: 'De Loutherbourg too would have dropped a melon'.

▶▶ *August 1967, South-East England*

A tableau. A first memory of sound as theatre. I was four years old. We had pirate Radio London on all the time at home and in the car. It was on in the background as I became aurally self-aware. My father was a radio enthusiast, and I had been taken to see the MV Galaxy, the former World War II minesweeper from which Radio London broadcast. Within the range of my hearing, outrage had been expressed about how the pirates were to be closed down, but also mild excitement about the new local and national BBC stations that would be started up in their place. Dad had someone climb onto the roof and retrain the aerial to Crystal Palace. Come the day of closure, we sat around the table as a family listening to Radio London's final show. There were recorded 'thanks and goodbye' clips from the Stones and the Beatles and the other pop stars of the time. I knew who these were. They'd been on and much discussed while I was learning to hear.

The station's familiar jingles and idents were given a final airing. As sound effects, these had been as much part of everyday life as the windscreen-wipers or blinking indicators that formed my sense of CAR, or the whistling kettle and my baby sister's wailing that formed my sense of KITCHEN.

When the moment came, there was dramaturgy and rhetorical panache. The final record was the Beatles' 'A Day in the Life', which I knew. *Sgt Pepper* had been released that summer on my birthday, and my father had brought it home from London. It had been on all summer, and I had spent hours poring over the pop-art packaging as though it were a child's comic. Now 'A Day in the Life' became the sound of my first tragedy. Time itself was sucked up in the final dissonant orchestral *glissando*, like the ocean into a waterspout. The final piano chord then slammed it down on the kitchen table in front of us. We sat around the table staring at it, gripped in a tableau. The whole moment – our kitchen, and that hazily magical space behind the loudspeaker of the Roberts radio set – was frozen on that table. The piano chord decayed and faded. The clock in our kitchen slowed down and got louder. Eventually, on exactly the right beat of the inaudible rhythm, the final line: 'The Big L Time is three o'clock, and Radio London is now closing down'.

II

The next thing I remember was Tony Blackburn and the crash of thunder. Noakes and the watermelon must have been soon after, as I remember it in black and white, and colour was standard by 1969.

⏮ For Gainsborough, the obvious artifice of *our* thunder made the superstitions of those who went to the foyer to complain about it seem outmoded. Its obviousness as an effect, and its miniaturist precision, made it better than the old all-shaking thunder of Shakespeare's time, and better than the real thunder over London too. But the other thing the dissensus of the aesthetic regime did, and which impressed Gainsborough most about *The Eidophusikon*, was to present sounds as art, liberated from the semantic pedantry of the representative regime.

⏭ The lives of children who grow up with the radio, TV or computer on in the room are shaped by art objects and aesthetic productions at the same time as they are shaped by the semantic logic that the whistle of the kettle means the water has boiled. Each is part of the same aurality. I understood that the sound effects on the Beatles' *Yellow Submarine* (1966)[2] were not trying to present a submarine any more than the BANG! written on a flag that unfurls from the barrel of a novelty toy pistol is trying to be a gunshot. I knew that the space between the comic-book bubble SMASH! and the sound of a real window breaking was a real space that I would live my life negotiating. Drama was a space to be explored between the Castle Thunder

---

[2] Raided from the effects store at Abbey Road that George Martin had accumulated for his early novelty records, also the source of the alarm clocks on 'Time' on *The Dark Side of the Moon*.

on Scooby-Doo or Radio One, and the thunder that had us scurrying into the school pavilion from the cricket field.

Pop began with sound effects. The word 'pop' itself is one: a plosive syllable that stands on its own as an aesthetic production, an onomatopoeia that pop life used to shape itself. The OED's etymology attributes the earliest use of the term to George Eliot, who said 'there is too much "Pop" for the thorough enjoyment of the chamber music' in 1862.[3] It became the standard term for the teen-oriented, easy-listening audio product in the 1950s. Pop was formed in the space between chamber music or the playhouse, and the electric ballroom or the radio on the fridge. Sound effects were part of its form from the start, as I discussed back in Chapter 1. It was the native popular artform of the audio age.

'Revolution 9'

The other side of a wall to the sonic art of pop, the avant-garde was also exploring the audio age. The wall was thin, and one often overheard what the other was doing. The Goons, whose influence on the development of the 1960s pop art of sound I have mentioned, had been demobbed from the army and were working variously in dance-band and jazz music when they met in 1950 through an aleatory art game they called 'Tapesquences', played with an early tape machine owned by the landlord, after hours at the bohemian pub the Grafton Arms in Victoria. Perhaps naturally, the show they went on to make, inhabited a sonic world between music hall comedy and *musique concrète*. Principal writer Spike Milligan had suffered shell-shock during the war and was compulsively obsessed with sound, often haranguing the BBC effects department for its failure to realize the unrealizable effects he heard in his head (McCann, 2006: 74, 205). This contributed to the formation of the BBC's experimental Radiophonic Workshop, a key development in electronic music, sonic art and sound design (Lewis, 1994: 162–3). As shibboleths of rebellious teenagers like Lennon or Townshend, the Goon's nonsense sayings, sometimes extended way beyond the throwaway catch-phrase to the surrealistic poetry of Arp, Marinetti or Schwitters (e.g., the recurring motif 'psstt, tick, voung' in *The Case of the Missing CD Plates*, 1955, or the line 'the pling plang toof, nobitty nibbitty noo, pleta omnivorous plethora, pletty plom plom tartity to to tooee, fit plor tong tang tit putt putt' from *The Call of the West*, 1959). The same year as millions were listening to this on the BBC Light

---

[3] 'pop, n.8 and adj.', *OED Online*. Oxford University Press, December 2018 [accessed 22 February 2019].

Programme, in 1959, Stockhausen was creating *Kontakte* for a far smaller audience in the electronic-music studio of a radio station in Cologne.

No wonder when John Lennon and George Martin created the *musique concrète* track 'Revolution 9' in 1968 for the Beatles' *White Album*, it was not shocking in the Situationist way Lennon had hoped. People found his intended revolutionary incursion into the pop format far less revolutionary than Milligan's incursion of silly surrealism into the world of light entertainment. Nevertheless, 'Revolution 9' did have an impact, in normalizing sonic art as a recognizable 'arty sound' that became available to sound designers and future pop, as a sound effect. While it is often celebrated as the most skipped-over song the Beatles ever made, everyone who knows *The White Album* has heard 'Revolution 9' at least once. Beatles' chronicler Ian MacDonald estimates that within days of its release, around a million households owned *The White Album* and therefore maybe twice that number would have heard 'Revolution 9'. At the time he was writing this account, in 1994, Macdonald calculates that it would have been heard by hundreds of millions (2008: 287). Today, over half a century after its release, this may well be billions.

As McDonald puts it, 'in one of the most striking instances of the communicative power of pop, "Revolution 9" achieved a global exposure never imagined by the artists who pioneered its techniques' (ibid.). It does not matter that many never listened to it again. The point is that through the pop medium, the contemporary audimus got to know what sonic art sounded like, was able to draw coordinates from that knowledge in hearing other things and to use it as part of a dramaturgical web of practices and references when it made new performances. Much has been made of the influence of the avant-garde in theatre's 'sonic turn' (Curtin, 2014) and postdramatic theatre (Ovadija, 2013) which is valid, but perhaps what has been missed is the role of popular culture in distributing an avant-garde sensibility.

Spike Jones demonstrates your hi-fi

America did not have anything quite as nationally significant as the Goon Show, but it had far more media channels, and it had advertising, which British radio did not until the arrival of commercial TV in 1955, the radio pirates in the 1960s (whose commercials – as mimicked on the album *The Who Sell Out*, 1967 – were considered as cool as the pop music it framed), and then licensed commercial radio in the 1970s. Commercials not only provided a space where snappy, onomatopoeic repartee, sonic surrealism and instant aesthetics could be developed, but also placed a surreal frame around more serious programming. American art pop tended to parody this juxtaposition, along with audio products that were commissioned for commercial reasons (muzak to enhance productivity in retail and work spaces; stock mood music for restaurants or hotels; sound effects or exotica records to showcase hi-fi systems; and so on).

Spike Jones, the bandleader and 'sound effects man' of 1940s radio and the penny-arcade *soundie*, had moved on to making records like *Dinner Music for People Who Aren't Very Hungry: Spike Jones Demonstrates Your Hi-Fi* (1957) for Verve – the label that would, a few years later, sign Frank Zappa and the Mothers of Invention. Zappa would cite Jones as influential to his psychedelic mix of tightly scored and rehearsed arrangements, top musicianship and contemporary satire. Jones made several such albums – as did others – which, as the title suggests, parodied the sound effects albums produced to demonstrate hi-fis and promote proprietary hi-fi formats, while also performing that function. Recalling the taxonomy of sound effects in the 1913 Futurist *Art of Noises* manifesto (Russolo, 2009: 13), the rear sleeve of *Dinner Music* sets out the palette of the record with a mock seriousness, in sections:

> Space Ship Landing; Glugs; Pbrts; Skks; Garbage Disposal; Garbage Disposal grinding up violin; Garbage Disposal grinding up Violinist; 38 Calibre Pistol; Burpaphone; Kissing Trumpet; Ratchet; Trombone Fonk [sic]; 1911 Blackhawk Stutz; Airplane dropping bomb in river; Living Coo-Coo; Birds (Feathered kind) Tweets for your Tweeter.
>
> > Dying Coo-Coo; Champagne cork popping; Poontangaphone;
> > Brick through window; Klaxon; Electric Auto Horn; Police Whistle;
> > Cough; Emptying Wash-tub full of cowbells & assorted Kitchen Utensils; Snore; Bird (Un-Feathered kind); Whistle; 22 Calibre Pistol; Paris Taxi Horns.
>
> > 32 Calibre Pistol; Clinking Bottles (soft drinks); Slide-whistle; Clinking Bottles (hard drinks); Fight Gong; Breaking Bottle; Whistle; Hic-cough; Assorted Belches; Wind Whistle; Grunt; Barking Dogs in Hi-Fido; Assorted Sneezes; Pneumatic Pile-driver breaking Pavement; Two Bulb Horns; Anvil.

Together, they form the object framework of a strange cartoon modernity, whose difference from the lifestyle-framing list of sound effects Alexa told us she could play earlier is marked.

A no less strange pop nowness is represented on *Spike Jones in Hi-Fi: A Spooktacular in Screaming Sound!* (1959). The album showcases Warner Brother's 'Vitaphonic Sound' format, and the album commands its audience's attention with the word '*hear!*' emblazoned on the rear sleeve in a modernist font. The tracks include 'Dracula and his hippie Vampira singing love songs', a 'lament by Frankenstein' and a song by 'Dr Jekyll and the Ghouls'. There is thunder, of course, and other gothic sound effects aplenty, but the delight, which has always structured gothic sound, is now the knowing delight of the kitsch. The space within which *Spooktacular* sells hi-fis is a space that already knows that terms like 'hi-fi', 'stereo', '3D' and 'widescreen' were all marketing gimmicks used initially to sell horror movies. It is within the acoustemological recycling of these tropes as publicity, and ironic comments on that publicity, that the gothic sound effect became a meme of pop and as much a native part of its form as the electric guitar. Think of the sound effects in Bobby Picket's 'Monster Mash'; the ghoulish voice at the beginning of 'Wipe-Out'; the lunatic on 'They're Coming to Take Me Away', much of Alice Cooper's output, the thunder at the beginning of 'Flowers in the Rain' or Michael Jackson's 'Thriller'.

As an historical aside, it is noteworthy that on Spike Jones' album cover in 1959, the word 'hippie' is already being mentioned. Hippy culture would soon come to play its part in shaping the audibility of modernity as an arty and exotic picturesque, but we are not yet done with the nineteenth century, to where we now return.

The theatre we daydream

Drugs, foreigners and animals

If Charles Lamb's flight back into the noisy streets from the studious silence that had befallen the theatres where music was presented as art, set one course for the Victorian flâneurism that followed, then De Quincy's hugely popular column *Confessions of an English Opium-Eater*, which replaced Lamb's *Essays of Elia* in the *London Magazine* in 1821, set another. The fictional ontology that was now being modelled as aesthetic product, whereby situation is suspended and form is experienced for itself, led both ways. Lamb's flâneuristic path led to the soundscape: to Varèse's *Amériques*, Cage's *4′33″*, the World Soundscape Project, Hildegard Westerkamp, Janet Cardiff, and other such narrativized ecological scenographies, which engage the mind in a dialectic between the picturesque production of the world as an aesthetic, and its phenomenal topography. De Quincy's led to scenographies of the detached mind: to surrealism and psychedelia.

Lamb chose one way of fleeing the oppressive pretentiousness of the music auditorium, which I have argued, drawing on Attali, constituted a commoditized tableau of Pythagorean unity while pretending that it did not. The solitary, inscaped and fantastic auditorium suggested by De Quincy's description of how, under the influence of opium, 'a theatre seemed suddenly opened and lighted up within my brain, which presented nightly spectacles of more than earthly splendour' (De Quincy, 2005: loc. 1123), proposed another means of escape – or inscape.

The mistake of most people is to suppose that it is by the ear they communicate with music, and therefore that they are purely passive to its effects. But this is not so; it is by the reaction of the mind upon the notices of the ear (the *matter* coming by the senses, the *form* from the mind) that the pleasure is constructed, and therefore it is that people of equally good ear differ so much in this point from one another. Now, opium, by greatly increasing the activity of the mind, generally increases, of necessity, that particular mode of its activity by which we are able to construct out of the raw material of organic sound an elaborate intellectual pleasure. But, says a friend, a succession of musical sounds is to me like a collection of Arabic characters; I can attach no ideas to them. Ideas! my good sir? There is no occasion for them; all that class of ideas which can be available in such a case has a language of representative feelings. But this is a subject foreign to my present purposes.

ibid.: loc. 476

In relation to the Romantic abandon of Coleridge, the flâneurism of de Quincy or Baudelaire, the expanded consciousness of 1967 as represented in 'A Day in the Life' or Pink Floyd's album *Piper at the Gates of Dawn*, mind-altering drugs are usually characterized as a modern technology of the self. But there is a narcotic tradition in early modern drama and the classical epic, too, that underwrites the figuration of later drug culture – a heady metaphorical aurality of liquid air, exotic fauna and daydreams. Take these famous words, written in 1611:

> Be not afeard. The isle is full of noises,
> Sounds, and sweet airs that give delight and hurt not.
> Sometimes a thousand twangling instruments
> Will hum about mine ears, and sometime voices
> That, if I then had waked after long sleep,
> Will make me sleep again. And then, in dreaming,
> The clouds methought would open and show riches
> Ready to drop upon me, that when I waked
> I cried to dream again.

SHAKESPEARE, The Tempest, 3.2.136–44

Traces of hallucinogens have been discovered in clay pipes from the early seventeenth century (Thackeray, 2015), but more interesting than the question of whether Shakespeare may or may not have smoked weed, is the sense of exoticism and its figuration that is associated with narcotic abandon in the early modern and classical tradition. This passage is spoken by the Caliban, a 'savage' constructed for a Jacobean curiosity about the 'uncivilized' world beyond the familiar sensibilities of early modern England. In the oscillations of Caliban's speech patterns, cadence and onomatopoeia, the semiotic stability of the classical dramaturgy of sound breaks down. One moment he curses, to the offstage sound of thunder, in an abrasive, fragmented approximation of a hybrid Creole or Pidgin; the next, he speaks in flowing poetry. All Caliban's speech is intelligible to English ears, but in one moment, it is a part of the sonic picture, or soundscape, of the island, and in the next, a commentary on the play's metaphors. This speaks to a two-fold colonial fascination with exotica, as a sense of otherness that defensively reinforces parochial boundaries, but which is nonetheless sensually seductive and makes a strange kind of sense, encountered entirely in aesthetic terms.

The Tempest has a noticeably more pictorial aesthetic than in the earlier plays. Whether as an influence of the masque, a showcase for the popular Blackfriars' Consort, to cover interludes when the candles in the Blackfriars were re-lit, or all three of these, the music was more continuous than in earlier works. It was a long way from being the melo or underscoring of melodrama or the soundtrack, but was heading in that direction. Against the music and the picture was counterposed a sonic meta-text: the 'savage' lyricism, rhythm, timbre and cadence of Caliban's creole and the fauna of the island mentioned or insinuated in the folio text, which included chattering apes, hissing snakes, squawking jays, tittering marmosets, barking dogs, buzzing bees and whooping owls. While bees, birds and dogs had, since the Greeks, held a traditional place in the classical dramaturgy of sound, this was a more exotic, less European menagerie. Shakespeare's word 'twangling' has an onomatopoeic exoticism – like Caliban's Creole, a dehumanizingly generic sense of other or foreign; of strange microtonal harmonics and unfamiliar tuning. There is a characteristically colonial mishearing in this, a wilfully lazy, mocking approximation of non-familiar sounds and modalities that remains a familiar part of the micro-aggressive behaviour of white, European privilege. As Stoever puts it, this 'underlines the aurality of race and the unspoken power of racialized listening' (2016: 7). There is also, perhaps as part of this power structure, a theatrical delight about the word's attempt at a foreign sound. The sonic meta-text of *The Tempest* is a metaphor for the picturesque pleasures of colonialism, but also its condescending aurality. Before Ariel was freed, the only sounds of the island had been his tree prison's groans which 'did make wolves howl' (Lindley, 2006: 230–1). It is the arrival of European travellers that aestheticizes, and therefore tames and controls, the wild world beyond Western acoustemological boundaries. 'It was mine art / when I arrived and heard thee, that made gape / the pine and let thee out', says Prospero. 'I thank thee Master', says Ariel (1.2.294–6).

Like Dorothy stepping out from her relocated house into the land of the munchkins, the white invaders colourize the island with their artful hearing.

Which brings us back to poppies and opium. Narcotic seduction and the risk of getting lost on foreign quests – not just geographically but mentally – is both part of the dramatic peril of the epic, and part of its theatrical appeal. Think of the poppy fields in Oz and the perennial popularity of pre-Homeric legends of islands inhabited by wide-eyed, melancholy lotus-eaters. We yearn to get lost on a magic island, but we fear our yearning. Caliban says that when he awakes from a long sleep, the noises of the island make him cry to dream again, and in Act 1, Scene 2 (375–95) Ferdinand hears the song 'Come unto these yellow sands', 'dispersedly' echoed by spirits in the air, as though this kaleidosonic effect were real. In fact, Ferdinand has been drugged:

> This music crept by me on the waters,
> Allaying both their fury and my passion
> With its sweet air. Thence I followed it
> Or it hath drawn me rather;

1.2.380–4

The association between 'sweet', musicalized air and narcotic effect particularly appealed to the Romantics at the turn of the nineteenth century. Druggy tropes ranged from the intoxicating Germanic rush of drowning in the torrent, to Coleridge's opium dream of a musically liquefied, light in sound:

> How, by the desultory breeze caressed,
> Like some coy maid half yielding to her lover,
> It pours such sweet upbraiding, as must needs
> Tempt to repeat the wrong! And now, its strings
> Boldlier swept, the long sequacious notes
> Over delicious surges sink and rise,
> Such a soft floating witchery of sound
> As twilight Elfins make, when they at eve
> Voyage on gentle gales from Fairy-Land,
> Where Melodies round honey-dropping flowers,
> Footless and wild, like birds of Paradise,
> Nor pause, nor perch, hovering on untamed wing!

COLERIDGE, 1997: 87

Or, in the first Choric Song from Tennyson's poem 'The Lotos-Eaters' (1832):

> Music that brings sweet sleep down from the blissful skies.
> Here are cool mosses deep,

And thro' the moss the ivies creep,
And in the stream the long-leaved flowers weep,
And from the craggy ledge the poppy hangs in sleep.

2004: Loc. 4312

While we are about it, I should also mention that the aurality of Romanticism's aesthetic products is not only indexed by narcotic escapism and a racialized auditory attitude, but also by a less than sublime, commercially packaged experience of wild animals trapped in small cages. Colonial expansion and trade with remote regions not only introduced drugs and foreign-sounding languages to European auditory culture, but also exotic animals such as birds of paradise, tigers and elephants. Coleridge wrote 'The Eolian Harp' around the same time that Wombwell was buying snakes from sailors at the Port of London to form his travelling menagerie, and Blake, Byron and Wordsworth all visited Polito's Royal Menagerie in the Exeter Exchange (perhaps taking in *The Eidophusikon* at the same time).

The archetypal montage of animal sounds, narcotic detachment and approximated 'ethnic' stylings, which one hears over and again as an estranging device in theatre sound designs and movie soundtracks even today, is a Romantic picturesque of dubious provenance. From *The Tempest* to Faust waking up in the forest to the sound of eolian harps at the beginning of *Faust II*, theatre routinely takes exotic fauna and disposes them against sweet, eolian or luminescent shimmers, and modulating drones. This combination of the organic and the ethereal – the instant atmosphere of resonating harmonics, exotic music drifting on the breeze, bird calls and the evocative rhythms of cicadas or frogs – remains an archetypal construct of escapist paradise in advertising, the audio relaxation industry, and much theatre sound design. It is a meme that still works, beyond its cliché. It is also a fabricated picturesque that, ironically, became associated with the terms 'hi-fidelity' and 'realistic'.

Hi-fi exotica

A precursor of more psychedelically trippy music, the long-playing, mood-programming Lounge Music sub-genre known as Exotica, with titles such as *Taboo, Le Sacre du Sauvage: The Ritual of the Savage,* or *Ports of Pleasure*, should be taken alongside the sound effects of pop singles, and 1950s experiments in *musique concrète*, as one of the means by which sound effects became normalized as part of the instrumentation and format of pop music. This strange development in the 'light' orchestral catalogue whereby sound effects began to appear as part of musical arrangements alongside vibrant, technicolour timbres, 'ethnic' rhythms and atmospheric moods reached massive audiences.

Perhaps Boulez was not wrong. Perhaps anecdotal sounds were incompatible with the dialectic between morphology and form that constitutes music. Perhaps what Exotica shows, was music becoming part of – being subjugated to – the dialectic between the morphology and form of a new, hi-fi art of sound effects. With the long-player format, new picturesque audio travelogues began to appear, whose illustrations were musical but whose linking texts were either recorded sound effect clips or practical impressions of sound. Gordon Jenkins' *Manhattan Tower* (1949) is perhaps the earliest identifiable 'concept album' to use soundtrack-style effects and narration as a continuity 'bed' between tracks. Stan Kenton's *City of Glass* (1951) or *This Modern World* (1953) used a stylized montage of musical sound effects counterposed against an avant-garde-sounding atonality, all arranged for a jazz big band. The sleeve designs for these albums make it clear that what is being offered is a 'modern-arty' mood. Charles Mingus' *Pithecanthropus Erectus* (1956) and *Tijuana Moods* (1962) each frame avant-garde jazz arrangements within picturesque travelogue conceits. All of these records, as well as original music soundtracks, such as 1958's *South Pacific* and new recordings of the classical repertoire, were sold as ways to enjoy realistic, hi-fi sound.

Exotica was a musical sub-genre retrospectively named after Martin Denny's 1957 album of that name. A strange concoction of sound effects and cinematically genre-based musical orchestrations, it was a musical form native to the soundtrack age and the recording studio, where sounds could move around without it being inauthentic, as it would be in a classical recording. It thus lent itself perfectly to showcasing record companies' latest advances in Hi-Fidelity LP production. Exotica was a representation of music as a sequence of tableaux, which took its picturesque from film. As David Toop (1999) has described, it was these fabricated soundscapes that provided the basis of the supposedly consciousness-expanding, psychedelic audio impressionism of the hippy era.

The sub-genre began with a string of albums by the light-orchestral bandleader, arranger and composer of soundtracks, Les Baxter. Like film music, it was characteristically a pictorial form of sonically framed musical states rather than structured musical development and progression. It introduced exotic audio 'tinges' (to use Gilpin's description of the picturesque function of sound) into the cocktail lounge, the space-age bachelor pad, or the male hi-fi Yogi enclosure, or cell. It was either music to be 'put on in the background', while cocktails were shaken, the tie loosened, dinner eaten, or seduction performed; or else music to put on in order to listen to the performance of your hi-fi. Either way, it was a music designed to be heard while attending to something else and not studiously listened to – what DeNora in *Music in Everyday Life* describes as 'a technology of the self', a music put on to 'get in the mood' for something else (2000: 46–74). To help, the album sleeve provided listening notes (the kind that Spike Jones had parodied on his hi-fi demo records). These were technical and informative, but also provided notes on the correct employment of emotional disposition required for the full effect. Again, they are largely male-oriented. Les Baxter's *The Passions* (1954, Capital, LAL-468) contains tracks called 'Despair', 'Ecstasy', 'Hate', 'Lust', 'Terror', 'Jealousy' and 'Joy', and briefs the listener thus (original ellipses):

HERE IS A CHALLENGE TO THE LISTENER
   a powerful conception that plumbs depths of human emotion. Here is a picture of woman's passion painted with strokes of shocking brilliance . . . vital music written and performed with bold imagination . . . daringly executed for those who can sustain the most stimulating of listening sensations.
   For the High Fidelity enthusiast the Passions is a truly exciting exploration into the realms of recorded sound. It is a musical entertainment displaying the fantastic range of tonal colour that the finest of recording techniques can now capture; it is an album designed for the ultimate in satisfaction when reproduced on fine audio equipment.
   In this album also is an attractive booklet which includes a track-by-track analysis of the recording from the high fidelity standpoint, together with other pertinent technical information.

The accompanying booklet did indeed go into precise, illustrated detail about microphone types and recording techniques used, and details about Baxter's musical arrangements, all framed in a somewhat aggrandizing way by quotations from Shakespeare. Toop suggests there was a subtext here that stroked ruffled male egos: 'a failure to understand the extreme emotions of women could be amply compensated by a den equipped with a well-balanced Hi-Fi system' (1999: 70). In case the same ruffled egos were concerned that this was all a bit fey, there were also men's men, on hand, like John Sturges, director of *Gunfight at the O.K. Corral* (1957) and *The Old Man and the Sea* (1958), to reassure them that it was not:

Maybe you've wondered what-in-the-world kind of fellow he is to have cooked up these fantastic sounds. Maybe you have in mind a pale, aesthetic type who flutters his hands and uses mystic four-hundred-dollar words to describe what he is doing. Surprise . . . he's a great big husky guy who looks like he could make bow knots out of iron bars. He is very shy, completely genuine and, first and foremost, a fine musician who plays piano like crazy.

Rear sleeve, *Quiet Village: The Exotic Sounds of Martin Denny*,
1959, Liberty – LST 7122

It's OK, the marketing people are saying, it's man's music, as are the Hawaiian tiki lounge stylings of Arthur Lyman which, the sleeve notes invariably stress, are principally an exposition of state-of-the-art recording techniques undertaken at the industrial magnate Henry J. Kaiser's Aluminum Dome in Honolulu. If one listened past the Hawaiian music and the vocal impersonations of jungle fauna, one could hear acoustically engineered quality that was

> unmistakably modern, the product of 20th Century construction genius [and the] ingenious simplicity of [its] structural design and ideal sound form; [which has] no 'peaks' and allows a pleasing 'easy' sound reproduction with natural room acoustical reverberation [. . .] Oh, yes, the ocean sounds heard are real Pacific salt water waves. Native cries are, well, weird but real.

Rear sleeve, Arthur Lyman's *Taboo*, 1958, HiFi Records – R 806,
author uncredited

Technical details ensue, of Austrian microphones and stereophonic tape recorders. It may all be weird, but you had to admire the engineering.

Toop charts a genealogical link between this strange music and Californian hippy culture. Brian Wilson of the Beach Boys developed his orchestration skills at the Capitol Building, where Baxter and other exponents of the genre worked on the Exotica production line. One of them, Eden Ahbez, titillated the Californian bourgeoisie in the late 1950s with his media persona of long-haired, bearded, alfresco-sleeping, itinerant wild-man artist – the original Californian hippy. A composer of new-age ecological exotica, Ahbez is pictured sitting next to Wilson during the infamous, drug-fuelled 1967 *Smile!* sessions. The arrangement of that legendary unfinished project was an exercise in collage, of vocal animal impersonations, trains, bicycle bells and musical fragments spliced together on tape. Wilson suffered a breakdown trying to make it all hold together as the coherent album its predecessor *Pet Sounds* (1966) had been, whose sound sits somewhere between Arthur Lyman and Phil Spector, and which spurred the Beatles on to make *Sgt Pepper*.

There are many books on the studio techniques and every other aspect of *Sgt Pepper*. For want of space, I will touch here only on the sitars, since they relate to the theme of exotica. While the peace and love, and Harrison's musicological interest, were undoubtedly genuine, it is hard not to hear a relationship between them and the 'ethnic' flavours and fabricated 'world' picturesques of Exotica. Sitars are a part of the sound of hippy culture and a meme in global audio-visual culture for Indian 'mysticism' and the expanding effect it was portrayed as having on white, Western consciousness. These kinds of meme work effectively in theatre sound design, as part of an object framework that, in Gilpin's phrase, tinges the imagination this way and that, because as memes they do their work without begging distracting questions such as 'why are there sitars?' In other words, they have become normalized, in a picturesque way, as part of the scenery in the space of a particular set of practices, meta-discourses and sensibilities. This is a form of dissensus – like Appia's light, it defaces the sitars and turns them into forms that no longer speak principally to their original contexts, but to something else.

In *Acoustic Interculturalism: Listening to Performance* (2012), Marcus Cheng Chye Tan problematizes the unintended colonial, intercultural utopianism that is woven into the aurality of modern theatre in this way. He points to Goethe's Weimar Classicism, Rheinhard, Brecht, Brook's *Mahabharata* (1985) and Mnouchkine's Japanese-influenced Shakespeare of the early 1980s as examples. This is not to stigmatize this work. I am suggesting only that it should be recognized that by drawing tropes, or using exotic flavourings eclectically, the sonic collage might get an instant hit out of cultural association, but in doing so defaces the sound a little bit more within the memic index or genome of 'global' aurality. This is true of figures of speech too, and I would reflect similarly on Carpenter and McLuhan's 'Acoustic Space', published in the same year as Eden Ahbez's arty and exotic 'new-age' album *Eden's Island: The Music of an Enchanted Isle* (1960) – an ecological concept album narrated in a Beat Poetry style, and illustrated with filmic mood music that twangles on the ear with exotic "ethnicity" and sound effects. Both Ahbez, and Carpenter and McLuhan, propose a theoretical acoustemology that draws casually on exotic tropes of generic non-Western mysticism. That the onto-theological holism in the idea of sound's supposed immersivity must be inspected for evangelistic agendas, I have already mentioned. Similarly, theories or dramaturgies that employ exotic tropes to create an evocative or picturesque auditory space of thematic allusion should be aware of the unspoken power of racialized listening, and its potential to deface and exclude.

II

But now hear this: a wolf is howling in the distance, calling us back from California to nineteenth-century London. So *without* the twangling flourish of a non-specifically Eastern European, approximately Transylvanian zither, we head back to the Strand and some other strands in the genome of the contemporary theatre we hear.

Thunder on the ear

> There are such beings as vampires, some of us have evidence that they exist. Even had we not the proof of our own unhappy experience, the teachings and the records of the past give proof enough for sane peoples. I admit that at the first I was sceptic. Were it not that through long years I have trained myself to keep an open mind, I could not have believed until such time as that fact thunder on my ear.
>
> STOKER, 1897: 220

The gothic adopted the Picturesque as its house aesthetic and expanded its tropes beyond ruined abbeys and the traditionally melodramatic Alpine picturesque of Frankenstein, to a broader picturesque plundered from mummies' tombs, voodoo zombie rituals and the 'sinister' 'Orient'. The definitive expression of the gothic, though, is the journey to the Transylvanian castle, which takes as its point of departure a stock melodramatic picturesque of disrupted domesticity amid the wind, wuthering and ruined abbeys of the north of England, a touristic excursion through rustic villages and Romany folklore and a precarious alpine bridge crossing the waterfall and leading up into the mountains where nemesis awaits. It then tinges it with suggestions of narcotic and erotic seduction, hallucination, and the sounds of wolves, bats and the disarmingly sexy voice of a polite but slightly foreign-sounding aristocrat.

Bram Stoker's novel *Dracula* (1897) is full of sound – of siren-like voices, echoes, wind and waves, and all the noises that familiarly characterize the cinematic sense of gothic 'horror'. The plot turns, though, on thunder: *our* thunder. Thunder appears at moments of realization and at the situational apexes of key scenes. The figurative use of the verb 'thunder' in the quotation above illustrates just how the effect had become a literary trope for marking of turning points in plots. It is both a trope and a dramaturgical device, which gothic fiction adopted from earlier nineteenth-century gothic melodrama.

Thunder is the delightful, almost orgasmic promise of melodramaturgy, which charges the plot with desire, fear and potential energy from the start. We know as the curtain rises on any melodrama that there is a storm of one kind or another coming, and that it will eventually arrive, perhaps several times. In *Dracula*, there are several passages of oncoming storm, and several thunderous realizations, whose descriptions recall the differentiation Uvedale Price delineated between the sublime of the threat, and the picturesque of the arrival: 'that prevailing intensity which, on the approach of thunder, affects persons of a sensitive nature' (Stoker, 1897: 72). Or: 'there were dark, rolling clouds overhead, and in the air the heavy, oppressive sense of thunder. It seemed as though the mountain range had separated two atmospheres, and that now we had got into the thunderous one' (ibid.: 7–9).

And then, at 'strong points' in the scenic narrative, as Mayhew called them, there are pyrotechnic displays where the sublime fear is realized as pleasurable thrill:

> the sea for some distance could be seen in the glare of the lightning, which came thick and fast, followed by such peals of thunder that the whole sky overhead seemed trembling under the shock of the footsteps of the storm.
>
> ibid.: 72

After the realization, the drama reboots itself. Our gothically bewildered hero wakes up to the sound of gently lapping water, tinkling eastern wind-chimes, or birdsong, before the suspense builds again. Thundering realizations are the archetypal turning points of melodramaturgy and imprinted in our modern sense of dramaturgical rhythm, cadence and dynamics. Thunder is thus a key sound effect of modernity as it had been in the acoustemology of classical antiquity, but for different reasons. We know it as a cliché, a joke about trite theatricality, and an effect. But despite all our knowing, it still works. (This is what defines a sonic meme.)

The Count himself makes only rare appearances, as is typical of villains in the horror genre and in gothic melodrama. The visibility and audibility of Dracula himself is analogous to the oncoming storm – a teasing inevitability and a constantly present potential energy from the start. Gothic villains are acousmatic beings, whose unseen presence can be heard in the wolves, the rumbles of oncoming thunder, and the mountain echoes, and in the febrile minds of the perilous heroine and the addiction-controlled factotum (Renfield). In this ominous state, there is no limit to their power. They are what Chion calls '*acousmêtres*', which I shall discuss further when we come to the acousmatic operation of audio-objects of the loudspeaker age (1994: 129–31). Where the audio *acousmêtre* might be heard in voiceover, Dracula is omnipresent in his ability to 'direct the elements, the storm, the fog, the thunder' (Stoker, 1897: 220). He finally appears with a Germanically Romantic *rausch*, or rush, of orgasmic asphyxiation: 'There was a red cloud before me, and a noise like thunder, and the mist seemed to steal away under the door' (ibid.: 261).

Dracula was written as a novel to be read; its effects heard in the mind. However, before it was published, Stoker adapted it for a rehearsed reading at the Lyceum in 1897, to secure the stage adaptation rights in a year when vampirism had suddenly become a thing (the kind of 'thing' people say when they recognize something that encapsulates the *Zeitgeist*). There had been the scandal of Philip Burne-Jones's erotic painting *The Vampire*, the Kipling poem of the same name, which it inspired, and Florence Marryat's novel *The Blood of the Vampire* (about the vampire daughter of a mad scientist and an exotically mixed-race voodoo priestess). Stoker had based his debonair portrayal of the Count on Henry Irving's depiction of Faust in the production for which Colonel Gouraud had provided the electric sword effect. He asked Irving to read the part at the Lyceum, but he refused.

The novel, however, can be read as a theatrical text, as part of a history that stretched back to the late eighteenth century. Stoker had learned his dramaturgy and aural sense of theatre as the manager of Irving's Lyceum. Irving had learned his from Charles Kean at the Princess Theatre, formerly the Royal Bazaar, where Clarkson Stanford's British Diorama had continued to test the borderline between the gallery exhibition and the scenic stage in De Loutherbourg's tradition (Stanford had revived *The Eidophusikon* as a homage to De Loutherbourg at Zoroaster at Drury Lane in 1824). Ludwig Chronegk, Stoker and Irving's contemporary and the stage director of the Meininger Players, had also learned from Kean and disseminated an epic theatrical picturesque of sound around Europe through extensive touring between 1874 and 1890. Chronegk's fabricated picturesque was a key influence on Stanislavskian naturalism and what we might now recognize as director or regie theatre, and was known particularly for his use of sound in reinforcing the spectacle of his vast crowd scenes. Reputedly the stage effect known as 'rhubarb' was an anglicization of 'rhabarber', which Chronegk would have his backstage chorus of noise-makers say to create a background murmur, although this is disputed (Brown, 2009: 69–73). However, he was also known for his gothic stage atmospherics. This contemporary description of his 1878 staging of Grillparzer's 1817 gothic play *Die Ahnfrau* lists sonic tropes that became the stock-in-trade of the twentieth-century gothic horror movie:

> the creaking of the weathervane, the howling of the wind, the flickering of the fire, the whining and wailing, the moaning and groaning in innumerable places, the squeaking of the doors at the entrance and exit of the Ahnfrau, and the strange and melancholy sound at her appearance.
>
> KOLLER, 1984: 101

The genealogy of this stock palette can be traced back through gothic fiction and ghost stories that had adopted the melodramaturgy of situation and effect, and through Chronegk and Irving, Kean, Clarkson Stanford, Macready, Edmund Kean and Madame Vestris to De Loutherbourg's Picturesque of Sound and the first peal of *our* thunder.

Gothic melodrama

Having referred to it enough, let us now address English gothic melodrama of the early nineteenth century. Holcroft's *A Tale of Mystery*, an uncredited translation of Pixérécourt's *Coelina* (1800) performed at Covent Garden in 1801, is generally considered to be the first. Its denouement is set in the Alps, which, as a 'lonely region full of rocks, caverns, and echoes', provided the formulaically correct picturesque disposition of rough, jagged and abruptly changing visuals, atmospheric aural circumstances, and the ever-present potential for thunder, waterfalls and avalanches (Gilpin, 2014: 133). The following stage direction from *A Tale of Mystery* is an encapsulation of how picturesque principles formed the basis of the gothic *mise-en-scène*, with all the prescribed ingredients present, from the rustic miller's cottage framed by dark rocks, to the storm effect and the diegetically framing presence of music. In it, we can also see how the backstage reverberation of the still relatively recently reconfigured picture box stage was now being used for effects of distance (the Holla!):

> Thunder is heard, while the Scene changes. Music
> Scene: the wild mountainous country called the Nant of Arpennaz; with pines and massy rocks. A rude wooden bridge on a small height thrown from rock to rock; a rugged mill-stream a little in the back ground; the miller's house on the right; a steep ascent by a narrow path to the bridge; a stone or bank to sit on, on the right-hand side. The increasing storm of lightning, thunder, hail and rain becomes terrible. Suitable music. Enter Romaldi from the rocks, disguised like a peasant, with terror; pursued as it were by heaven and earth.
> *Rom.* Whither fly? Where shield me from pursuit, and death, and ignominy? My hour is come? The fiends that tempted now tear me. (*dreadful thunder*) The heavens shoot their fires at me! Save! Spare! Oh, spare me! (*falls on the bank*).
> Music, Hail, &c. continue; after a pause, he raises his head. More fearful claps of thunder are heard, and he again falls on his face. The storm gradually abates. Pause in the music. A very distant voice is heard. [Holla!] Music continues. He half rises, starts, and runs from side to side; looking and listening; Music ceases. Voice again. [Holla!]
> HOLCROFT, 1802: 40–1

If the repertoire of sound effects in early melodrama seems somewhat limited to storms (compared with the later melodrama of Boucicault or Bruce 'Sensation' Smith, which had exploding steamboats, train crashes, fires, and earthquakes), then one must not forget that melodrama was not played against a background of silence. Fronting the stage, with its almost continuous, filtering materiality, like an audible gauze or scrim, was the music, or melo. As the above excerpt shows, it offset both the vocal sound and the noises-off, with carefully orchestrated timing.

Melo

The melo is not audible on stage: an obvious point perhaps, but formally paradigmatic in terms of melodrama's departure from the scenography of classical theatre, where there was no demarcation between the apparatus of the diegesis (the music, the separation between auditorium and stage reinforced by the conventional 'art' of seeing, as Gilpin described it). Melodrama is also different to masque, Italian opera, or musical theatre, where music subsumes the scene and must be audible there because characters dance and sing along to it, and are thus musicalized figures. In a melodrama, the stage is not musicalized. The music accompanies and shapes the emotional response to the drama *in the auditorium*. The pit orchestra is situated on the audience side of the curtain line, under the stage apron, which serves as a kind of altar at the threshold between auditorium and stage. The melo, on *our* side of the altar, underscores and structures the hearing, and not the stage performance, which is structured by the pictorial dramaturgy of situation and effect. Melodrama frames the scenery, gestures, voices and noise with music. It frames the spectacle with hearing. The interior of the scenes is not musicalized – it is disposed, not composed by the musical auditorium.

English melodrama was the production of a range of influences from equine circus, pantomime and different forms of illegitimate musical drama and opera (Mayer, 1980); but formally, the melo remained in the service of the pictorial Effect, as it had on De Loutherbourg's stage and in Garrick (and Diderot's) tableau-oriented reconfiguration of dramatic sensibility. In the first French *mélodrame*, Rousseau's *Pygmalion* (1770), acted, spoken exposition alternated with passages of pictorial exposition framed by specially composed music. These used mime as well as poses drawn from classical gestural rhetoric (traces of which can be seen in the relationship between the gestural acting and inter-titles in early silent film). A section of *Coelina* retains something of this original format, where a deaf and mute character relays, in mimed interludes, the story of a terrible crime he has witnessed (and whose retribution eventually plays out in the Alpine storm). This is retained in Holcroft's plagiarized adaptation, but the script annotations and Thomas Busby's score indicate that it is merely a set-piece sequence within a far more interwoven musical picturesque, where the melo does not simply frame a dumbshow but orchestrates and underscores the building of suspense and the formal construction of pivotal situations and their aesthetic Effect. There are musical punctuations to accompany reveals and specially composed hurries, tremolos and agits to assist what Mayhew called 'the flow of interest', from situation to situation (Meisel, 1983: 39), but which the historian David Mayer perhaps more aptly describes as the 'momentum of the play's headlong rush from sensation to sensation' (1980: 51).

Other than the timeless, breathless, dramaturgically pivotal and regenerating *coups de théâtre* at the apex of each scene, the melo tends only to stop to assist the transformation of the stage into exterior scenes – forests, windswept moors, mountain passes or coastal scenes. Here, stage sound effects take over. Mayer notes that in Pocock's early gothic melodrama *The Miller and His Men* (1813), there are only two scenes that are 'bare' of music:

> Act 1, Scene 2, has none at all, but its setting is 'The Forest', and the opening stage direction designates the dominant sound, 'distant thunder'. The scene to follow is also played without music until the closing sestetto, but again the storm sounds outside Kelmar's Cottage.
>
> MAYER, 1976: 119

Even in these scenes, the absence of music hangs translucently in front of the scene and delimits its hearing space, as an invisible front wall, through which the sonic picturesque appears, conditioning the aural mood.

The drama between the audible and the inaudible

Theatre is an art of establishing conventions and then breaking them for effect. And thus, having established that the stage is not musicalized, and musical underscoring from the pit is inaudible on stage, a caveat soon appeared. This demarcation between musicalized auditorium and musically silent stage space remained the rule *except* when one of the protagonists became psychologically unstable and suffered auditory hallucinations. In such circumstances, the auditory two-way mirror of the fourth wall dissolves, and the music, usually the audience's diegetic framing or commentary, becomes the agent of a vicarious, first-person subjectivity, within the scene. During these scenes, the audience hears the music *through* the protagonist's febrile mind. The source of the music seems to move from the pit onto the stage. In such febrile states, the category boundaries between music and sound can also become permeable.

In the following example from a letter from Charles Dickens to the French actor-manager Charles Fechter, rehearsing the Paris production of *No*

Thoroughfare (Dickens and Wilkie Collins, premiered in London the previous year, 1867), we see an elaboration of these two ambiguities, and an interplay between pictorial stage sounds and the emotionally orchestrating function of the melo. In it, we see one of the fundamental principles of modern sound design – the hyper-real ability of sound effects to equivocally take on the diegetically musical function of emotional underscoring, within the scenic tableau.

> I have an idea about the bedroom act which I should certainly have suggested if I had been at our 'repetitions' here. I want it done to the sound of the Waterfall. I want the sound of the Waterfall louder and softer as the wind rises and falls, to be spoken through – like the music. I want the Waterfall listened to when spoken of, and not looked out at. The mystery and gloom of the scene would be greatly helped by this, and it would be new and picturesquely fanciful.
>
> DICKENS, 2011: loc 6087

It is Act IV, Scene I, and we are inside a rustic chalet. The protagonists, Obenreizer and Vendale, and the audience can hear the unseen waterfall through a window (the full exterior picturesque with the precarious alpine bridge leading to the mountainous nemesis is revealed later). So far, so orthodox: a sound effect which gives a sense of the not-so-new and fanciful, stock Alpine picturesque outside. However, the musical modulation of the sound, which Dickens is suggesting might underscore the mood, is not simply the effect of the wind rising and falling in the way Gilpin prescribed as atmospherically apt for the melancholic gaze. The 'fanciful' part of this picturesque is that the waterfall is conducted, as it were, by Obenreizer's modulating mental state, as he recalls a disturbing childhood memory. The audience thus hears the waterfall *through* Obenreizer. His subjective emotional psychology changes the auditory fabric of the mimetic onstage world, rather than simply applying a translucent filter in front of the scene, as pit music would:

Vendale How still the night is! I hear a rushing sound somewhere in the distance. Is it a waterfall?

Obenreizer Yes. A waterfall on the lower slopes of the mountain.

Vendale The mountain that lies between us and Italy! The mountain that we cross to-morrow!

Obenreizer (*stopping in his walk, and pursuing his own train of thought*) It sounds like the old waterfall at home. The waterfall which my mother showed to travellers – if she *was* my mother!

Vendale If she *was* your mother?

Obenreizer (*still pursuing his thoughts*) The sound of that waterfall changed with the weather, as does the sound of all falling waters, and flowing waters. I remember it as sometimes saying to me for whole days – 'Who are you, my little wretch? – Who are you, my little wretch?' – I remember it other times saying, when its sound was hollow, and a storm was coming up the pass – 'Boom! Boom! Boom! Beat him! Beat him! Beat him!' like my mother in a rage – if she *was* my mother.
DICKENS and COLLINS, 1867: IV:1

Theatrical thunder and lightning are thus no longer only picturesque realizations that tap into the awe of the sublime for their effect. They can now also be realized delusions, the picturesque results of psychological derangement and disintegration – no less awful prospects. The symphonic correspondence between a waterfall or the storm coming up the pass and Obenreizer's mother complex sets course the symbolism of Ibsen, Maeterlinck and Freud, and the modernity of the 'Age of Anxiety'. However, in the breaking of the different spaces of audibility – of the musical auditorium and the non-musical stage; in the auditory punning Dickens and Collins are clearly using here, between thunder, violence and a beating heartbeat; and in the juxtapositions of scale between the figuration of the mind, the room and the mountains: drama sets its course towards the age of the microphone, the amplifier, the loudspeaker and the movie.

8

Inside out
(Symbolism, cinema and *The Bells*)

The soundtrack, its prehistory and audiovisual morphology

It is tempting to narrate theatre history in relation to broader historical narratives. I could suggest the 'boom, boom, boom' of the new storm was the quickening pulse of modernity just as I could read this earlier passage from *Faust* Part II as a prophecy of the twentieth-century soundscape of combustion engine and amplified music:

> Granite gates jar open, grating,
> Apollo's car drives up, wheels rattling –
> Oh what a din it makes, the dawn!
> Glittering trumpets loudly blaring
> Dazzle eyes and ears dumbfound
> With sounds unheard of, past all hearing.
>
> GOETHE, 1998: 2–3

One could hear the 'boom, boom, boom' coming up the pass as foreshadowing war, and the 'common world of great slaughter and much sorrow' that W. H. Auden identified as the keynote of the twentieth-century 'Age of Anxiety' (1968: 261). It could be the sound of the nemesis of Romanticism approaching, and the new music of 'dissonance, density, difficulty and complexity' born in the Nazi prisoner-of-war camp Stalag 8 on 15 January 1941, in Messiaen's *Quartet for the End of Time* (Ross, 2009: 387–90). All of these would be good narrative conceits, but what these seemingly prophetic passages really do is show how new ways of hearing were becoming imaginable. This is not insignificant. It is the countenancing of new sensibilities that sets the conditions whereby changes can then happen in the *technē* of audibility.

While melodrama's form continued to develop and find new picturesques for its headlong rush from one sensational situation to the next, at the beginning of the twentieth century, a pan-European New Drama (as historians have designated it) became discernible, which was no less a drama of sensation and aesthetics, but in a less musically reinforced way. In London, the critic William Archer's championing of Ibsen and Granville Barker's staging of Hauptmann, Galsworthy, Maeterlinck and Schnitzler at the Royal Court, amid much discussion of developments in Russian drama, created the sense of a movement that broke away from the musically demonstrative melodramatic paradigm.

It was characteristic of this new drama that significant events happened offstage rather than in full view, and the continuous auditory programme of the melo and sound effects of the weather were replaced by a dialectic between the spoken word and what Osip Mandelstam, speaking of Stanislavsky's productions of Chekhov, calls 'nothing other than a holiday of pure tactile sensation. Everything grows quiet, and only a silent tactile sensation remains' (quoted in States 1985: 74).

Bert States adds how, within verbal pauses,

> The tactile world, the visible world (which the talk is aimed unconsciously at keeping at bay), this history-in-objects, quietly encroaches on the human [. . .] Suddenly you can hear the ticking of objects and the ceaseless flow of future into past: the world is no longer covered by conversation.
>
> ibid.

It seems unlikely that this turn of events happened in isolation, simply as a rejection of melodrama, but arose from the kinds of artistic convention-breaking I have described. In the rearview mirror of the New Drama, the 'boom, boom, booming' might be credibly argued to have been the beginnings of a symbolist turn on the popular London stage. This brought with it a new kind of sound effect, whose indeterminate significance seemed to reside in a resonance between an idea, memory or delusion in the minds of its protagonists, and something outside the picture frame.

II

We have now reached the point where we left things at the end of Chapter 5, with Gouraud and his electric mansion on the hill, next to the rotting ear of the neo-classical Georgian crescent. 'Anathema maranatha!' – let it be damned to perdition! – Clement Scott, was saying when we left him, referring to Edison's phonograph, in his review of Law's *The Judge* at Terry's Theatre (Scott, 1890).

While Scott was hardly the most progressive of critics, neither did Gouraud's wax-cylinder recording, when replayed offstage at Terry's Theatre, seem to add anything new to the drama which merited all the hype. The baby in front of the phonograph's recording horn may have been real enough, but the sound effect was far from realistic. It was obviously out of place, but, more to the point, this obviousness did not seem to have any purpose; it was just a mistake. Plus, it was too quiet.

▸

1904 also happened to be the year that John Ambrose Fleming, a consultant to Edison's Electric Light Company in London, invented the thermionic diode valve. This rectified AC current to DC, through the emission of electrons from a heated filament in a vacuum. This so-called 'electronic' process would lead to a communications revolution, but also the distribution of a new sensibility. In 1906, Lee De Forest's prototype *Audion* triode grid tube introduced power gain and the ability to control or modulate the amount of signal passing through the valve. This simple device changed the world. It led to telephone repeater amplifier, which by 1912 allowed analogue signals to be relayed over long distances and became one of the defining technological and cultural advances of the twentieth century in enabling networked telecommunications.

Over the next decade, De Forest continued to develop the amplifier as we know it, and to play a pioneering role in radio transmission and the optical film soundtrack. Amplification became not only a way of hearing things louder and disseminating them more widely, but also a way of hearing things differently. The network would turn the globe into a village; records, radio and film would become its village theatre. By January 1926, *Popular Science Monthly* was full of advertisements for the latest valve-amplified sound equipment for the home. 'If Zimbalist plays, it is Zimbalist – as if you were actually in the studio' reads a full-page ad for the six-tube Kolster Radios on page one, continuing that 'there is no interference, no muffling, no exaggerations or repressions. If the President makes a speech, if McCormack sings, if Lopez jazzes, if Godowsky plays the piano – whoever or whatever is broadcast is reproduced faithfully.' In such ways, the ethic of fidelity was introduced to the aurality of the age.

On page three, there is then an advertisement for an Audio Transformer. The root of De Forest's term *Audion* had been retained but the *n* had been dropped, identifying the purpose of the new technology with a first-person singular form of the Latin *audire*: *I hear*. 'The Audio Transformer amplifies at an unusually high ratio of 1 to 5', the ad reads. 'Two steps of amplification may be used without transformer distortion' (ibid.: 3). The audio age had arrived. The technicalities were of specialist interest, but by the 1930s, radios, gramophones and visits to the talkies, or 'audible pictures', had woven audio through people's lives. With this came nothing short of a new mode of sensory being specific to everyday existential counterpoints of acoustic life and a selectively amplified *I hear*.

II

We will come to those, but I want to discuss how theatre countenanced the second great reconfiguration of the sensible in the audio age, and for that we need to stay in the Alps and the nineteenth century a little longer.

|◄◄

Delusional situations and effects

Four years after Dickens and Collins' 'new and fancifully picturesque' waterfall, the inside-out aurality that not only characterizes symbolism but the psychological horror genre found one of its earliest iconic expressions in the deranged auditory hallucinations of Mathias in the Lyceum production of Leopold Lewis's *The Bells* (1871). It was the role that made Henry Irving famous, but sound was his co-star. Its central image of the actor angularly contorted with terror, his hands over his ears, desperately trying to block out the sound of his inner demons – or maybe to keep them *in* his head – became an instantly recognizable trope of psychological melodrama:

> MATH. (Who has sat in chair R. of table L. rises – walks quickly R. fingers in ears which he removes when R. then runs up to window, tears curtains open and looks out and closes them again.) No one on the road, no one! (Down C.) What is this jangling in my ears?
> MUSIC 4.
> Ah, the very night – the very hour. (*Clock strikes ten.*) (*Down to chair R. of table.*) I feel a darkness coming over me, a giddiness seizes me. (*Staggers, hand on chair back.*) Shall I call for help? No, no, courage, Mathias, courage. The Jew is dead – dead – ha ha ha – dead! (*Drops into chair, head in arms on table – vision slowly revealed. Mathias rises.*) It's nothing, the wind and the cold have overcome me. (*Walks down R.*) It's nothing, nothing, nothing.
> (At the third 'nothing' Mathias has walked up C. and is confronted with full view of vision.) Ah, ah!
> (Loud cry dying away and falling C. as curtain descends.)
> Stop MUSIC 4.
> END OF ACT 1
>
> MAYER et al., 1980: 49

Like the modulations of Dickens' waterfall, the audibility of the eponymous bells is a production of the mind. There *are* no bells in *The Bells*, other than in the audience's manipulated aural empathy with the protagonist's psychotic state – his deluded first-person auditory presence in the scene. Set, like a ghost story, on Christmas Eve, 'an occasion consecrated to domesticity', as Clement Scott put it (1897: 4), *The Bells* has the trappings of a traditional gothic melodrama set, once again, in the Alpine picturesque of Alsace. However, rather than building towards the thunderous recognition and unmasking of the villain, the protagonist himself is revealed to be the murderer, early on.

Mathias (Irving) is a burgomaster overcome by hallucinations derived from a guilty secret: his murdering of a travelling salesman for gold, fifteen years before. The production's *coup de théâtre*, fully realized at the end of Act I and then referred to and reprised as a motif until a second full realization at the denouement, was a special-effects 'vision' sequence, heralded by auditory hallucination of the bells on the salesman's sleigh. It begins faintly. Are we all hearing things? Or is it real? Then it builds, with music, towards a crescendo as a lime-lit tableau of the snowy murder scene appears through the painted scrim. We reach what we think will be the tableau's apex and expect a scene-ending blackout, but Mathias fights back and regains control. Henceforth, each time we hear the bells effect, we join Mathias in his battle to hold the apparition back. He believes that if he can hold off his demons until the forthcoming wedding of his daughter to the local police chief, all will be sacrificially atoned, and the ghost laid to rest.

However, in a departure from the usual supernatural ghost story, Mathias understands the apparitions to be psychological artefacts. He is worried by a visit he has made to a fairground 'Mesmer', or hypnotist, whose act is to place people into trances whereby they vocalize their innermost secrets. The visit plays on his mind. He is worried that one of his hallucinations might, if witnessed, inadvertently reveal his secret. The night before the wedding, he dreams he is in court, being tried for the murder. In the dream, the Mesmer is summoned and hypnotizes him into re-enacting the crime before the court. The stage effect is reprised. He is found guilty and sentenced to be hanged. His family wake him from the nightmare as he is clawing at an imaginary rope around his neck, and he dies in terror.

Sonic apparitions are part of a long tradition of stage magic in drama (Butterworth, 2005; Brown, 2009: 90–6), but here is a critical difference. Mathias' visions are not supernatural phenomena. The big scenic effect gives the audience its stage magic, but at the same time it is party to Mathias' understanding that they are delusional psychological artefacts. Unlike the ghost voice from under the floor in *Hamlet*, say, there is no doubt that these sounds are imaginary. The point is that these are sounds that Mathias *cannot* get out of his head, and *we* the spectators have been drawn into the subjectivity and delirious aurality of Mathias' crisis. We are inside his mind. As Mayer puts it, *The Bells* 'offered to theatre audiences the opportunity to share vicariously the experience of criminal action, guilt, fear of discovery, and eventual retribution' (Mayer et al., 1980: 5).

Crucially, the effect was not only an impressive accomplishment of stage technology, but a rehearsed scenographic interplay between Irving's acting (or reacting) and the sound effect. Of this, we have the modern first-hand account of Jones-Evans, who saw the production several times as a boy and describes the 'visual-auditory' experience the first time the bells appear. Mathias is at dinner, about to drink a glass of wine, when the missing 'Polish Jew' is mentioned. Irving pauses in the act of raising the glass to his lips, and peering into it, pretends to remove a fragment of cork with his little finger. This tiny act and slight pause draws the theatre in to Mathias' first-person space like a push–pull camera zoom, and then, as Jones-Evans recounts:

> 'So, you were talking about that, were you?' he murmured, wiping his finger on the table-cloth. Wipe, wipe, wipe. 'You were talking about that, eh?' It was at that moment that he heard, and so did we, the far-off jingling of sleigh-bells. 'Bells' he whispered. 'Sleigh-bells on the road.'
>
> ibid.: 22–3

Like the miniaturist intensity of *The Eidophusikon*, the whisper and the scale of gesture are quintessentially cinematic. This minutely rehearsed timing, between the actor and the cueing of the effects – there is another where Irving looks up from tying his shoe when the Mesmer's powers are described – created the synchrony of performance and *mise-en-scène* that would soon become the work of the film-editing suite. It made the main bells effect even more breathtaking. Clement Scott was not convinced this stagecraft should be called acting, but Scott's editor, also in the audience on the opening night, overruled him, ordering him to 'write about it so that everyone shall know he is great' (Harwood, 1984: 210). Scott complied, but was a little mealy-mouthed:

> Weird enough is the story to be sure, but there is a strange fascination about horrible things, and for many reasons, 'The Bells' is a play, which those interested in the drama as an art should not fail to see.
>
> SCOTT, 1897: 7

Irving became a star.

The popular science of sound

Harwood (1984) notes in his discussion of *The Bells* phenomenon that 'in the century of Doctor Jekyll and Dorian Gray, a character who led a successful public life but nursed a criminal secret was a resident in the popular imagination' (209). Strange, perhaps, but the idea that inner secrets could mesmerically be uncovered with ticking watches, through 'tells' triggered by other sounds or through the power of resonant suggestion, was indeed a fascination in the late nineteenth century, as Scott remarks.

The play on which *The Bells* was based, *The Polish Jew* by the horror writers Erckmann and Chatrian, had been a hit in France in 1867, the same year as *No Thoroughfare* and also the year John Tyndall's *Sound* made available to English readers a synopsis of the theories of Helmholtz's *On the Sensations of Tone*, published in German in 1863. Tyndall's *Sound* became a surprise bestseller, on the back of some public Royal Institution lecture-demonstrations that involved spectacular visual demonstrations of acoustic waves affecting large flickering gas flames (it was through a similar experiment that De Forest would also observe that electromagnetic pulses flickered a flame, and would therefore release energy in a thermionically heated, ionized near-vacuum, which led to the Audion). *Sound* was followed by Lord Rayleigh's two-volume bestseller *Theory of Sound* (1877–88).

To communicate its principles to a lay readership, the new popular science of sound employed familiar Romantic tropes such as the eolian harp to explain the principle of sympathetic vibration and complex tones. Helmholtz too had compared the wiring of the ear to the neural network as a kind of 'Frankenstein's piano' whose vibrating strings animate the consciousness (Picker, 2003: 91). In George Eliot's *Daniel Deronda* (1876), which takes the contemporary popular science of sound as a metaphorical framework, the musician Klesmer (a Yiddish parody of Mesmer) plays with people's minds through his piano, in a reference to Helmholtz's trope. The enigmatic sound of the breaking string in Chekhov's *The Cherry Orchard* (1903) asks to be read not only against the Pythagorean symbol of cosmological unity, the monochord, but also against this new figuration. *On the Sensations of Tone* was fully translated into English in 1875 by Alexander Ellis, on whom Bernard Shaw partly based Henry Higgins in *Pygmalion* (1914).

The fragile workings of the mind constituted, if not a new sublime, then certainly a very real anxiety and a dramatically motivating form of peril. As James Sully observed in discussing the new sonology and its figurative uses in George Eliot:

> Modern tragedy differs from classic in its conception of the conditions of human nature. We have substituted for the old idea of an external divine necessity an internal psychological necessity, for an objective Retributive Justice, a subjective Nemesis.
>
> 1881: 385

This was an invisible nemesis, but it could be heard.

By the late nineteenth century, according to the artist Rudolf Lehman, also part of the social circle that included Dickens and Eliot, sound had 'assumed the status as an ideal function that sight had earlier held' (Picker, 2003: 91). In the 1890s, the Russian physiologist Pavlov began experimenting to make dogs salivate as a conditioned response to the ringing of the dinner-bell. Amid the interest in the theatricality of mentalism and its relationship to the secret science of sound, Symbolism emerged across the arts. The young Freud began to study the physiology of voice and speech, and Breuer began his work with hypnotism with the patient Anna O, two starting points from which they would develop the 'talking cure'. Writing in 1924, Freud's friend, the psychoanalyst Charles Baudouin, remarked that 'symbolist art is like Helmholtz's resonators[1] which isolate the overtones of a musical note, and make them perceptible in isolation' (Baudouin, 1924: 203).

It was through sounds that the new subjective nemesis made itself apparent in symbols: enigmatic sounds like birds or breaking strings from the sky or axes falling, offstage, in the cherry orchard. Maeterlinck's night birds exulted suddenly in the gloom. His grandfather clock ticked louder and more slowly, and the silence in between each tick, like the partial vacuum in De Forest's tube, became the space of a thermionically amplified subtext. 'Sleigh-bells on the road', whispers Irving, as the whole of the Lyceum hangs on a hair he has found in his wine glass. 'Boom boom boom', goes something new coming up the pass.

My God, it's coming out of your ears!

Stevenson wrote *Jekyll and Hyde* in 1886, at the height of the popular fascination with sound, psychological auscultation and criminal secrets. It perfectly encapsulates Sully's observation of the switch from divine dramatic retribution to internal subjective nemesis.

The first time Jekyll transformed into his nemesis Hyde in Mamoulian's 1931 film version, the audience watched it in a mirror, and while it was happening, something completely new was heard. Technically ground-breaking and years ahead of later experiments in the montaging of recorded sound as *musique concrète*, what it heard was known at the time among the Paramount technicians as 'Mamoulian's sound stew'.[2] Created before magnetic tape, it

---

[1] A hollow chamber tuned to resonate at a particular frequency according to the relationship between the size of an aperture on a short neck, the length of that neck, and the volume of air in the chamber. As when one blows across the top of a bottle, the effect is surprisingly boomy and loud.
[2] See https://binged.it/2urpT1m

consisted in an abstract sonic creation made directly on the optical soundtrack of the film, overlaid with memories of dialogue. The effect placed the spectator vicariously inside the traumatized subjectivity of Jekyll's noisy body as his nemesis emerges and the room spins around him. Its focal point and rhythm, sandwiched between a high-pitched sinusoidal tone like tinnitus, resonating metallic sounds and a low-frequency, organic drone, was a sound usually only heard before by doctors or in moments of personal stress or interpersonal intimacy. This was the disembodied, now electronically amplified, sound of a human heartbeat.

So commonplace has the use of a heartbeat become as a way of building dramatic tension in films like Ridley Scott's *Alien* (1979), or as a montage element (e.g., Pink Floyd's *Dark Side of the Moon*, 1973), that it too has transcended cliché and become a sonic meme like the Castle Thunder. So familiar is this kind of inside-out, first-person sonic perspective that it is hard to imagine that in 1931 it had not been heard before. And yet so it was, that in the same year that James Whale gave the world the Castle Thunder in *Frankenstein*, Mamoulian gave it the heartbeat effect in *Jekyll and Hyde*. Mamoulian was often asked about it in interviews, such as this one from a 1973 special edition of *Film Journal* dedicated to his horror production (note, in relation to our earlier discussion, how exotic 'world' instruments already form part of the stock audio effects cupboard):

With such a fantastic transformation what sound do you use? Do you put music in here? God, it's coming out of your ears, the scoring. I thought the only way to match the event and create this incredible reality would be to concoct a mélange of sounds that do not exist in nature, that a human ear cannot hear. I said, 'Let's photograph light.' We photographed the light of a candle in various frequencies of intensity directly transforming light into sound. Then I said, 'Let's record the beat of a gong, cut off the impact, run it backwards.' And we recorded other things like that. But when we ran it, the whole thing lacked rhythm. I'm a great believer in the importance of rhythm. I said, 'We need some kind of a beat.' So they brought in all sorts of drums, a bass drum, a snare drum, a Hawaiian drum, Indian tom-toms. But no matter what we used, it always sounded like what it was – a drum. Finally in exasperation I got this wonderful idea. I ran up and down the stairway for a few minutes, and then I put a microphone to my heart and said, 'Record it.' And that's what is used as the basic rhythm in the scene – the thumping noise which is like no drum on earth because it's the heartbeat, my own heartbeat. So when I say my heart is in Dr. Jekyll and Mr. Hyde, I mean it literally.

ATKINS, 1973: 42–3

As fascinating as the sonic stew may be now to sonic art historians, the headline at the time was the heartbeat. This was anticipated by Paramount's marketing department, which made a puff about it in the press pack for the film:

> The beat of the human heart recently was recorded in Hollywood for talking pictures for the first time. The sound effect was secured by Rouben Mamoulian, Paramount director, for a scene in 'Dr. Jekyll and Mr. Hyde,' in which Fredric March plays the dual personality role and Miriam Hopkins and Rose Hobart have the leading feminine roles. This remarkable picture dramatization of Robert Louis Stevenson's weird story is the feature picture at the___ theatre for___ days the___ part of next week. To obtain the 'boom, boom' of the heart-pump, the microphone was held over March's heart [although as Mamoulian says in interviews, it was actually his]. The sensitiveness of the instrument boosted the sound past that which one naturally hears while holding an ear over a heart to the quality attained by listening through a stethoscope. The heart-beat was conceived by Mamoulian as one of his novel effects in the Stevenson story; by use of this, the director will obtain the sensation of one's own heart pounding in one's ears as he chronicles the experiences of Jekyll in transforming for the first time into Hyde.
>
> 1931 press release, quoted in Neil Learner's *Music in the Horror Film: Listening to Fear*, 2010, loc. 1709

This 'sensitiveness of the instrument' was down to tube amplification, which changed the way the world was heard, not only by making sounds louder, but also by disconnecting sounds from visual perspective. Far-away sounds needed no longer to be distant and quiet, and small, even internal sounds like Mamoulian's heartbeat, could be larger than life and place the hearer, as the press release suggests, not only into a vicarious first-person psychology, but a physiology too.

This was the microphonic effect.

The microphonic 'Wonderland': amplification and the rescaling of the world

Amplification did not simply turn the world's volume up. Controllable amplification and modulation in transmission and reception circuitry made audio more malleable to processes we might now think of as sound design. Microphone signals are weak, only energized by tiny diaphragm movements as they resonate in sympathy with acoustic vibrations in the air around them.

The triode tube was used to 'pre-amplify' this signal before it entered the analogue, electronic signal chain. Henceforth, all along the chain, tubes were used wherever the signal needed to be 'tuned', controlled or transformed. Hi-fi radios are still called 'tuners', because the radio signal is used to tune and control the amplification in the triode tubes. Asa Briggs attributes the 'transition from wireless to broadcasting' to the valve (tube), which he saw as 'the greatest invention since fire, the lever and the wheel' (1961: 28). It was also the 'vital spark that brought the talkies into being' (Hepworth, 1930, in Macpherson, 2011: 117).

The proportionality between sonic scale, auditory effect and aurality itself, as a personal and social subjectivity, became mutable in ways that are perhaps now so routine as to be taken for granted. The development of potentiometers (volume controls) meant audio could be faded in and out and modulated manually. In the home and elsewhere, audio could now be operated dynamically, and this was one of the things that enabled the transformation of the everyday hearer of sound into an everyday user of it as a technology of the self. Loud sounds could be turned down, oceans and thunderclaps shrunk, so that they could be heard from radio sets on the fridge or on the car dashboard. Conversely, small sounds could be made to resonate the whole body, in voluminous radio and movie theatres.

This disruption of familiar aural scale reconfigured auditory space in the 1930s, but this reconfiguration had been countenanced over the preceding century. The first use of the word 'microphone' was in the formulation 'microphone effect', attributed to the physicist Charles Wheatstone. He had observed tricks of amplification in theatrical automata shows, which used the transmission of vibrations down wires to what would later be known as 'Helmholtz resonators'. This inspired first experiments in telegraphy in the 1830s, only a decade after Pyne published his account of *The Eidophusikon*. Forty years after that, David Hughes developed the carbon-based transducer used in ear-pieces in telegraphy and analogue telephone mouthpieces and revived Wheatstone's term 'microphone' to name it. To demonstrate the microphone effect, he fitted one to a closed box filled with insects, whose scratchings and movements, he explained, when heard in an earphone pressed to the ear, were perceived to be 'amplified' (Macpherson, 2011: 118). The only power involved was that produced by the kinesis of the sound. The tube-driven audio amplifier stepped up the power. It enabled the scratchings of insects, and the whole infra-world of little sounds usually only audible, if ever, in very quiet, personal, intimate situations, to be fed not only directly to an individual ear, but through circuits and into celluloid soundtracks that were distributed to, and replayed in, vast auditoriums.

With the added control and power of the Audion, the microphone effect and the network together revealed a parallel sonic continuum of intimacy, of rustling clothes, sighs, sniffs and breathing. It estranged the familiarities of scale. In 1931, the clavichordist and teacher Dorothy Swainson remarked that:

> when a clavichord recital was broadcast from Daventry on April 16, the volume of sound reached Paris at least three times life-size. I am so accustomed to the voice of my clavichord in the privacy of my chamber that it was an uncanny experience, as though this clavichord from London had been tasting the cake that made Alice grow large in Wonderland.
>
> SWAINSON, 1931: 397

The new audio reality was also pre-edited. Within the audio framework that now overlaid the acoustic, the *asyndeton* of psychoacoustic 'unhearing' was taken care of by sound editors or designers. Only sounds deemed dramaturgically or aesthetically necessary were put on the soundtrack or the radio programme. There was no background noise for the hearer to unhear other than the inherent hiss or crackle of the medium. If there were background noises in the mix, they had been put there to be heard as atmosphere. In the terms we discussed in Chapter 1, this was a dissensual process that brought 'back into play both the obviousness of what can be perceived, thought and done, and the distribution of those who are capable of perceiving, thinking and altering the coordinates of the shared world' (Rancière, 2009: 49). The microphonic dissensus called into question the obviousness, and therefore the reliability, of binaural sound location and the cognitive map of the auditory scene that forms the basis of hearing. It destabilized the disposition, habits, techniques and discussions that constitute auditory space, the auditory habitus, or audimus, and the aural being.

There is a scene in Hazanavicius' film *The Artist* (2011) which expands on a similar scene in *Singing in the Rain* (1952). It is 1929 and Valentin and a group of studio executives are watching some 'audible picture' rushes. We see him laughing mockingly at silent actors struggling to be vocal actors. 'If that's the future, you can have it', he says, via inter-title, as he leaves the viewing room. From this, we cut to him in his dressing room, like Mamoulian's Jekyll, looking into his mirror, in a way that merges us into his first-person subjectivity. The musical underscoring fades out. The movie falls 'silent' for the first time, save for the analogue hiss of the soundtrack. Valentin wipes his hand with a cloth: no sound. But then, suddenly, the sound of the glass tumbler on the table. Valentin stares at it in disbelief. The joke is that in his world he has never encountered a sound before. He starts to experiment, tapping the glass on the table again, knocking over a makeup brush, dropping a comb.

As he does this, the sound of the outside world fades very quietly up in the background – at first, a gentle ambience of distant car horns, indistinct talk, and the familiar booming artefacts of wind in an effects microphone. He hears it and gets up. He tries to speak in the mirror; no sound comes from his mouth. The mirror wobbles and makes a wobbling noise, but his visibly speaking reflection is mute. He hears, and we hear, the screech and clatter of his chair as he kicks it back in panic; his dog barking; his phone ringing. Each of these sounds is giant, fulsomely recorded and individually foregrounded in a way that is familiar to our practised screen aurality, but which clearly terrifies Valentin. He glances up at the sound of what we assume is an electric fan in the ceiling. There is more background noise now, the sound of someone bumping about upstairs, perhaps, the sound of a door opening. Valentin is shouting again, but still has no voice. We hear the door opening and the background sound snaps out. Silence again; save for the hiss of the analogue medium. The noise that seemed to come from outside has disappeared in the cut from interior to exterior. We hear Valentin's hard heels on the wooden deck as he rushes outside; then, slightly pre-empting the visual cut, the giggling of one, three and then more chorus girls passing by, each with the artificial warmth and presence of a valve mic and the immediacy of an acoustically baffled vocal booth. This literally 'deranges' a space which the visual cue tells us should sound more reverberative and set further back than the close-miked voices suggest. We hear the wind gusting and see a palm tree blowing in it. The camera then cuts to a feather falling from the sky, and the wind fades to silence, or rather, it fades again to the analogue hiss that stands in for silence. We know what is coming. It is an audio joke. When the feather lands, it is to the sound of a huge explosion. Valentin wakes up with a jolt. The silent film music returns, and it has all been a nightmare.

Electro-acousmatic being

The audio signal chain inveigled its way rhizomatically into people's lives like knotweed. It enmeshed the world and insinuated itself into millions, and then billions, of homes and workplaces, through the cables and over the radio waves of the global communications network. As Valentin realized, it was not a passing fad but constituted a new reality. All sounds now had audio within the mereology of their structure of audibility. Hearing itself – the process of figuring out what is going on in the acoustic plenum as an auditory scene – now had to account for audio, and audio's laconically symbolic, pre-edited way of knowing. Every siren and thunderclap – every voice – was now comparable to a radio or screen version. Even when switched off, the loudspeaker presided over acoustic life with a simple message: 'you heard it here first'. Just as the reverberations of flies and wings of the reconfigured picture box stage had provided a new sense of a resonant 'beyond', a new, implicit backstage area suggested itself, from behind the loudspeaker.

It was like a limbo. The microphone removed sounds 'from the flow of life, allowing for their magnification and manipulation' (Macpherson, 2011: 118). The loudspeaker reintroduced transformed versions of them into the flow of life as audio objects. In between, the sounds existed in a dimension beyond the senses – a space where sound no longer decayed but was held in electronically suspended animation:

> The electric ear of the microphone and the electric mouth of the loudspeaker, established the conditions for an electric space, like the telegraphic space of the previous century, a mysterious zone where the transmitted information resided.
>
> MACPHERSON, 2011: 128–9

The audio network of transmission and storage media was an electromagnetic reservoir. Every kitchen, car and theatre was plumbed into it through its loudspeakers. The idea of it shrouded the sensible world in a new aura; a new theoretical musica; an ethereal store of electroacoustic potential. Audio objects appeared from it in cars, movie houses and living rooms, as if through a wormhole from a different dimension. Sounds picked up by a microphone at one point in time and space could rematerialize from the electric limbo at another – in the vibrating paper cones of the loudspeakers. It could be milliseconds, weeks or decades after the acoustic event and thousands of miles away. Such audio apparitions commanded the attention as does any sound whose source is hidden from view, but with the added, metaphysical authority of this inapprehensible and quintessentially modern space.

The command of sounds from unseen sources beyond the immediate scene is one of the principle effects of theatre and of accoustemological ways of knowing governed by good sound metaphors. While social sounding reiterates auditory belonging, Lévi-Strauss and others have observed that the ritual construction of a perimeter fence in time and space between the deliberate world of a performance and the accidental world beyond (the auditorium wall; the beginning and ending of a ritual act of theatre) does the same (Brown, 2009: 82–90). Within the perimeter, performance of raucousness and the detritus of *logos* (vocal stumbles, slang, mispronunciations) along with the power exercised in representing or wilfully misrepresenting foreign sounds – all this social noise-making enables communities to reassert their boundaries through, as Lingis puts it, 'struggling, together, to jam the unequivocal voice of the outsider' (1994: 104). People are territorial about sound.

This is why unseen sounds from beyond the perimeter command a special attention. The peril of the space beyond is the motivational basis for much of the dramaturgy of sound. The earliest sites of ritual sonic practice had hidden chambers where sound could be performed or resonated out of sight, and then defeated through the summed energy of chanting. When the first thespians put their audiences in front of, rather than inside, hillside caves and burial chambers, it was in part to use the dark, reverberative space behind them for an effect of the realm of the dead – the effect that sounds performed behind or under the skena replicates (Brown, 2009: 149–60).

Thus, the acousma – the audible but unseen thing; the sonic outsider – has a special privilege within the schema of human aurality and within acoustemological schemes of social knowing. It is a diegetic sound effect. In appearing within the sensible scene from beyond the construct of its sensibility, it frames the scene's reality and tells a story about the wider world beyond. It is frightening, but it is also pedagogic. The term *acousmatic* is often used in sonic art theory simply to describe a sound that has been dislocated from the visibility of its source, but it is important to also understand that the term originally related to the pedagogic value of this disembodiment. It is associated with the ancient Pythagorean practice of delivering lectures from behind a screen or curtain, to *akousmatikoi* – students who were tasked with learning from the lessons of sound alone, without any visible demonstration. The term was adopted by Pierre Schaeffer to describe the auditory task of *musique concrète*, and the term *acousmaître* was assigned to the unseen sonic pedagogue, the voice that carried the theatrical authority and command of an acousma.

In the audio age, the voice of the *acousmaître* (an audio announcement, narration or any diegetic audio) no longer implies a presence hidden behind a physical screen (a source that may have spoken years ago or miles away). The sound is electronically absented from the flow of life and reintroduced to it through the loudspeaker, from the mysterious, electric zone. It becomes what the film theorist Michel Chion instead calls the *acousmêtre* (1994: 129–31) – a portmanteau that combines *acousma* and the French verb *être*, to be. An *acousmêtre* is an *acousmaître* that now exists only in audio and whose command as an outsider comes from the inapprehensible electric aura. In film theory, Chion's term is usually limited to vocal apparitions. I would suggest it can be expanded to include any kind of audio-object that uses its power to give diegetic instruction – to frame the present moment as a learning space, with information from beyond. As an audio-object, the *acousmêtre* is omnipotent. The screen can no longer be knocked over to reveal the mundane figure of Pythagoras or the small, human Wizard of Oz behind it. The loudspeaker curtain cannot be parted to reveal the stagehand shaking the thundersheet or playing a pair of coconut shells. It is in the absence of these implicit figures that the *acousmêtre*'s power resides. The *acousmêtre* is only a sound. There is nothing else to it.

The free ear

Audio reprogrammed the dramaturgical logic of the acoustic world. By the late 1920s, electro-acousmatic voices and audio-objects could serve as *acousmêtres*, instructing the hearer as diegetic narrators or commentators, implying neither that there was a visible source hiding off-screen or offstage, nor that the sound was some kind of hallucination. This revolutionized audio-visual dramaturgy. The fixed relationship between the ear and the eye around which the tableau stage and end-on auditorium had been configured was not so certain now that the electric ear of the microphone could roam around beyond the visible world of radio reception, and free of the camera's viewfinder. While radio drama came first by a few years, as a form it was seminally shaped by the arrival of the soundtrack, so I am going to take the talkie, or the 'audible picture' as it was also known,[3] first.

Rouben Mamoulian (1897–1987) – he of the recorded heartbeat – was of the theatre and of a symbolist disposition. No one was more responsible for making sound work aesthetically and dramaturgically in cinema. Brought in by Paramount to their Long Island studios in 1929 from a successful career in theatre, he was given the task of figuring out a new, cinematic relationship between the eye and the ear, in order to save the talking picture project from an early failure. By 1927, the movies had the technology, but not yet the technique, to make sound work as an artful counterpoint to the fluid, sophisticated cinematography that had developed during the later silent era. Cumbersome microphones had to be hidden in the set near the dialogue, which meant the actors' mobility was limited, and cameras had to be encased in massive, sound-muffling 'blimps' so that the microphone did not pick up their noise. This meant the camera became immobile. The coming of sound had led to a stage-bound *mise-en-scène* that, for all the hype, was seeming like a backward step in the cinematic art. Mamoulian's approach to audible pictures was, radically, to make them more like silent pictures – to worry less about imitating the auditorium view of theatre, where eyes and ears were conjoined in a fixed view of the stage, and to return to a visual *mise-en-scène*, with audio providing a diegetic framing:

> Talking pictures up to now have been merely substitutions, stage imitation, mirrors of acted plays – and that is not their purpose. They should be motion pictures always using the old motion picture technique, but substituting dialogue for subtitles.
>
> MAMOULIAN, 1927, quoted in LUHRSSEN, 2013: loc. 779

---

[3] See Luhrssen (2013: loc. 797).

An Armenian, born to an artistic family in Georgia, Mamoulian had been to school in Paris with René Clair, and then trained at the Moscow Art Theatre. He began directing professionally in 1918 in Tbilisi, moving to London in 1920, where he directed Austin Page's Russian Revolution drama *The Beating on the Door* (St James Theatre, 1922) in a naturalistic style: 'you know, utter realism – chopping wood, real wood, naturalistic action and all that' (ibid.: loc. 343). After this, he determined never to work in that mode again, instead moving towards symbolism, and 'rhythmic and poetic stylisation' (ibid.). He moved to America, keen to pursue opera, and directed several conservatoire student public productions at the Eastman Theatre in Rochester from 1923 – most notably Gounod's adaptation of Goethe's *Faust*. However, it was a professional 1927 production of Der Biggers' 'melodramatic farce' *Seven Keys to Baldpate* at the Garrick in Manhattan that brought Mamoulian to the attention of the Theatre Guild, where he would make his name.

Maybe what attracted Mamoulian to this 1913 potboiler, adapted for the stage by George M. Cohan, was the way it played knowingly with the sonic conventions, clichés and tropes of old-fashioned theatricality. The Alpine setting, the howling wind outside, the three-act structure with every scene ending in a cliffhanging tableau of suspended animation – all the formulaic components of gothic melodrama are present, although so familiar have they become that they now lend themselves more to farce. In twentieth-century melodrama, the continuous musical agits, hurries, tremolos and suspended chords of the melo had all but ceased and given way to the more symbolic sound effects that had first started to be used in the 1860s. Silence and noises now underscored the emotional subjectivity of the scene – or, rather, they rehearsed it within the formal knowingness of genre and convention, which, to Mamoulian, was more interesting. The story shares the same basic premise as King/Kubrick's *The Shining* (1980). It centres on a writer who has bet he can write a novel in twenty-four hours, in an isolated mountain resort (the Baldpate Inn), shut up for the winter. He is assured that he has the only key to the place, but during the night receives several visits (or visitations) from others – six of them, as the title suggests. The sound of the exterior weather, of the protagonist's typewriter from other rooms, of clocks striking out the passing of the twenty-four hours, knocking, and the sounds of keys locking and unlocking of doors all weave through the text.

The rehearing of silence

Silence, not music or sounds, is the programmatic figure of symbolism. Words, noises and sound effects are its ground; the materials of its form. This is why it provides the most unbearable tension in modern theatre, as the audience's future passes through the suspended moment of drama into its past. This is what suspense is: time running out and nothing being done about it. *Baldpate* opens with a bare stage and only the distant noise of howling winds (a wind machine) outside, which the script stipulates must be held for thirty seconds. This is a very substantial period of stage time, although not unprecedented; there had been a whole silent scene in Galsworthy's *Justice* (1910), three years earlier (Brown, 2009: 77–8).

Thrillers and symbolist plays share a common interest in the effect of silence, and the virtuoso of symbolist silence was Maurice Maeterlinck, whose work Mamoulian encountered in Yevgeny Vakhtangov's studio at the Moscow Arts Theatre. In the year before *Baldpate*, 1926, Mamoulian had directed Andreyev's 'symbolist farce' *He Who Gets Slapped* and Maeterlinck's *Sister Beatrice* at Rochester, with an early organ score by 1940s electronic and tape-music pioneer Otto Luening and choreography by Martha Graham.

William Becvar's programme notes for *Sister Beatrice* described how:

> The Music completes the action and [was] used throughout the whole play, not as an incidental accompaniment. The Spoken Word [was] treated not as the main element in the drama but as additional to theatrical action. Scenery, Costumes, and Light [were] used in the same way of Music and Word, supplementing theatrical movement and joining with it to form an artistic unit.
>
> Quoted in LUHRSSEN: loc. 466

The techniques Mamoulian brought to the screen combine this kind of stylistic *Gesamkunstwerk* with a knowing delight in old-fashioned theatricality and the proven effectiveness of melodramatic stagecraft. But the most marked departure from wearingly continuous noisy dialogue tracks of the early sound films of the previous two or three years is the way he used sound, as he explained, in a way analogous to silent film inter-titles. The *mise-en-scène* of *Applause* (1929) and, even more, *City Streets* (1931) is influenced by the silent films of Murnau and Lang, but what is really striking about them, compared with the early talkies, is the way in which sound is confidently withheld or separated from the visual action and silence is used as an element of the soundtrack. Mamoulian understood from his theatre training the stagecraft and dramaturgy of foregrounding silence. It is likely he would have known from Vakhtangov's studio what Maeterlinck said about it: that 'we stand in so deep a dread of silence', that we can bear, when need must be, the silence of ourselves, that of isolation: but the silence of many – silence multiplied – and above all the silence of a crowd – these are supernatural burdens, whose inexplicable weight brings dread to the mightiest soul. We spend a goodly portion of our lives in seeking places where silence is not.

MAETERLINCK, 1897: 7–8

Silence in theatre is this social kind, and it is a powerful effect available to the scenographer. In cinemas, or even more so, on radio, the suspension of sound can be even more powerful.

Mamoulian's *Applause* was not the only audio media event in 1929 to realize this. In Britain that year, the BBC began broadcasting the two-minute Armistice Day memorial silence, and it rapidly became one of the most popular programmes in the schedule. As the *Radio Times* put it a few years later, 'there is probably no moment in the year when broadcasting has a more communal aspect' (1935: 7). It then quotes one of the BBC's original pioneering engineers, H. H. Thompson:

> Its impressiveness is intensified by the fact that the silence is not a dead silence, for Big Ben strikes the hour, and then the bickering of sparrows, the crisp rustle of falling leaves, the creasing of pigeon wings as they take flight, uneasy at the strange hush, contrast with the traffic din of London some minutes before. Naturally, vigilant control of the microphone is essential. Audible distress near to the microphone would create a picture out of perspective as regards the crowd's solemn impassivity and feelings. Our job is to reduce all local noises to the right proportions, so that the silence may be heard for what it really is, a solvent which destroys personality and gives us leave to be great and universal.
>
> ibid.

In the post-sublime world of audio inscape, the silence constituted by sparrows, falling leaves and pigeon wings is not the negative shape left behind by the *découpage* of sonic symbols. It is the desired object – the fetish – of sonic symbolism (and symbolism is what sound editing, sound design and the dissensual process of lifting an aesthetic scenography up and away from the predetermined semiotics of mimesis are engaged in). Audio inscapes silence. As Maeterlinck said, we can bear the silence of ourselves, that of isolation. What we cannot bear but are fascinated by is what Paul Farley, in his poem 'A Minute's Silence', describes as the social silence of 'the dead, the never-born, the locked-out souls scratching on the thin shell we have grown around ourselves' – the sublimely feared silence (Farley, 1998: 334–5).

Popular modernism

In the inter-war years, theatres such as the Theatre Guild in New York and the Old Vic/Sadlers Wells in London found, much as the BBC had with its silent broadcast, that the public were fascinated by the sparse, stylized auditory *asyndeton* of European modernism, which unheard all but the most enigmatically oblique sonic symbols. In his book for amateur sound effects makers, *Noises Off*, Frank Napier, the Old Vic's 'effectsman' during the late 1920s and stage director from 1931, provides tips on how to approach these curious sign-systems, from the enigma of Chekhov's broken string to the sonic formalism of Čapek or Obey's modernist plays, and other *-isms*, 'the precise meaning of which are so hard to determine' (Napier, 1936: 106–7). His advice is brilliantly simple and begins by disarming any populist anxiety about pretentious artiness. Don't imagine 'artistic youths armed with drumsticks doing arabesques from bass drum to thundersheet', he jokes (ibid.). All that is really required is that the noises-off be 'tidied up' into a pattern of sound that fits whatever style is required. 'Tidy up', he explains, is what 'formalize' means (ibid.). This is not dissimilar to what Baudouin said in 1924 when he likened symbolist art to Helmholtz's resonators which isolate the overtones of a musical note, and make them perceptible in isolation (see above).

It was Mamoulian's quantised, synoptic formalism – Luhrssen describes as his 'characteristic stylized, rhythmic manner' (2013: 32) – that the Theatre Guild liked about his production of *Baldpate*. This is how he therefore approached his first production for them, Heyward's *Porgy* (1927) – the production from which the Gershwins and Mamoulian later developed *Porgy and Bess* (1935). It cemented Mamoulian's reputation for sonic innovation and brought him to the attention of Paramount. For *Porgy*, Mamoulian staged an overture of noises: a fugue built from the sounds of Catfish Row waking up and coming to life. Although set in Charleston, South Carolina, rather than a city of motor engines and sirens, this overture has much in common with Edgar Varèse's symphonic soundscape *Amériques*, which had premiered in Philadelphia the previous year. It was recreated for the beginning of Mamoulian's Rogers and Hart screen musical *Love Me Tonight* (1932), as a follow-up to the celebrated *musique concrète* transformation scene he had included in *Jekyll and Hyde* the previous year.

It begins with the sound of a bell striking six o'clock. A workman enters pushing a wheel-barrow, and starts pounding the stage with a pickaxe, setting up a downbeat. Next, we hear a homeless street-sleeper snoring on the third beat, setting up common time (4/4). A woman appears from a door with a brush to sweep her step on the second and fourth beats. Windows begin to open, babies start crying, there are sounds of cutlery on plates, shutters going up, children in school uniforms skipping across the stage, carpets being beaten, and street cobblers and tinkers sharpening knives and hammering out counter-rhythms. More and more people appear, on bicycles, honking horns, ringing bells. There are sounds of traffic, more sirens and, finally, music – but music is now just another section in the orchestra of city noise; another sound in the orchestral disposition of modernity. 'It all had to be conducted', said Mamoulian of the sequence (Milne, 1969: 13). 'I think I came close to being fired for trying out some of my pet theories [. . .] Only later could [the Guild] appreciate a stage full of actors snoring, hammering and making other homely noises', which is to say, when it came together with the expressionistic visuals of huge, expressionist shadows from the concealed footlights, as a 'modern-arty' aesthetic (in Luhrssen, 2013: loc. 618).

After *Porgy*, Mamoulian continued to direct a modernist repertoire at the Theatre Guild for another year or so before Paramount called. After a mere five weeks' induction into the film-making process at their Long Island studios, Mamoulian directed *Applause* (1929). He did the job he was hired to do, transfiguring film sound and reanimating the lugubrious audio-visual *mise-en-scène*. He put wheels on the camera blimps (sound-insulating enclosures) and insisted that they *could* be moved despite their weight, and made the stage crew practise doing this gracefully, and silently so as not to be picked up by the microphones. He insisted that it was not necessary for the microphone to follow the camera around, as had been the assumption, and to share its viewpoint. Instead, he introduced a first-person point of audition that could depart and roam separately to that of the camera, creating audio and video tracking shots that wove a counterpoint to one another.

Sometimes the eye and the ear would meet up in a synchronous take on a scene, but often they would attend to different things. The audio track might move from foreground to background within the same scene or into the psychological perception of a character and then back again to a third-person view. Passages of dialogue are sometimes played out acousmatically, without seeing the speaking actors, the camera cutting instead between visual symbols: caged birds and mundane domestic ornaments. In the gangster melodrama *City Streets* (1931), a long, fixed shot of the unfairly imprisoned protagonist's face is juxtaposed against sounds of her cellmate sleeping and a swirling sound montage of her inner turmoil. Mamoulian faced resistance on set when creating this effect, as he often did: 'No one thought audiences would be able to accept this kind of audible inner monologues and reminiscences combined with a silent face', he said later. '[But] the audience understood and accepted it quite easily' (Luhrssen, 2013: loc. 971).

Mamoulian also brought music back to the talkie, in a way that immediately made stylistic use of this interplay. Since the advent of the soundtrack, music – which had stood in lieu of sound on the silent screen – had largely been limited to the opening title and closing credits. The intertwining journeys of audio and picture in *Applause* (1929) create the scenic space of the film, a sinuous counterpoint of different sonic, musical and visual lines of diegesis. The central character, April, leaves her convent school for the big city to be reunited with her showgirl mother, in a long tracking shot, set to the music of Schubert's 'Ave Maria'. We assume the music is extra-diegetic, in the familiar manner of silent film music and most sound film underscoring. We then discover that it originates from within a chapel, which the mobile camera visits *en route*. The music continues, uninterrupted, over multiple montaged shots of April departing her serene, cloistered convent life and taking a train. Finally, it abruptly cuts to the sound of her arrival in the industrial noise and cathedral-like reverberation of the big city station. A modernist sonic montage, like Varèse's *Amériques*, with claxons, traffic and car horns then takes over, in parallel to a montage of city shots.

In *The Artist*, Valentin is shown reeling from the disorienting effect of audio's artificially synoptic and out-of-scale sonification of the world, but audiences were able and willing to accept the fluidly dispositional audio-visual morphology of the sound film; to accept, too, the wordless pedagogic instruction of the audio-object whose source they could not see. Different pictures could be audible to the ones that were being projected on the screen; different pictures too, in the sound of the words and the spaces between them, to those that the words described. In fact, to picture the drama, one did not really need visual aids. The audio – the sound of words, and maybe a few effects and a little music – was all that was really required.

9

Audio drama

The art of moving, audible pictures which De Loutherbourg had first prototyped in 1781 was now established reality. Cinema was now an art that consisted, like music, in a dialectic between its form and a morphology that comprised the audiovisual counterpoint between the soundtrack and the cinematography. Disposed against the visual montage and the literal meaning of the text, the soundtrack represented a new way of hearing the world, and film sound editing became the defining sonic art of the twentieth century. While theatre had rehearsed the symbolist process of 'tidying up' that characterized sound editing, the soundtrack's audio format could hear (and unhear) the enervating everyday chaos of engine noise and audio sign-systems as scenery in a way that the kinetic acoustic stage simply could not. The movies aestheticized the destabilized aurality and growing noise of modernity by quantizing it into audio effects and clips that could be reconstructed, not to imitate acoustic auditory experience, but to reimagine it. Once it was imaginable, one could shut one's eyes and live the movie.

The sound effect in its widest sense (the stuff of radio)

The subjective effect – the cracking open of the obviousness of the given – as portrayed in *The Artist* related not to the audibility of onscreen dialogue, but to the sudden audibility of small, mundane things within the movie's scheme of meaning. The audio arts responded to the roar of modernity not with wattage and decibels, but by harkening to the existentiality in what States called the history-in-objects quietly encroaching on the human (1985: 74). Valentin's sense of himself is completely changed by the sound of a shaving brush. The bickering of sparrows and the crisp rustle of falling leaves provided the solvent to destroy personality and gave listeners leave to be great and universal within the broadcast memorial silence. One is reminded of W. H. Auden's line from *The Age of Anxiety* (1947): 'But now the radio, suddenly breaking in with its banal noises upon their separate senses of themselves' (1968: 261).

In his foreword to the 'effectsman' Frank Napier's *Noises Off* (1936), Tyrone Guthrie lauds his colleague's lateral thinking and ingenuity, approaching it through what was by now already a meme of old-fashioned theatricality, the clopping coconut-shell:

> A horsehoof by the river's brim to most Stage-managers is a simple coconut and nothing more. Not so to Frank Napier; he will offer you hoofbeat realistic, or, equally readily, hoofbeat surrealistic – the Inner Meaning of the hoofbeat.
>
> Someday I hope to produce a one-act play by Maeterlinck, called 'Les Aveugles'. The scene is in a dark forest at night. One of the stage directions reads: 'The nightbirds exult in the tree-tops.' I shall feel that life has not been entirely empty when Frank Napier, requested to produce this effect, does so, immediately and with complete success, aided by an empty matchbox and three bent pins.
>
> 1936: v

It was Tyrone Guthrie who brought the modern European *-isms*, 'the precise meaning of which [were] so hard to determine', as Napier put it, to Lillian Baylis' Old Vic as resident producer (artistic director) in 1933. It was he who threw down the challenge of Chekhov's breaking string effect to Napier; he who charged him with finding a sonic *mise-en-scène* for the abstract formalism of Čapek and Obey. Guthrie had begun his career in radio, joining the infant BBC in its Belfast station in 1924, then moving to its Savoy Hill headquarters in London. Here, he had become part of a seminal debate about what distinctive form the microphone drama, as he called it, should take, in the new world of audible pictures, where already the development of live, broadcast television was considered inevitable.

A symphonic form

Guthrie understood that sound is how you hear things. The advent of the film soundtrack meant you heard it differently: not only in counterpoint to the visible world, but also with an artistic style (his comments about 'hoofbeats' are humorous but have substance). In the BBC's review of the year from 1 November 1929 to 31 October 1930, the year in which Mamoulian's *Applause* had appeared, Guthrie contributed to a section on sound effects in radio drama. Much as Gilpin had approached the picturesque landscape in 1794, he invokes the technique of audience – but this time, of movie audience:

> there is a technique to listening, just as there is a technique of looking at moving pictures. Do you remember in the early days of [silent] films what difficulty one had in telling one character from another, in following devices like fading and flash-back, in quickly adjusting one's mind to the location and time of the various 'shots'? Now all that has, by use, become almost an unconscious mental process. Similarly with listening.
>
> BBC, 1931: 186–7

Guthrie had recently produced two experimental 'plays for the microphone' for the BBC at Savoy Hill: *The Squirrel's Cage* (1929) and *The Flowers Are Not For You to Pick* (1930). He saw opportunity in the audio-only form for a scenography that transcended the dull monumentality of the visible stage, in an auditorium that was both intensely concentrated and diversely scattered:

> The listener is dependent upon one sense only for his impression – the hearing – and in this lies both the strength and the weakness of the broadcast plays: weakness inasmuch as the effort of concentration required by the listener is considerable and is more than many people can consistently achieve; strength inasmuch as the impression, if it reaches the listener at all, will reach him in a highly concentrated form. [. . .] An imaginative writer can build up a scene by subtle and ingenious word pictures, and for an imaginative listener he will create illusions infinitely more romantic than the tawdry grottos of the stage. [. . .] Now, not only is the broadcast play invisible, and therefore highly concentrated, it is also played to an audience who are not clumped together in one mass in an auditorium, but who are scattered over an area of hundreds of square miles and who are listening to plays under the most diverse circumstances.
>
> ibid.

The anticipation that television would soon arrive and steal radio's mass audience gave an urgency to the debate about what distinctive form radio drama should take. Between the differing views of Val Gielgud (who ran radio drama at the BBC from 1929), and Guthrie and Lance Sieveking, a staff producer of drama and educational features, it could become heated. Gielgud, like his brother John and his cousin Edward Gordon Craig, was born into the theatre. He established drama's place in the radio schedules and in the British public's listening habits by pursuing short, simple dramas that configured minimal uses of music, sound effects, narrator and actors' voices – as recognizably separate formal elements – around the primacy of the writer's words. Gielgud's prime directive, still the credo of the BBC today, was that whatever the actor or the producer might wish to try with sound, the words must be intelligibly audible above all else. Sieveking, on the other hand, who came to Drama from Features, whose output characteristically had a more ambient, documentary sensibility, saw only one formal element: the sound. Sound was the 'stuff of radio', he argued in a book of the same name (Sieveking, 1934): the sound of the music, the voice and dramatic world; sound as the disposition of audio objects, unified in their resonance together.

Much like Mamoulian in relation to film, Sieveking believed that if radio drama were to have a future as a distinct artform in the oncoming televisual age, then radio must be used as more than the imaginary, pictorial stage for literary drama. It should be the medium of a new, phonic, dramatic form. While over the Atlantic in Long Island, Mamoulian was also demanding Paramount sound technicians develop a way of mixing two microphone signals onto the film soundtrack (Milne, 1969: 24), the BBC invested in a state-of-the-art, valve-driven radio mixing console, the Dramatic Control Panel. The sound of effects, music, announcer, narrator and cast could be separately fed into it from multiple discrete studios or booths, each on its own individual channel, dynamically mixed together, and put out to the transmission amplifiers and circuits as one, mono signal. Sieveking advocated that rather than being deployed in the construction of audio-only stage plays, this technology should be played like a musical instrument, creating a tonally expressive, symphonic drama.

Like Sieveking, Guthrie also saw little point, given what people like Mamoulian were now starting to do with film, and with television on its way, in radio pursuing a radio dramaturgy that simply tried to restage theatre plays within imaginary box sets and scenery laid out with sound effects (a room with a door, a clock, a window with cows outside it). Such prosaic semantics were surely redundant:

> One feels that only by attacking the subject from a symphonic angle is it possible to rid the mind of unwanted literary and theatrical conventions; and, furthermore, that, in the inevitable and fast-approaching fusion with the talking films, the contribution of broadcasting to the new artform will be a symphonic one and that, therefore, it would be wise to approach the problem symphonically at the outset.
>
> BBC, 1931: 189

Guthrie's views on radio drama are followed in the 1931 *BBC Yearbook* review of 1929–30, by an article – unattributed, but probably by Sieveking – entitled 'The Use of Sound Effects'. This takes the familiar format for such magazine pieces. Fun secrets about how sounds are made are revealed, followed by some analysis and a taxonomic 'scope', wherein different uses for sound effects are delineated. But Sieveking, assuming it is he, also impresses that it is sound's overall *effect* that is the 'stuff' of radio. Radio drama must learn from the early mistakes of the talkies. Everything which comes out of a loudspeaker should be regarded as programmatic:

> Just before its temporary death [following the hype around *The Jazz Singer*, he is writing at the same time that Mamoulian and others were figuring out how to use sound effectively and save the talkie format], the silent film had begun to realise that it must aim for what was proper and peculiar to its medium; that it must not allow itself to be bound within the limits of the old theatre; that, in fact, there were a thousand new things which it alone could explore and exploit. And this is just beginning to be true of talking films. In the same way, those people who deal with a certain side of broadcasting are realising that they must not only use things created for other mediums in the past, but must constantly endeavour to develop and use that which can only be attempted in the medium in which they are working, namely, the Sound Effect, *in its widest sense* (the essential stuff of broadcasting).
>
> BBC, 1931: 194

The word 'effect' suggests that the essence of broadcasting is what sound does, not what it is: the acoustemological knowing it rehearses, the technique of hearing it involves, and the social space it produces. Sound is not the stuff; it is the effect, the thing accomplished, the difference made. As the radio historian and practitioner Gregory Whitehead puts it, writing from the perspective of the transmitter rather than the hearer:

> Radio happens in sound, but I don't believe that sound is what matters about radio, or any of the acoustic media. What does matter is the play among relationships: between bodies and antibodies, hosts and parasites, pure noise and irresistible fact, all in a strange parade, destination unknown, fragile, uncertain. Once you make the shift from the material of sound to the material of the media, the possibilities open to infinity, and things start getting interesting again. Each broadcast takes place inside an echo chamber of informations, histories, biographies, life stories – and inside the echo chamber resounds the most unnerving question of all, the ghost question: who's there? Is anybody out there on the other side of the wall, on the other side of this broadcast.
>
> WHITEHEAD, 1996: 96–7

A kaleidosonic form

In the commercially driven local American radio schedules of 1929–30, there was little place for extended drama. As the 1931 *BBC Yearbook* superciliously explains, American broadcasting was 'apt to restrict [itself] to the beaten track of successful features', predominantly 'those kinds of music which make the loudest noise head[ing] the list in popularity – that is, orchestras and dance bands', interpolated by non-musical sketches 'comparable with certain serial cartoon features in English newspapers' ('The American Listener: A British Impression', in BBC, 1931: 132). These supplied 'a snappy little commentary of five or ten minutes' every evening, telling stories of 'the ordinary experiences of the ordinary man'. Typically, these valorized the capitalist American dream of social mobility 'from Log Cabin to White House', epitomized by the comic serial 'Amos 'n' Andy', concerning the progress of their 'Fresh Air Taxicab Corporation' (ibid.).

America's early radio stations adopted a fast-paced popular variety format, based more on the ad-friendly, quick-paced presentational format of the informally hosted vaudeville, than the more educational, public service broadcasting of Reith's BBC. There was, however, some minor interest in modern drama at the Columbia Broadcasting System. At the end of 1930, Georgia Backus, an actress whose career would be ended by the Hollywood blacklist and who ran the CBS's tiny Dramatic Programming Division, introduced the Columbia Experimental Dramatic Laboratory. This began a twenty-six-year run of experimental drama programming on CBS, which, although never a high priority for the commercially driven network, would eventually provide it with the single highest number of North American Radio listeners in history – an estimated seventy million for Norman Corwin's VE Day dramatized documentary *On a Note of Triumph* (1945) – making radio the largest auditorium for a live theatre drama that there ever was.

As Le Bruit's 1948 article comparing it to the Picturesque suggests, the way of hearing disseminated by 'golden age' American radio drama, before TV took over as the principal broadcast medium, took a 200-year-old dramaturgical frame of historical reference and combined it with contemporary modernist influences (much as the soundtrack had done, in drawing on the traditional diegetic know-how of theatre-craft, and the stylistic quantizing of modernist formalism). The short, sharp vaudeville format of 'Amos 'n' Andy' developed not into a symphonic form, but a dispositional news item or vignette-based format, or what Verma has called a 'kaleidosonic' radio dramaturgy (2012: 70–1, 75); one which Jacob Smith describes as 'a mode often heard in news dramatization . . . [which] created the feeling of a shifting sonic world, by aurally leaping from place to place' (Smith and Verma, 2016: 105). Odd as it may sound, this format, the generally warm tone of its populist American dream agenda and the relaxed informality of its studio announcers, represented a distinctively American form of the epic diegesis Brecht and Piscator were developing in Europe.

But it was also the theatricality of its scale – of the artifice and ingenuity of a small studio reaching out over thousands of networked square miles – that captured the moment. The much publicized (and exaggerated) 'panic' to which Orson Welles' *War of the Worlds* 'faux-news' conceit had reportedly led in 1938 suggested a new pan-American community theatre in the big broadcast – the live, national, networked event. It updated the community-forming Picturesque fascination with artifice and backstage secrets (the '*our* thunder' effect, which Le Bruit astutely identifies as part of radio's fascination) within a dialectical space that juxtaposed the state-of-the-art modernity of the audio age against the romance of what Gregory Whitehead calls 'a kind of Grotowskian "poor" radio, a simple organizing concept surrounded by a few cheap sound effects and a small ensemble of improvising actors' (1996: 98).

An interactive form

The idea of creating an auditory theatre space where the artifice was declared, and which played knowingly with radio conventions and Whitehead's 'ghost question' about the separation of audience from production, had begun in Backus' Experimental Dramatic Laboratory in 1931. While in London, Sieveking and Guthrie were imagining a more symbolist, symphonic drama to be the distinctive radiophonic form, in America, the innovation was to make it a medium-specific interrogation of radio and its workings as a theatre space. As quoted in *The Brooklyn Daily Eagle*, Backus' first production, 'Murder in the Studio' (broadcast 28 January 1931), begins with the announcer reading the following:

> Ladies and gentlemen, we present another play in the series which comprises Columbia's Dramatic Laboratory. These radio dramas are designed to stimulate an interest in experiments made in that art and tonight we are presenting a murder mystery that is baffling the minds of the greatest detectives in the country. We are doing this in the hope that some one of you who are listening in may be able to give the authorities the solution.
>
> On the night of Dec. 3 Dave Cross, announcer of Station WTAZ, of Newton, Ill., was alone in the studio. A few minutes before midnight someone entered the announcer's booth and killed him. Although there were no sight witnesses, many people were listening to WTAZ on their radio sets that night, heard the events that led up to the tragedy.
>
> SKINNER, 1931

Backus's formal conceit of creating a theatre space through letting the audience in on backstage secrets became the house style of the Columbia Workshop under engineer-turned-radio-auteur Irving Reis. Its mission, initially stated by the announcer at the top of each broadcast, was to 'dedicate itself to the purposes of familiarizing you with the story behind radio [. . .] and to experiment in new techniques with a hope of discovering or evolving new and better forms of radio presentation, with especial emphasis on radio drama; to encourage and present the work of new writers and artists who may have fresh and vital ideas to contribute' (Oakland Tribune, 18 July 1936: 12). The 'workshop' element was intended to work as follows:

> During some of the broadcasts, the listening audience will be asked to participate in offering constructive criticism of new production methods. It might be a series of five sounds, with the audience being requested to determine which is the most pleasant to the ear. Then again, they will be asked comparative opinions on five-minute one-act plays, presented first by a carefully rehearsed group of actors, then by a second group which has simply 'read over' the lines individually.
>
> ibid.

There may have been an intent to develop audio drama on the basis of such interaction. However, by declaring it, an effect was created – a mode of attentiveness that treated the audio drama as a vast, acousmatic, dialectical learning space. The publicity (or propaganda) apparatus of popular journals and local newspapers are part of the dispositive of theatre 'as an exemplary community form', as Rancière puts it, where community is an idea of 'self-presence' (2009: 5). The various discussions of sound effects techniques in the press considered in this book – the *Wine and Walnuts* column (Pyne, 1823), the *Strand Magazine* (Vincent, 1904), the *Radio Times* (BBC, 1931), *American Notes and Queries* (Le Bruit, 1947), the *Blue Peter* item – are all examples of this. They are part of what Sterne refers to as the meta-discourse that is required for auditory space production (2013: 183–4).

Reis's idea for the Columbia Workshop in 1936 resonated with one proposed by Brecht in July 1932 in an article entitled 'Der Rundfunk als Kommunikationsapparat':

> Radio could be the most wonderful public communication system imaginable, a gigantic system of channels – could be, that is, if it were capable not only of transmitting but of receiving, of making the listener not only hear but also speak, not of isolating him but of connecting him. [. . .] What [traditional radio drama] finds in front of the set is the individual – and of all alcoholic excesses none is more dangerous than solitary drinking.

[. . .] Were there a theatre of epic drama, of didactic documentary performance, then radio could carry out an entirely new kind of propaganda for the theatre, namely genuine information, indispensable information. A commentary of this kind, closely bound up with the theatre, a genuine, worthy complement to drama, could develop entirely new forms and so on. Direct collaboration between performances in the theatre and on the radio could also be organised. Radio could transmit choruses to the theatre just as it could broadcast publicly the decisions and productions of the audiences at the meeting-like collective performances of didactic plays.

BRECHT, 1980: 25–7

Corwin

What eventually convened a vast audience for live radio theatre in America, and the star-studded 'Big Broadcast' format (named after Frank Tuttle's 1932 movie about one, staring Bing Crosby), was the threat of war, and as it approached, the Columbia Workshop was joined by a new creative force.

Norman Corwin was discovered producing a poetry programme in New York in 1937 and took Columbia's experimental drama from relative obscurity within the schedules, to a high-water mark (possibly for any form of live theatre) of seventy million VE-day listeners in 1945. Combining a rich historical knowledge of literary and dramaturgical convention, with a rhetorical panache, a disarming wit, and a politically left-leaning common touch, Corwin was the ideal wartime propagandist to unite America's diverse, far-flung and worried domestic audience. He was also a sonic innovator who, according to Smith and Verma, belongs in a pantheon of genre-transcendent 'sound auteurs' that includes 'Lou Reed and Yasunao Tone, Sun Ra and Laurie Anderson, Emile Berliner and Dylan Thomas, Alan Lomax and Nina Simone, Janet Cardiff and Miles Davis, Christian Marclay and Bjork, Brian Eno and George Clinton, Paul Robeson and Pauline Oliveros, David Byrne and David Lynch, Walter Murch and Hildegard Westerkamp' (Smith and Verma, 2016: 4). In terms of the reach of his work, the shared, live moment it convened across the nation, its influence on the way America heard itself and its relationship to the world and the great sociopolitical issues of the day, he was arguably more impactful than any of them.

The theatre Corwin heard

In what follows, I describe my audition – disconnected by seventy-four years from that live moment – of Corwin's VE Day production, *On a Note of Triumph* (broadcast 8 May 1945). I describe how Corwin configures a theatre for the mind's ear, which dialectically engages his audience the ways in which theatre is configured as the aesthetic or sensible constitution of the 'common' populace. Corwin takes control of the space in which the drama is heard – the aural disposition of the listeners. He is not authoring a drama or an imaginary movie, he is authoring a hearing. I describe how he controls space through a series of sonic 'cues' plotted against a matrix comprising, on one axis an acoustic spectrum that ranges from the closely microphonic voice through to more ambient sound and spatially reverberant speech, and on the other, a spectrum of performative registers that ranges from the radio announcer through studio-actorliness to theatrical projection. The quotations are transcribed from the original audio, which was released as a vinyl album in 1975. Now hear this.

*

▸

My kitchen. A Bluetooth speaker on a fridge: an overture and then a voice, in the rhetorical register of an orator; around it, the reverberation of a hall or theatre.

> 'So, they've given up. They're finally done in and the rat is dead . . . Seems like free men have done it again!'

The voice is addressing the 'common men of this afternoon' who defeated the supermen of tomorrow.
   There isn't any surround sound in my kitchen, and of course none encoded in the signal chain that began in 1941 and which emerges here in 2019; just a voice and some music coming from the mono radio set. I am alone in my hearing today, although when this was first broadcast, there were as many as seventy million 'I's, set together – and apart – by their ears.
   I do not exactly visualize it, but in some other way behind my eyes, I picture myself in an auditorium, among others; somewhere like a drill hall. The overture is reprised and then . . . a different voice. Or certainly a different register and phonic persona.

> 'By popular request the Columbia Broadcasting system presents On a Note of Triumph.'

A studio announcer's voice in friendly radio space. The auditorium evaporates. I am a solitary radio listener – the sense of public space now gone. For a moment, the familiarity of the announcer's tone and cadence makes the radio just another domestic appliance in a scenography of sound-emitting objects. There is no more hall to the announcer's voice. The only space indexed by this new sound is the electric space, the vacuum in the warmly distorting amplification valves of its radiophonic signal chain seventy years ago, into which my transistorized speaker and modern Wi-Fi now opens. As it happens, I am doing the dishes.

The voice introduces Martin Gable as narrator and Bernard Hermann as composer. Hermann's music picks up and leads, with VE Day bells ringing, back to Gable's voice. It is different to before, closer to the microphone; not the radio announcer persona – radiophonic or cinematic rather but still actorly in a new performative register. A patriotic newsreel narrator. The effect is I am part of an addressed congregation, a we again. We know where we are and the kind of program to which we are going to be listening: a documentary propaganda drama.

The narration continues, the music dies away, and the narrator's voice begins to acquire an oratorical cadence. As he gets into his stride, Gable becomes yet more theatrically actorly, moving back from the microphone. More of the reverberation of the performance space is revealed. The signal-to-ambience ratio decreases. Within this acoustic ratio but also between the rhetoric and resonance, a theatre space forms again and I am imagining a figure on the forestage of a proscenium arch theatre. However, as before, it deflates the instant the scene switches to a folk song about dancing on Hitler's grave ['Rally 'round Hitler's Grave', performed by Pete Seeger and the Almanac Singers]. *We are now looking into a scenic vignette – of a barn dance. If Gable had previously sounded as though he was hitting the back of the circle from the forestage, this scene is upstage of that, in the softer, smaller, and more contained acoustic of a furnished set (this is how I imagine it; it was most likely a separate studio). The barn dance fades as Gable's forestage voice returns, with its warm halo of reverberation. This voice steers the listener through a sequence of folk songs in different languages.*

II

Up to this point, the spatial configuration has matched a fairly standard format for American radio drama from this period. An announcer – a radio voice – introduces a show. There is a musical framework, like that of movie or a pit orchestra, providing a formal framing from an extra-diegetic space. After this, the actorly voice of the narrator, combined with the acoustic reverberation of the studio, suggests a theatre configuration to my mind, a sense that I am being configured as a *we* from a forestage between the lively acoustic of the auditorium and the smaller acoustic of the stage scene, where a series of vignettes is being presented.

▸

We think that Gable has reached the end of his introduction and we have settled into this format, but then comes a strange command in his actorly rhetoric: 'fix your eyes on the horizon, swing your ears about, size up the day and date'.

From this point onwards, the format becomes less of a hosted series of radiophonic tableaux, and more the 'kaleidosonic' trip I mentioned above.

Our ears are, indeed, swung about around by a switchback narrative, a pirouetting stream of consciousness from which we glimpse a fragmented scenography, flashing before our mind's seeing ear. Our seat in the imaginary auditorium becomes unfixed. We are going on a ride.
   'Listen. Listen closely', *Corwin instructs, through Gable's narrator's persona, as though he is about to perform some close magic. He is. The voice remains constant on the forestage as the auditory scene changes behind it, like the sonic projection of a microphone that has grown wings and taken flight. The theatre ceases to be statically end-on and becomes a microphonic wonderland of mercurial reconfigurations of scale and perspective. We are guided from the personal intimacy of the whispering of our own internal monologue, to a bird's-ear view of the theatre mundi heard from the clouds . . . no: now through the headphones of the navigator of a B-29 bomber.*
   Swinging about from scene to scene, our microphonic proxy-ear is paraded, under Corwin's instruction, through voices, sound effects, and music, across a map of Europe and beyond. And then: '. . . in just a moment now' *the voice of the conqueror is trailed. We expect, perhaps, the note of triumph of the play's title, but this is Corwin's point:*

> 'Don't expect to hear metallic speech from the rosette of amplifying horns on the high poles of the public address system. But listen for a modest voice as sensible and intimate to you as the quiet turning of your own considered judgement.'

Regular listeners in 1945 would have then recognized Hank Peters, the everyman soldier and one of the 'common men', *of Corwin's earlier propaganda drama* Untitled *(1944):* 'this boy, that boy, any boy at all with war still thumping in his ears'.
   We do not hear triumph but the concerns of our auditorium resonating in his words: 'who did we beat and what did it cost to beat him. Is it all going to happen again?'
   Quickly we are whisked back into the drill hall space again: 'can it be, that our soldiers are footnoting the surrender?'

As if to answer this question, we are switched back to the intimacy of the electrified radiophonic vacuum tube again, only this time Corwin instructs us to imagine we are *the microphone, on a stand, in front of which a prisoner of war is hauled.*

'I'm a soldier, a little man, I merely obeyed orders.'

The narrator now becomes interrogator and the microphone – we – are now mounted on the dock of a war-crimes hearing.

Back in the auditorium of oratory, suddenly a new voice: an ethical acousmêtre, *not from the stage, but seeming to come from everywhere:*

'Observe him, note him well!' [BIG REVERBERATION!!!]

Who speaks this?

And so, it continues: the 'reversible' microphone that embodies our point of audition flips us up and down, back and forth; the music, the dynamic registers of performance, their acoustic signatures and the instruction 'listen, listen, listen' – all snaking around each other in an aural counterpoint, within the frame of a kaleidosonically cubist composite of multiple aural viewpoints. But all the while, and finally, the present-day noises and hums of a kitchen, 2019, and a speaker on a fridge.

■

Immersivity and the mono loudspeaker

Before returning to the political rhetoric of Corwin's radio theatre, I want to talk about the space of the auditory imagination, especially since the spatial configuration of the 'intracranial' head theatre constituted by the podcast and live-event theatre formats now being produced for headphones lends the phrase 'theatre of the mind' new meaning. Unpacking this term in his book of the same name, Verma describes how 'dramatists [of the late 1930s depression era] became preoccupied with suggesting plastic settings in the listener's mind, encouraging listeners to explore imaginary space just for the sake of doing so' (Verma, 2012: 19). Identifying Corwin's as a 'People's Radio Aesthetic' that 'attempted to meld intimate and kaleidosonic designs into a rhetoric befitting the New Deal era's rituals of unity, drawing stirring pictures of America itself in the mind of the listener', Verma notes how Corwin transformed these 'exploratory celebrations of exteriority into tales of interiority, and dramas of space and time taking place in the mind [into a form that] truly became a theatre about the mind' (ibid.).

My audition of Corwin bears this out, but also that this 'theatre about the mind' seemed to configure, in my mind, something like a traditional, end-on playhouse – albeit with an impossibly mercurial stage/auditorium configuration that could snap back and forth, at Corwin's authorial will, to the electric vacuum of the valve microphone and radiophonic signal chain. Maybe this, rather literally, shows how, within an artistically governed distribution of the sensible, theatre provides the metaphor and thought-model for understanding community 'as a way of occupying a place and a time' (Rancière, 2009: 6). If so, I would argue that theatre's metaphor and thought-model is principally an aural one (just as theatre is, principally, an aural situation). Although I 'pictured' theatre settings in the audio of *On a Note of Triumph*, these were only fleetingly and vaguely visual, as my eyes remained open and active in the world of my kitchen. Nevertheless, as I 'fixed my eyes on the horizon and swung my ear about' on the switchback ride around Europe, I clearly felt I was in an impossibly mutating theatre that related to a visual sense of front (the front of the head being where the eyes are).

Martin Welton has described how theatre's traditional auditory configuration is 'sutured' to this ocular determination of forward or front.

> Even upon taking one's seat in an auditorium – where that seat faces towards a separated stage – one's spatial orientation and relationships are defined by their subservience to the mechanics of seeing. Not only the flow of sound, but the manner by which one orients oneself and prefigures one's receptiveness to it, are shaped by a visual engagement with one's surroundings.
>
> WELTON, 2012: 77–8

My audition of Corwin shows that given a number of acoustic and verbally suggestive cues, the ocular orientation of my head theatre can become fluid in ways that would be impossible in perceptual space. I can imagine myself in a shape-shifting world, while also remaining upright and spatially functional in my kitchen, because one of the basic, self-preserving abilities of the mind is to be imagining space in different ways to those that the senses make it available – all the time. Thus, even though the sense of front might be an optical determination, humans can see things in the rear-view mirror of their imagination as part of their cognitive mapping of an auditory scene. It is the visualized imagery associated with a sound that provides the self-preserving impulse to turn the head to see whether there is really a predator there. There is no basis for this rear-view world in perceptual experience. While the sense of front might be an optical determination, the visualization of the rear world is aural. The spatial imagination is different to the perceptual realm, with vision – the mind's eye –

sutured to the omnidirectional ear. Don Ihde illustrates this with a simple mind game. He imagines a small red horse galloping on the floor behind him:

> I seem to be able to place [this] visually imagined object in any position in relation to the surrounding imagined space. And if this is possible – let each try for himself – then the space of visual imagery parallels in at least one aspect the space of the auditory field and not its visual counterpart.
>
> IHDE, 2007: 209

Audio drama releases many such small red horses into the mind.

Clive Cazeaux comes at this using Merleau-Ponty. As he puts it, even when attending to a 'sound-only' medium, other senses are potentially active in 'invitational' relationships with one another. Accordingly, radio should be understood not as 'a series of inadequate clues from an unlit world' but as 'a medium that opens onto and generates a world and, as part of this world-generation, enjoys interaction and conjunction with the other senses' (Cazeaux, 2005). In opening onto such a conjunction of sensory modality, radio requires no surround-sound, or even stereo, to create a sense of immersivity. Audio generates an immersive picture. Mono will do. When Corwin fixed seventy million pairs of eyes on the horizon and spun as many pairs of ears about, turning a nation into one soaring, pirouetting, electric ear, stereo was in any case not available. Disney's Fantasound project had literally been torpedoed by a German U-boat, and most people had never heard the effect. Corwin did it with studio microphone placement and technique, verbal cues and one vibrating cone of treated paper and glue, hidden behind the grill of a radio set.

The hole in the wall

All the acoustic information needed to suggest the dynamic spatial configurations I describe above came through one mono speaker. This need not seem so improbable if one imagines the loudspeaker as a small window that opens onto the space of the concert hall, the studio or the fabricated space of the radio drama. If the radio producer works consistently to this thought-model, a coherent sense of the performance space will appear in the audience's room, regardless of whether it is an intimate bedsit or an echoey hall. Picture yourself in the room. If an actor were to come right up close to the window and speak through it, you would hear none, or very little, of the space of the room that they are in. You would hear the actor's voice and the reverberation of your room only, however big your room is. The further back the actor stands, the more the ratio of resonance and reverberation from the actor's room increases in proportion to their voice. If the actor stands beyond a certain tipping point, the sound coming through the window can no longer be described as an actor in a space, but as a space with an actor in it. However, whatever the acoustic of your listening room, the balance between voice and space coming through the window will be the same, and even though this single, combined programme of sound may take on the secondary reverberation of your small bedsit or large drawing room, the original spatiality of the performance is now built into it.

Several different kinds of mic were developed to facilitate a range of distances from the window, and therefore different ratios of voice (or sound effect) to circumstantial ambience. Having an actor speak very closely into a cardioid microphone (a kind which privileges the sounds in a heart-shaped and sized area in front of it over the ambience further away) produces the up-close radio-voice sound (the person speaking directly into the audience's space through the window). Having them speak further back from omnidirectional microphones, which pick up the ambient resonance and reverberation coming back from the room on all sides (or in the case of a 'figure-of-eight' microphone, mainly from the front and back) sets the voices in bigger spaces. By speaking into a directional figure-of-eight or hyper-cardioid mic off-axis, there is a tonal change that the mind will read it as lateral or vertical displacement, even if there is no binaural information. By the 1940s, there were microphones and practised techniques to convey a wide range of subtle spatial suggestions through the loudspeaker 'window'. Artificial reverberation and echo could be added too, using springs or resonant metal plates which could extend the studio or radio theatre beyond the dimensions of the studio space (as De Loutherbourg had done with his whalebone spring and drums).

It was P. G. A. H. Voigt, the young Edison-Bell engineer from near the Crystal Palace, mentioned in passing back in Chapter 5, who first suggested the hole-in-the-wall model for making sense of the new, unintuitive, acousmatic presence of loudspeaker sound in people's living rooms. Voigt went on to design cinema loudspeakers and high-end hi-fi equipment but proposed this 'mental picture of ideal reproduction' to the BBC's first chief engineer, Captain P. P. Eckersley, at a public meeting in 1924, when the BBC was only about eighteen months old (Voigt, 1932). As a model, it now seems obvious, but loudspeakers that relayed the radiophonic sound of remote, unseen studios or theatres into the home were an entirely new proposition. Nobody was sure quite how people would listen to – or through – them within the auditorium of domestic life. Fearing the destabilizing effect of presenting different microphone positions and registers of space, the weight of opinion was that the radio set should represent a single, fixed auditory perspective on the studio or stage at the other end of the signal chain, like that of a fixed seat in a stage-facing auditorium. It was Voigt's suggestion that provided a stabilizing logic for programming to switch between different perspectives and intimacies in the malleable way we now take for granted.

'The Loudspeaker' as a voice

Whether or not Corwin was directly influenced by Brecht and Piscator's *epic* theatre, Corwin admired Brecht and was keen to work with him. This would almost happen in 1946–7, when Brecht, in exile in the US, was struggling, under House of Un-American Activities (HUAC) scrutiny, to find a producer for the American version of *Galileo*. FBI notes on a bugged phone call between Charles Laughton and Brecht's wife describe how Laughton says that he had just read two scenes of the play to Corwin, who immediately said he would like to direct it. Laughton points out that this is a good thing. Corwin 'is a tremendous personality in the country and is a number one patriotic American [. . .] It would be advantageous for such a man to produce this play of Brecht's, who might be called a Communist' (Lyon, 1983: 225).

Corwin's 'people's' aesthetic and New Deal-era rhetoric was, in fact, more socialist than the patriotic framing of his wartime propaganda might suggest. His documentary style and use of the microphone persona of the newsreel narrator – alternately theatrical and personable – is resonant of the Federal Theatre Project's epic style, particularly that of the *Living Newspaper* series. These community productions began in 1935 and were originally intended to provide work for unemployed journalists and theatre professionals as part of the New Deal. They were produced across America until terminated by HUAC for their socialist sensibilities in 1939. They were notable for their innovative use of projected images, amplified effects and soundscapes, and introduced a new figure to the dramaturgy of sound – the immersive *acousmêtre* simply as 'Loudspeaker' or 'The Voice of the Living Newspaper', which placed and organized *The Living Newspaper*'s 'articles' *within* an editorial 'voice from the dark' (Woodruff, 2013: 1).

The Living Newspaper's sound designer, Harold Burris-Meyer, describes in a 1977 interview quoted by Woodruff, how the FTP innovated with loudspeaker positioning and filmic uses of audio that brought the contrapuntal independence of hearing and viewpoint of film and radio back to the theatre. The vocal persona of the Loudspeaker not only provided a linking commentary on the scenes (the newspaper's articles), but also, as an *acousmêtre*, staged the ubiquity of audio as a spatially organizing presence:

> we used the sound of an aircraft as it approached and circled over the audience and then landed. And the place it landed was up stage left . . . it was a very realistic reproduction. However the voice of the Living

Newspaper ['Loudspeaker'] was really the important element and this voice was reproduced [from all directions at once]. That is, the voice was there, but no place to which you could point. And this made it at once intimate and all pervasive . . . All you needed to do was to make it come from everywhere . . . in the Ritz Theatre where we worked a good deal, we had loudspeakers which were pointed up at the ceiling so that the audience heard the sound as reflected down from the ceiling. And since one's sense of direction is not accurate in altitude, since you can't tell very well . . . the audience found it rather easy to accept what was logical.

ibid.: 5

Just over a decade after radio became a mass medium, theatre was modelling the space of a community occupying time and place according to the now-familiar sensibilities and techniques of domestic audio.

The totalizing voice of 'The Loudspeaker' was something like the internal monologue of this audio mode of being. Rather than thinking of it as a disembodied voice, it might be more apt to think of the audio 'voice from the dark' or *acousmêtre* as an embodying voice, which placed the immediate, physical, acoustic theatre within the command of a figurative manifestation or avatar of the audio meta-space I described earlier as a mysterious zone or electric limbo. 'Loudspeaker' was presented in the *dramatis personae* and publicity, as a cast-member in the *Living Newspaper* productions. Its legacy within the dramaturgy of sound outlived the FTP and remains one of the principles of sound design: the acousmatic being, the audio-only entity, *as actor*. Its creator, Burris-Meyer, presents it as such in his seminal 1959 textbook *Sound in Theatre*, in listing the functional dramaturgical scope of sound (original emphasis):

1. To transmit the human voice in speech or song; (adequate audibility is always the first requisite).
2. To establish locale; (bird songs, traffic noises).
3. To establish atmosphere; (wind and rain).
4. To create and sustain mood; (combinations of devices used for locale and atmosphere; distortion of speech; soft music).
5. As an independent arbitrary emotional stimulus; (music).
6. As an actor; (the voice of the LIVING NEWSPAPER).
7. To reveal character; (the unspoken aside).
8. To advance the plot; (sound bridges between scenes or episodes).

BURRIS-MEYER and MALLORY, 1959: 2

Common sound

Norman Corwin often switched to this 'everywhere' expository, embodying voice – the voice of the audio circuitry of the network itself – when he instructed his listeners to 'observe' what he is about to do. It cued a theatrical gravitas, which contrasted the otherwise relaxed, colloquial style of his exposition, which should be understood within the context of a national agenda to develop educational, spoken word programming across the networks. There was a concern on behalf of those networks and their sponsors that radio drama might seem elitist and alienate a pre-war radio audience that was largely blue-collar and still taking to the new medium (Douglas, 2004: 141–4). Regional America was wary of federalism, and of a federalization of the airwaves by a metropolitan intelligentsia, although by the end of the decade, the threat of war made the nation eager for up-to-the-minute news and reassurance from Washington, and there was a surge in radio ownership and interest in spoken word content on national issues. Corwin's folksy, didactic style relates to this political agenda for networked radio to have a people's aesthetic (quite unlike the formality and King's English of the BBC), but is also characteristic of the Brechtian epic form, which, as Benjamin describes, was a dialectical diegesis that required a relaxed auditorium (Benjamin, 1973: 15–22). Also Brechtian is Corwin's referencing of and playfulness with the radio format and medium, which continued with Irving Reis's 'workshop' conceit of 'familiarizing [listeners] with the story behind radio'. The first programme in CBS' *26 by Corwin* was an episode called *Radio Primer* (1941).

The Anatomy of Sound, which we shall now consider in detail, followed in the same year. It was an easily accessible, entertaining 'treatise' in the ever-popular 'backstage secrets explained' vein, on sound, audio and contemporary aurality, which, like Le Bruit's article, located radio drama in the tradition of De Loutherbourg's picturesque of sound. Literary allusions to Romanticism and satires on melodramatic clichés are interspersed with illustrated discussions of amplification and perception, and philosophical sections on silence and music. While the tone is generally easy-going and humorous, there is a propaganda message – a passionate plea for *our* common aurality to overcome the rising age of despots and demagogues, which is underlined with thunder.

The Anatomy of Sound, by Norman Corwin

In the following account, the quoted sections are a partial transcription (made with the kind permission of the Corwin estate) of my audition of a low-fidelity audio recording of *The Anatomy of Sound*, broadcast by CBS on 7 September 1941. Where passages are inaudible, I have referred to a fascinating copy of the working production script, covered in Corwin's handwritten annotations, held by the American Radio Archives at Thousand Oaks Library in California, which also owns the recording and much of the Corwin archive. Into the account, I have woven a commentary that serves as a summarizing recapitulation of some of the themes we have considered in this book's own epic narrative.

▸

The broadcast begins, in typical Corwin, epic style, with a succession of diegetic framing devices to establish an auditorium within whatever everyday context the listener is found. The voice is female. She has a colloquial chatty style (the script only refers to this voice as 'Narrator').

'How would you like to get up before an audience of four million people and introduce yourself?'

It is a soft opening. There has been no formal introductory announcement. How would I attract their attention, if I were in her place, the voice asks me? Would I use a spoon on a glass?

I hear the tinkling of metal on glass.

'Do you think that would quiet such an audience?'

Now I understand I am at a social gathering.

'Would you clear your throat like this?'

I hear a throat being cleared, loudly and performatively.

'Or would you try to ride over their various noises by shouting through a public address system the traditional salutation?'

I hear the sound of a PA 'as though trying to top a great noise', the working script says, although Corwin has then crossed out 'great noise' and replaced it with 'hubbub'.

'Ladies and gentlemen', *says the sound of a loudspeaker in the world through my loudspeaker's hole in the wall.*

Corwin's working script then notes a switch to a 'normal' cardioid, studio announcer's mic. The voice recommences, but still in the dramaturgical rhetoric of a prologue intended to set the dispersed audience together by the ears. She is continuing to preface the programme, talking now about the 'ghost effect' Whitehead refers to in my quotation earlier. She is talking from one dimension to another, not really knowing if there is anyone there.

'Suppose some of your audience were playing bridge and others were arguing and others were lying down reading newspapers – would that terrify you? It would me, I know . . . Except at this moment when I am addressing four million people and thousands of them are playing bridge and talking across my voice and riding in automobiles and reading things – I'm not at all terrified. That's because there are four bare walls of a radio studio around me and I cannot see your faces. I cannot see a hundred thousand cigarettes light up in the dark across 8 million square miles of curving continent.'

I hear the sound of a bell, as between the rounds of a boxing match.

'Thank you', *she says, in a new more formal tone – that of radio announcer.*

'From Hollywood, the Columbia Workshop presents me, Gale Sondergaard, in a treatise for solo voice entitled *The Anatomy of Sound*.'

I hear the bell again and realize it is a recurrent motif or punctuation device. It has the effect of switching Sondergaard back from radio announcer to lecturer. The original script had the line 'two bells and so far all is well', but Corwin has crossed this out. The sound reads well enough on its own. The voice continues like this. The crossed-out sections are from the working script and did not make the broadcast:

'Now, how shall we anatomize sound for you? With formulas and scientific talk? Well, hardly. To us, you see, a sound wave is a sound wave ~~and not a form of vibrational energy propagated by progressive longitudinal disturbances~~. What do we care if the intensity of a sound varies directly as the square of the amplitude of the vibration? Let the Bell Laboratories worry about that.

'We are concerned tonight with the anatomy of *common* sound, your sound and my sound and everybody's sound, because sound is *common* and let's not forget that. ~~The sound of my voice at this very moment is common to four million listeners (or else the prologue written for me tonight is a liar).~~'

I then hear her explain that by 'common sound' she means 'unpatented, royalty-free, public domain and non-ASCAP' *sounds made by* 'man and beast and wind and rain and crickets and dynamite'. *This seems no less specialist than the scientific definition, but whether Corwin's audience was familiar with the way sounds had become licensed as audio objects since the early 1930s, the point is clear and is the same as Cowper's when he had his 'free man' survey the land and its glittering mansions, as his scenery.*

'After all, our lives are full of sounds and furies signifying everything from the coming of dawn, as in the cockerel to the coming of doom, as in the tolling of the sexton's bell in Gray's Elegy.'

There is undoubtedly a populist rhetoric in Corwin's repetition of the word 'common', but there seems little doubt that Corwin the poetry scholar intends to evoke something of the revolutionary subjectivity of Romanticism. He continues with a section about poets who connect with their reader's through aural tropes, giving examples beginning with a paraphrasing of Wordsworth's 1806 sonnet on materialism 'The World Is Too Much with Us':

'Sound is always with us late and soon . . . and all our days can easily be traced by ear'

and then breaking off to describe how there is such a thing as an average sonic life, and how it would be easy to

'log a day's career in decibels.'

I then hear a simple demonstration: a spoken narrative of an ordinary day, diligently illustrated with sound effects: an alarm clock, breakfast dishes, a newspaper being opened and turned, a coffee percolator, a toaster popping up, a front door opening and shutting, steps on a staircase, street sounds, whistling, boarding a bus, clocking-in, factory whistle, a cash register, key and lock, the home door opening and closing again, the winding of the alarm clock, the creaking of the bed.

'Those are the ordinary sounds' *I am told*, 'footsteps and doorknobs turned and typewriters and dishes and the sound of brushing teeth and autos starting up in low gear.'

Then the voice revisits the alarm clock, back in her easy-going conversational mode – 'a mean and ordinary little sound and yet it rules your life, and it's the first thing that you hear each day'. *She takes me on a romantic, escapist version of the same day. Big Ben chimes and I am asked whether, awoken thus, I would* 'go forth to epic deeds . . . ride off on a white Arabian charger instead of a bus, . . . punch not clocks but dragons. Or take that factory whistle, whistling noon a while back.' *I hear a factory whistle, an* 'uninspiring sound', *it is suggested, but am then shown how whistles* 'can be more romantic than a full moon in Tahiti'. *I hear the sound of a great liner bound for Cathay or Singapore.*

'Do you argue that it's not the idea of escape which makes a ship's whistle romantic, but the suggestion of luxury? Of salons and lounges and tea on deck and officers in white uniforms? Nonsense! Here is another romantic whistle, without any possible association of evening gowns or black ties.'

A freight whistle as if in the distance, an instant American picturesque: a night train winding its boxcars through the vast landscape. 'That's the kind of sound Tom Wolfe would write seven chapters about.' *Corwin then gives us a taxonomy of train whistles, each with its own picturesque, before moving on to whistles* 'sober and romantic, utilitarian, ridiculous'. *I hear each: peanut whistle (blown by vendors at sports events), traffic whistle, slide whistle (the clown kind), bird box (warbling bird whistle), whistling with fingers in the mouth, and then a swerve: the whistle of a shell followed by an explosion. On this cue, a decade before John Cage's 1951 visit to the anechoic chamber at Harvard, whose legend provided a cornerstone for modern musicology and sonic art theory, Corwin addresses silence:*

'So much for common sounds, but what of common silences? Do you protest "all silence is the same?" It isn't though, not for the living. There's not a man alive who has ever heard complete and perfect silence. Not deaf men, for they hear hums and pulses; not men shut up in silent rooms, for there is their own breathing and the beating of their hearts.

'The perfect silence is of course the grave, for in the grave, as far as we know in our ~~unmystical~~ *[Corwin's hand has substituted 'amateur']* way, there are no worthy noises. All is a deep and ultimate silence - profound, inscrutable, surpassing anything the living ear can testify to having heard.'

There is a beat; and then the narration restarts in a lighter vein with a sonic joke about the silence of the countryside, which Corwin demonstrates is anything but, with sounds of insects and nocturnal fauna building to a nightmarish crescendo. Other silences follow of a crying baby going to sleep; of embarrassment; a dentist's drill stopping. Then three dramatic silences. The first, we have discussed in relation to Baldpate Inn – 'the eerie silence, usually found in ghost stories and unpleasant places, *Wuthering Heights* and *Manderley*'.

'And then we have the twin favourite of writers, without which they'd be sorely handicapped if not ruined. These are, these are the Tense silence and the Electrifying silence. Whenever two or more people in the story are afraid and confront each other without speaking a word, in fact confront each other head-on – well, that is tense silence.'

Electric silence is demonstrated with a vignette. The interior of a wood cabin in the forest. It is dark out. 'Our heroine', *played by Sondergaard (Sondergaard tells us) is alone, walking up and down in the cabin.*

I hear walking up and down on wood. The space has switched from that of a closely miked voice, to a room with an actor in it.

'Suddenly there is a knock on the door.'
I hear a knock on the door. Then a pause.

Sondergaard steps back to her lectern position (I imagine from the change of tone in her voice) to explain how that was the first of a series of four electrifying silences, she then returns to her narrator persona, I hear more steps, and Sondergaard talks me through the remaining three. A door opens with a great creak.

Silence.
Scream.
Silence.
Gunshots.
Silence.

'That was the fourth and final electrifying silence.'

'Now we must tell you about radio silence. Radio silence is the only sound which can cover so much ground and be in so many places at the same time. As a free sample, suppose we stop now for a few seconds and transmit only what is known as dead air:

A three-second silence

'You have just heard silence, ~~racing~~ whipping around the world at the speed of light – a silence cutting through the tangled ethers of the globe, straight into your living room. I hold my tongue a moment in studio B, station KMX, Sunset and Gower, Hollywood California – and little whirlpools and eddies of silence play on every rooftop in America. An unexpected silence in the midst of any network programme such as this would shock preoccupied technicians. Engineers in master-control rooms around the country would look up in alarm – stand-by organists, announcers, production men would jump to their feet or to a microphone or both – thinking a line had failed, a link dropped out of the great chain, a wire in the circus gone haywire. Silence is a strange and out of place phenomenon, in such a talkative and busy channel of communication. Just *how* strange it is you can gather for yourself, from a simple illustration. Take a small quantity of dead air and place it where it doesn't quite belong . . .'

Nine-seconds of silence.

'See what I mean? How long was that? Nine seconds, long enough for a fast man to run 90 yards, or a fast plane to fly a mile, or a radio engineer to have a fit. Nine seconds doesn't seem long in casual seconds, but in a radio studio would amount roughly to forty years.'

Then there is a sequence of sound effects, linked together as many-a HiFi Sound Effects record would later do to demonstrate the stereo effect, in a travelogue. Moving from Times Square and a cab with electric windows (a novelty at the time) to the jungle in the Belgian Congo, I hear a steam locomotive at Grand Central Station (with an explanation that while trains are all electric now, poetic license allows for the steam train effect); Niagara Falls; Chicago Stock Yards; Native American Dances, and so on to Hollywood (swimming); Hawaii (volcano) and Australia (kookaburra).

Corwin has mapped out the kind of audio object framework of memes and tropes within which the acoustic everyday can be heard, if the hearer is so minded, as soundscape, scenery or theatre. He continues thus:

'Now you may have noticed that this thesis hasn't covered the common matter of music. It certainly comes under the heading sound. ~~That's because we think music bears the same relation to sound as the brain to the body – it's another program, another time, another station.~~

'Oh well, we have a platform regarding sound. Let it, like music, captivate the sense by metaphoric utterance; by moodstuff and far-ranging concepts. Let it say things in terms of other things, dissolve and modulate and set up new vibrations in the deepest chambers of imagination.'

This is where I began this book: the sound effect of a crowd. They – Sondergaard, Corwin and all the team in that imaginary room on the other side of the loudspeaker (she has slipped from the first person singular to plural) play it for me straight and then they pitch it down so it becomes the wind of people's voices blowing in a mighty chorus, that can become a hurricane and topple tyrants – a wind 'of protest, of opinion, of determination'. *I hear a crowd of people turn to surf and the restless drama of renewal, of* 'wave and wave and wave and wave, upon the planetary shore'.

I hear the bell motif.

There sounds a signal for the final phase: Concerning Amplification.

'We are living, my good and far flung friends, in the age of amplification. Practically everything today is amplified . . . the man who calls out numbers in the beano concession . . . the auctioneer, giving away the beautiful, unbreakable fountain-pen at less than cost . . . the keynoter at the political convention . . . the president at his inaugural . . . the sound-truck on Main Street, advertising the circus has come to town . . . the counter man relaying orders to the kitchen . . . all sounds, you see, can be amplified. A heartbeat can be made to sound like far off drums in Africa!

I hear this done. And then, in Corwin's working script, a cut paragraph:

~~Even a silent radio studio can be cupped to the ear like a sea-shell. Our engineers to demonstrate this point, have arranged to amplify the normal room tone of the studio. To anybody standing in the studio, no sound would be apparent; but to the blasé amplifying tube, it sounds like this.~~

~~Sound 85: amplified room tone~~

By blasé, I assume he means indifferent, the unselective hearing of the microphone, which cannot unhear background noise. His point is that that there is a human hand – and ear – within the amplifier-repeater tube chains of the global audio network; there is art in the machine that allows it to hear discriminately.

'Here is another specimen: a man bites some celery. It makes a little noise, but unless he is an exceptional biter or the celery is unusually crisp, you can't hear his chewing more than two feet away. Take an ordinary microphone like the one I'm speaking through and place it at this man's jaw and you won't hear much if anything.'

I hear a quiet chewing effect in a room.

'But put a little *contact* microphone against his cheek, and you'll get this.'

I hear an explosive sound. 'It is positively thunderous', *says Corwin's annotation on the production script.*

And so to thunder – our thunder; the effect by which De Loutherbourg's tiny Eidophusikon *conquered the sublime and by whose history the audimus can be traced from ancient times through to Scooby-Doo and the object-framework of auditory memes that constitutes the present.*

'Now, if celery can sound like thunder, what can *thunder* sound like? A blast, no doubt, to shake down twenty-seven thousand stars from heaven. Man's amplifying ear would hear the respiration of the tadpole, count dust-motes as they knocked against his pillow in the night, awake in winter to the thud of snowflakes on the roof. The very air, when tranquil, will disclose new harmonies; the clash of kissing lips makes towers totter and suspension bridges sway like birches in the wind.

'Will *Truth* be amplified one day? Will man's *humanity* to man make joyful noises, shouting down the tyrant's cannon? Will the handclasp of two honest men be louder than the clink of hoarded gold? Will song and laughter roll unmitigated down the soundways of the world? How soon, O Engineers of man's society, before the grosser sounds are banished from the hearing of the race? The venal cluck of greed, the roar of despotism, the bluster of the deadly braggart?

'Let bursting bombs fade eventually to the Choruses announcing Victory; let Independence's cracked bell ring out again for all enslaved peoples; let the groaning of the persecuted rise to shout of jubilation . . . to the Hallelujahs of a world made free. Let one decisive crash of thunder cleanse the sentient earth!'

A great clap of thunder, with full reverberation.
I press STOP.

10

Conclusion

Audimus: the theatre we hear

⏭

▶

We are back in the theatre, 2019.
   Thunder reverberates around us as we listen at the actor standing on the forestage.
   This is a state-of-the-art thunder. It sounds good. The actor speaks within it, unamplified other than by the room, which tunes voice and thunder alike with its warm, designed resonance. But the sound effect is more than this. An inner shell has built up within the auditorium walls, a patina of everything that has been heard here. Literally speaking, scenography, more or less, means the art of writing on the skena, but there is also writing on these auditorium walls. A history that shapes and tunes what is heard here. There is history too in the patina of personal memories and associations in the room: of cabbages and watermelons, Sean Connery narrating an orchestra, nonsensical shibboleths of sound, favourite sounds and musical subcultural identities.
   Now hear this, the thunder says, delivering the actor's voice to us. Now hear all of this.

*

This book has taken a diegetic form and has been epic in its coverage. I have tried to summarize as I go and to relate its stories to the themes of the book, but will conclude now by drawing together a few key points.
   Firstly, as McBurney says in the artfully (artificially) informal but dramaturgically necessary soft beginning to *The Encounter* at the Barbican in 2016, 'stories are real – whatever those two words mean'. This has been one historical avenue of this book: that the sense of the audibly real is the stories

that are told and heard about *our* sense of things (whichever *we* the auditoriums of our stories convene). Our stories, as McBurney also establishes with some comedic onstage business involving his camera phone and videotape cassette, tend to be episodic and contained within pictures – both audio and video. This is the paradigmatically intransitive, serial discontinuity of modern dramaturgy to which Meisel drew our attention; the picturing of the world in scenes. Filters, however, are applied. The options, settings and preferences of our self-dramatizing pictorial narratives are adjusted aesthetically, and so is the reality they constitute. This is as true of the way we represent sound, through the delimitations we place on our hearing and what we unhear. *Our* shared life is not entirely honest (I will not say it is not true), and we are comfortable with that. *Our* sense of truth, as we rehearse it in our various theatres, is known to take artistic license in order aesthetically to reconfigure lived experience, such that audible effect and causal action are not necessarily linked in a transitive way. Theatre is the constitution, or Organon, of the living community. It forms the basis by which, whatever community it convenes (whichever 'we') understands its occupancy of space and time. What it rehearses and stages, and what the community hears, understands and then resounds, are productions of an object framework of sonic and audio phenomena, inscribed in the patina of personal, social and institutional memory and the genome of our auditory memes that fronts the skena. These productions are bound together as a travelogue, a picture-book reality of aural and visual dispositions. In the sixteenth century, Rabelais had imagined a fantastic place where words and noises could be frozen in the air (Zegura, 2004: 87). Theatre cannot freeze sounds, but it quantizes them into pictorial and aesthetic units; it shows us audible pictures, and this is how we, in turn, hear and inhabit the world.

Secondly, it has been characteristic of the modern era that the expansion of horizons by travel, science, new media networks of communications, have been matched by an inverse process of diegetic inscaping, a contracting of the auditory sphere and its horizon of silence around the stuttering voice of verbalized consciousness. I have argued that the term 'immersive theatre' is misunderstood – that it is not the theatre that immerses the spectator, but the other way around. In our picture-book narrative, we have seen how the picturesque disposition immersed the scene in the aurality of the viewer; how the melo of melodrama did it; and how the crafted mono audio stream of radio drama that came into the home through a hole in the wall, created a mind theatre where the same immersion – and subjugation – of the pictured world in the aestheticized, auditory imagination took place. This, however, is not an immersion in the liquid musical soul or the eolian resonance of the romantically conceived subject, but an immersion in a space of representation, according to the object framework and mnemonic delimitation I describe above. The inner human subject is a space of auditory representation, constructed by and limited to a matrix of artistic products and aesthetic concepts (in the way Barthes describes non-mimetic representation as a geometrically delimited outlook). Theatre today, which occupies space and time topically, under rubrics such as 'Sound Design by', 'Soundscape by', or simply 'Sound by', rehearses this sensibility. By 'topically', I mean relating to *topoi* or synecdochally significant features, as in *topography*. Such theatre cuts a tableau out of the sonic continuum by attributing the symbolism resulting from its temporary and topical unhearing of noise (which is what sound design is), to a process of art. Sound design is arty sound, hard to define, but one knows it when one hears it because artiness is not affectation, it is a sensible mode of being.

Within the acoustemology of picture-book auditory reality, music no longer stands against the image, because music itself has been reformatted by the same diegetically inscaping process of modernity that reduced the unimaginable sensibility of the sublime to an imaginable picturesque. Music is no longer an ideological meta-organization of self, time and space. It is a sound effect. Boulez and Barthes perhaps betray an inadvertent romanticism in deploying words like 'anecdotal' or 'trite' to dramatic music that frames the aural theatre spectator (not the stage) for pictorial effect – which is what the melo does, and which the musical collage of a sound design or soundtrack usually does too. Barthes in particular refers to music resisting the tableaux (the 'strong point', as Mayhew called it, on which the pictorial diegesis turn) in Pythagorean terms. The resonant things, or acoustically audible music sounds of *musica instrumentalis* within the Boethian trinity (and in the liberal arts quadrivium that provided the top-level rubric for classical European acoustemology) were once the *topoi*, or iceberg tips, of a universal mathematical ideology. However, they only made musical sense as part of a process of unhearing everything else – the noise of life. When capitalism insulated music from noise (and Charles Lamb fled the artificially, uncheerfully silent auditorium, back into the noisy Victorian street of organ-grinders and gypsy fiddlers where music, as he understood it, made sense), only the tips were left, and not the invisible ontological mass below the surface. The totalizing condition of music (to which all Romantic art aspired according to Pater) became an old story: an epic retelling of the quadrivial theory, filtered and framed with artistic licence, and packaged in pictorial tropes. *Musica instrumentalis*, rather than being a self- and space-organizing effect of resonant and tuned things within everyday processes and frameworks of aurality, became either something one paid specially to hear in insulated conditions, or else a garden ornament imbued with poetic metaphor, that 'tinged' the atmosphere – wind chimes; the picturesque tableau encountered at Beulah Spa; the eolian harp; mood music.

The soulful *musica humana* Appia wished to flow through and saturate the organizations and processes of dramatic representation was no longer connected in a resonant unity either with *musica mundana*, which, as Lindley describes, had, even by the late Shakespearian period of early modernity, become an acknowledged poetic trope rather than a literal belief; nor with *musica instrumentalis*, whose audibility had been split between the fetishistically silent, ticketed auditorium, and the category of ambient scenery. Musical immersivity remained a well-loved story and a scenographic fixation of Romanticism, and it remains a powerfully persuasive diegetic device and marketing trope within the arts. In this sense, it continues to be a part of the constitution of the real, but as part of a diegetic story-system, not a belief-system or a scientific theory. The idea that people occupy a quasi-musical meta-space that is around them and in them, and through which they can spiritually access a space that is more universal than the visual space before their eyes, is a figurative one, a tableau of their self-dispossession, but nonetheless a part of the modern pictorial system of reality, which is a theatrical one.

A distinction was once made between music that serves the drama (melo) and drama that serves the music (opera), but all music is now theatrical effect, which does not 'debase' it, as Barthes suggested. Modern drama and stage design, since the late eighteenth century, has inhabited and pictorially realized a post-sublime world. Theatre is a dispositive of an aesthetic regime of art whose dissensual break from the regime of mimesis has been to reconfigure theatre's living community from being aural subjects of the natural world, to being spectators of it within the space of their aestheticized aurality. Music is part of the disposition of that space, but so is sound. Sound and music sound good together, because they are all parts of a collage of effects, and a collaged mode of being.

Romantic praxes such as the Picturesque, of which I argue the pictorial reconfiguration of the legitimate English playhouse in the latter part of the eighteenth century was a part; and the further reconfiguration of the sensible by audio in the 1930s, were a pictorial inscaping of old, subjugating schemes of universal aesthetics. They also determined that sublime effects of ruination and decay should be appreciable in terms of artistic pleasure rather than fear, which was a form of aesthetic emancipation. De Loutherbourg's thunder, the Castle Thunder, the thunder of *The Anatomy of Sound*'s final sound effect – these are not sounds that are diminished by the fact that they are not true to nature. On the contrary. *Our* thunders are the best. Nature has become true to them, or perhaps falls slightly short of their standards, as it did in Gainsborough's estimation. As Gilpin might have said, if nature doesn't sound real enough (according to the pictorial expectations of art), then hear it better. Theatre shows us how, but the real sound effect takes place as we leave the theatre and a storm breaks around us. If theatre has helped us hear it better, in more realistic higher-fidelity, that is how we know that theatre has been effective in changing the world (it has always been part of theatre's ritual remit to change, or at least repair, the world with sound – in an earlier era, theatre's performative resolving of the chaos of a storm with music was what kept the world turning in the Pythagorean cosmos).

Thunder, however, is no longer sacred but part of *our* soundscape. A geometrically delimited harkening as fetishistic in its way as Barthes' dioptric decoupage, the modern notion that the acoustic environment might be produced or reproduced as soundscape, continues to frame subjectivity and aestheticize noise within picturesque lines, and draws itself in, through 'immersive technologies' ever closer to the self-narrativizing internal monologue of our aural spectatorship. These immersive technologies included mono, stereo, surround sound, headphones, binaural audio, noise-cancelling headphones, and now neurally bespoke headphone systems such as Nura, that, we are told, learn and adapt to our unique hearing.

Earlier in the book, I introduced a conceit – the audimus. Audimus pointed to the fact that the word *audio* was the first-person singular form of the Latin *audire* – to hear. Later in the book, however, we discovered that the modern term 'audio' appeared in the 1920s, in the context of the revolution in communications and sound reproduction effected by the Audion amplification tube. It was after the heavily marketed Audion that other neologisms involving the stem *audio* – such as 'audiology' – began to appear, and the phrase 'audio signal' was shortened into the term 'audio'. At the beginning of the book, I argued that sound does not exist – only sounds. But audio demonstrably does exist. One can measure it with a meter and display its waveforms on a screen, whereas a sound pressure or level meter (SPL), as Corwin said of the microphone, is blasé – indifferent to the situational dramaturgy by which the auditory brain unhears the noise in the room to produce sounds. The Audion changed the world, such that aurality became indexed by a studio-produced audio object framework as well as by acoustic effects. As a result, all sounds were fabricated, and the voice of 'The Loudspeaker' became god, the voice of the creator. While theatre had countenanced the separation of the *I hear* and the *I see* with symbolism and psychological melodrama, it is the legacy of the Audion that, through mediatized forms, audio became a separate and free-roaming proposition to video, and a scenographic and an artistic space opened between the two modes of attending to a scene. It was cinema, like Mamoulian's, which separated audio – and thus the audio-framework of the acoustic word – from the cranial logic that sutured the orientation of the sonic world to the ocular front and to visual perspective.

Cinema too that took the silence that had become a material of drama – the substantive silence that symbolist unhearing had produced between the *topoi* of its synecdoche – and superimposed it over speaking faces and noisy scenes. This is in part how we can walk down the street with headphones in our ears and make sense of our situation, even experience the musical silencing of the world as pleasurable. The superimposed soundtrack inscaped and tamed the fear of silence in the way that picturesque theatre had done for the Burkeian sublime with thundersheets and an artful thumb on a tambour skin. Perhaps this is an extreme example of the dissensual process of aesthetic art, of lifting an indeterminate aesthetic truth off and away from any underlying determining causality or scheme of ideas. But while this cracking open the obviousness of the given might model a new scenography of the possible, there are risks.

I introduced the term *audimus* because the pictorial fetish or tableaux the rubrics of the audio age cut out from the space of everything else, can lead to a dangerous solipsism. The fact that audio means *I hear* in Latin may have been a coincidence, but audio's marketing – characterized by socially othering words such like 'exotic' and misleading words like 'immersive' – along with evangelical meta-discourses of aurality such as McLuhan and Carpenter's *Acoustic Space*, which resonated some of the problematic structures of this late 1950s sales patter, do fetishize a first-person singular experience.

Sound, even as an art production of the audio-object framework, is a socially constructed space, and it needs to be, for its bearings to be reliable and secure. One of the reality-narratives of the audio age – associated with the hi-fi cell, personal audio, the personalizable sound settings of the mobile theatre people carry about their technological selves and now neurally adaptive audio technologies – is that sound enables an ethically desirable selfishness. Hi-fidelity was a construct that sold realistic sound as an escape from humdrum reality (often signified in the sexist marketing campaigns of the 1950s by the figure of the scolding wife). It offered an illusion of escapism that was really an inscapism, into a fabricated and self-serving intercultural utopia where exotic meant an arrogant or wilful mishearing or approximation of cultural otherness. Or else it uses a trope of immersivity that assigns an infantilizing maternal metaphor to the aurality of the spectator (I gave examples from Pavis and of the New Age repurposing of the chant 'OM' or the Upanishad mantra *nada brahma* as a therapeutic performance of a mystical or exotic picturesque). The auditory sphere becomes a life-giving and nourishing, almost liquidly dense atmosphere that closes in on, immerses and permeates the body at its centre. Once, these narratives were located in a universal truth system that accounted for spirituality and society in an acoustemological cycle of sounding and resounding. In the world of noise-cancelling technologies of the self that began as Attali identifies, when music became monetizable art and a noiseless auditorium was guaranteed by the ticket price, this acoustic ecosystem is broken. Listening-in to the self in a noiseless world becomes a narcissistic obsession with a source-less echo that only leads to a crisis of the self, and ultimately to nemesis.

My proposition of the audimus counters this with its necessary first-person plurality. It dispels the pictorial narrative that aural subjectivity is a sphere filled with a liquidly atmospheric, pleasurably intoxicating, insulating substance called sound, which centres on the I. This pictorial conception subjugates the individual to its promotional narratives of individuality, and not only isolates the hearer from socially constructed sonic space but predisposes them against it. The industry sells audio as a liquor, and, as Brecht said, of all alcoholic excesses none is more dangerous than solitary drinking.

People hear sounds but tell each other about sound. As I described in Chapter 2 with reference to Leibnitz and Serres, people have an appetite to form unities between multiplicities of phenomena. This is because humans want to learn, and as Serres says, hearing is a model of understanding that takes the disposition – the multiple, as such – and not the composition, as its singular object (Serres, 1995: 7). The individual hears pluralities of sound. In the deliberations of our *epistēmē* and *technē*, *we* produce unities. *We* replay or resound these ideas and, by putting them out there, re-pluralize them. The only viable definition of sound is the dialectical, cultural process of re-defining sound.

I will offer my definition to that process. Sound is audibility. The sound of London is the audibility of London; the sound of a baby crying in the wings is the audibility of a baby crying, a book about sound is a book about audibility. Audibility is not a given, and nor can it ever be fixed as a set of expectations or international standards. It is a negotiation. It is our differences as hearers that define sonic space. I took time in Part One to describe the psychoacoustic cognitive mapping of auditory scene analysis, to demonstrate how the individual's process of hearing is reliant on auditory differentials, a culturally agreed object-oriented framework of knowing, and a situational dramaturgy that provides criteria for audibility according to topical imperatives of scenic utility and significance. Theatre, as a congregation of hearers, as an audience, works in the same way. It should be a place that celebrates the ways in which *we* do not all hear the same. Sonic aesthetics and the way of hearing that theatre models are characteristically epic or diegetic, and as such are didactic and constitute a community learning process. Theatre stages sounds as a form of sonology within a broader acoustemology. This is the civic function of theatre, as Bruce R. Smith identified in addressing the early modern era of Shakespeare's public wooden Os.

Drama and theatre are social and cultural resonators within an iterative circle of hearing and sounding. They are at once ears and amplifier-repeaters, like De Forest's Audion or Serres' trope of the black box. There is neither escape nor inscape into a solitary world of sound. For the space of audibility to be a living space, it has to be a social one, an audimus, a *we hear*. Theatre's next civic duty is to attend to who this *we* includes. And who it excludes.

■ STOP

References

Appia, A. (1962), *Music and the Art of Theatre*, Miami: University of Miami Press.
ASD (2018), *ASD* online, http://www.associationofsounddesigners.com/whatis [3 January 2019]
Atkins, T. R. (1973), 'Dr. Jekyll and Mr. Hyde: An Interview with Rouben Mamoulian', *Film Journal*, II(2), January–March: 36–43.
Attali, J. (1985), *Noise: The Political Economy of Music*, Minneapolis: University of Minnesota Press.
Auden, W. H. (1968), *Collected Longer Poems*, paperback edition, London: Faber and Faber.
Augoyard, J., and Torgue, H. (2005), *Sonic Experience: A Guide to Everyday Sounds*, Montreal: McGill-Queen's University Press.
Barenboim, D. (2008), *Everything is Connected*, London: Weidenfeld & Nicolson.
Barthes, R. (1977), *Image Music Text*, London: Fontana.
Baudouin, C. (1924), *Contemporary Studies*, London: Allen & Unwin.
Baugh, C. (1990), *Garrick and Loutherbourg*, Cambridge: Chadwyck-Healey.
Baugh, C. (2008), 'Stage Design from Loughterbourg to Poel', in J. Donohue (ed.), *The Cambridge History of British Theatre*, vol. 2, 309–30, Cambridge: Cambridge University Press.
BBC (1931), *The B.B.C. Yearbook 1931*, London: The British Broadcasting Corporation.
Benjamin, W. (1973), *Understanding Brecht*, London: NLB.
Berendt, J.-E. (1988), *The Third Ear*, Longmede: Element.
Berendt, E. J. (1991), *The World Is Sound: Nada Brahma (Music and the Landscape of Consiousness)*, Rochester: Destiny.
Bijsterveld, K. (ed.) (2014), *Soundscapes of the Urban Past: Staged Sound as Mediated Cultural Heritage*, vol. 5, Bielefeld: Transcript-Verlag.
Boethius (1989), *Fundamentals of Music*, New Haven: Yale University Press.
Boulez, P. (1971), *Boulez on Music Today*, Cambridge, MA: Harvard University Press.
Bower, C. (2001), 'Boethius', in *Grove Music*, online edition, Oxford: Oxford University Press. Available: https://doi.org/10.1093/gmo/9781561592630.article.03386 [27 June 2019].
Brecht, B. (1978), *Brecht on Theatre*, London: Bloomsbury.
Brecht, B. (1980), 'Radio as a Means of Communication', *Screen*, III(4), Winter: 24–8.
Bregman, A. (1999), *Auditory Scene Analysis*, 2nd edn, Cambridge, MA: MIT Press.
Briggs, A. (1961), *The Birth of Broadcasting*, London: Oxford University Press.

Brown, R. (2005), 'The Theatre Soundscape and the End of Noise', *Performance Research: On Techne*, 10(4): 105–19.

Brown, R. (2009), *Sound: A Reader in Theatre Practice*, Basingstoke: Palgrave Macmillan.

Brown, R. (2010), 'Sound Design, the Scenography of Engagement and Distraction', in J. Collins and A. Nisbett (eds), *Theatre and Performance Design: A Reader in Scenography*, Abingdon, Oxfordshire: Routledge.

Bruster, D., and Weimann, R. (2004), *Prologues to Shakespeare's Theatre: Performance and Liminality in Early Modern Drama*, Abingdon, Oxfordshire: Routledge.

Burke, E. (1998), *A Philosophical Enquiry into the Origin of Our Ideas of the Sublime and the Beautiful*, Oxford: Oxford University Press.

Burris-Meyer, H., and Mallory, V. (1959), *Sound in Theatre*, Mineola, NY: Radio Magazines.

Byron, G. G. (1901), *The Works of Lord Byron*, Vol. V, E. H. Coleridge (ed.), Kindle edition, London: John Murray.

Cage, J. (1978), *Silence: Lectures and Writings*, London: Marion Boyars.

Carpenter, E., and McLuhan, M. (1960), 'Acoustic Space', in E. Carpenter and M. McLuhan (eds), *Explorations in Communication: An Anthology*, Boston: Beacon Press.

Cazeaux, C. (2005), 'Phenomenology and Radio Drama', *British Journal of Aesthetics*, 45(2): 157–74.

Chion, M. (1994), *Audio-Vision*, New York and Chichester: Columbia University Press.

Cibber, C. (1889), *An Apology for the Life of Mr Colly Cibber*, London: J. C. Nimmo. Available: https://archive.org/details/apologyforlifeof01cibb [4 January 2018].

Coleridge, S. T. (1812), *The Friend: A Series of Essays*, London: Gale and Curtis. Available: https://archive.org/details/friendseriesofes05cole [24 March 2019].

Coleridge, S. T. (1997), *The Complete Poems*, W. Keach (ed.), London: Penguin.

Combe, W., and Rowlandson, T. (1812), *The Tour of Dr Syntax in Search of the Picturesque*, London: Ackermann.

Complicite/McBurney, S. (2016), *The Encounter*, London: Nick Hern Books.

Connor, S. (2009), *The Hard and the Soft*, 26 November. Available: http://www.stevenconnor.com/hardsoft/ [23 June 2018].

Copley, S., and Garside, P. (eds) (1994), *The Politics of the Picturesque*, Cambridge: Cambridge University Press.

Corwin, N. (1941), *The Anatomy of Sound*, radio play, Columbia Broadcasting Service, 7 September 1941.

Corwin, N. (1944), *More by Corwin: 16 Radio Dramas by Norman Corwin*, New York: H. Holt.

Corwin, N., Gabel, M., Herrmann, B., and Gluskin, L. (1945), *On A Note of Triumph*, vinyl album, US: Mark56 Records 704.

Cowper, W. (1785), *The Task*, online edition, London: J. Johnson. Available: http://www.eighteenthcenturypoetry.org/works/o3795-w0060.shtml [12 January 2018].

Curtin, A. (2014), *Avant-Garde Theatre Sound: Staging Sonic Modernity*, Basingstoke: Palgrave Macmillan.

Curtin, A., and Roesner, D. (eds) (2016), 'Sounds Good', *Theatre and Performance Design*, special edition, 3(4), Autmn/Winter.
De Quincy, T. (2005), *Confessions of an English Opium Eater*, Kindle edition, Urbana, Illinois: Project Gutenburg. Available: http://www.gutenberg.org/ebooks/2040 [22 January 2019].
Dekker, T. (2005), *Dekker, Thomas, Satiromastix*. Available: http://www.gutenberg.org/files/49636/49636-h/49636-h.htm [4 January 2018].
DeNora, T. (2000), *Music in Everyday Life*, Cambridge: Cambridge University Press.
Dickens, C. (2011), *The Complete Works of Charles Dickens*, Golgotha Press.
Dickens, C., and Collins, W. (1867), *No Thoroughfare: A Drama in Five Acts* (first correct edition), 9 April. Available: http://goldstraw.org.uk/no_thoroughfare.pdf [6 October 2018].
Douglas, S. (2004), *Listening: Radio and the American Imagination*, Minneapolis: University of Minnesota Press.
Du Noyer, P. (2002), *An Obituaray: Spike Milligan 1918–2002*. Available: http://www.pauldunoyer.com/pages/journalism/journalism_item.asp?journalismID=291 [8 February 2018].
During, S. (2007), 'Beckford in Hell: An Episode in the History of Secular Enchantment', *Huntington Library Quarterly*, 70(2), June: 269–88.
Edison, T. (1888), 'The Perfected Phonograph', *The North American Review*, 146(379), June: 641–50.
Erlmann, V. (2010), *Reason and Resonance*, New York: Zone Books.
Fantel, H. H. (1959), 'Take two! They're small!: jumbo bookshelf speaker systems – good sound for compact rooms', *HiFi Review*, April: 49–52.
Farley, P. (1998), *The Boy from the Chemist Is Here to See You*, Kindle edition, Basingstoke: Pan Macmillan.
Farnell, A. (2010), *Designing Sound*, Cambridge and London: MIT Press.
Fogerty, E. (1936), *Rhythm*, London: Allen & Unwin.
Frankin, A. (1997), 'Precious Lord (Take My Hand), Pt. Two', recorded 1956, on *Aretha Gospel*, Chess – MCD 91521.
Gilpin, W. (1794), *Three Essays: On Picturesque Beauty; On Picturesque Travel; and On Sketching*, 2nd edn, London: R. Blamire. Available: www.books.google.com [25 November 2017].
Gilpin, W. (2014), *Observations Relative Chiefly to Picturesque Beauty Made in the Year 1776, On Several Parts of Great Britain*, vol. 2, Cambridge: Cambridge University Press.
Goethe, J. W. (1998), *Faust, Part Two*, trans. M. Greenberg, New Haven: Yale University Press.
Goethe, J. W. (2003), *Faust, Part One: Dedication, Prelude, Prologue*, trans. A. S. Kline. Available: http://www.poetryintranslation.com/PITBR/German/FaustIProl.htm [1 January 2018].
Gouraud, C. (1888), *Toasts at Little Menlo*, audio recording. Available: https://youtu.be/R1f8pnmy4t0 [8 January 2018].
Harwood, R. (1984), *All the World's a Stage*, London: Secker & Warburg.
Helmholtz, H. (1885), *On the Sensations of Tone as a Physiological Basis for the Theory of Music*, 2nd edn, London: Longmans, Green & Co.
Holcroft, T. (1802), *A Tale of Mystery, a Melo-Drame*, 2nd edn, London: Richard Phillips. Available: https://archive.org/stream/taleofmysterymel00holciala [6 December 2017].

Holmes, D. (1977), *The Lawns: History of the Former Beulah Spa*. Available: https://www.norwoodsociety.co.uk/articles/115-the-lawns-history-of-the-former-beulah-spa.html [8 January 2018].

Home-Cook, G. (2015), *Theatre and Aural Attention*, Basingstoke: Palgrave Macmillan.

Ihde, D. (1970), 'Parmenidean Meditations', *Journal of the British Society of Phenomenology*, 1(3), October: 16–23.

Ihde, D. (2007), *Listening and Voice: Phenomenologies of Sound*, 2nd edn, Albany: University of New York Press.

Jay, M. (1994), *Downcast Eyes*, Berkeley: University of California Press.

Johnson, S. (1909), 'Prologue Spoken by Mr. Garrick at the Opening of the Theatre-Royal, 1747', in W. S. Braithwaite (ed.), *The Book of Georgian Verse*, New York: Brentano. Available: http://www.bartleby.com/333/76.html [10 January 2018].

Kahn, D. (1999), *Noise Water Meat: A History of Voice, Sound, and Aurality in the Arts*, Cambridge, MA: MIT Press.

Kahn, D., and Whitehead, G. (eds) (1992), *The Wireless Imagination: Sound, Radio, and the Avant-Garde*, Cambridge, MA: MIT Press.

Kahn, I. (2005), *Volume II: The Mysticism of Music, Sound and Word*, October. Available: https://wahiduddin.net/mv2/II/II_1.htm [20 February 2018].

Kaye, D., and LeBrecht, J. (1992), *Sound and Music for Theatre*, New York: Back Stage Books.

Keightley, K. (1996), ''Turn it down!' she shrieked: gender, domestic space, and high fidelity, 1948–49', *Popular Music*, 15(2), May: 149–77.

Kendrick, L. (2017), *Theatre Aurality*, Basingstoke: Palgrave Macmillan.

Kendrick, L., and Roesner, D. (eds) (2011), *Theatre Noise*, Newcastle: Cambridge Scholars.

Kilgarrif, M. (2015), *Henry Irving and the Phonograph: Bennett Maxwell*. Available: https://www.theirvingsociety.org.uk/the-voice-of-henry-irving/ [8 January 2018].

Koller, A. M. (1984), *The Theatre Duke: Georg II of Saxe-Meiningen and the German Stage*, Stanford: Stanford University Press.

Kornhaber, D. (2009), 'Regarding the *Eidophusikon*: Spectacle, Scenography, and Culture in Eighteenth Century England', *Theatre Arts Journal*, I(1), Autumn. Available: https://www.taj.tau.ac.il/images/stories/pdf/volume-1-issue-1/kornhaber.pdf [1 December 2017].

Lamb, C. (1923), 'A Chapter on Ears', in *The Essays of Elia*, London: Dent.

Le Bruit (1947), 'Notes on the Early Progress of the Picturesque of Sound', *American Notes and Queries*, VII(8), November: 115–19.

Lehmann, H.-T. (2006), *Postdramatic Theatre*, London: Routledge.

Lerner, N. (2010), *Music in the Horror Film: Listening to Fear*, Kindle edition, Abingdon, Oxfordshire: Routledge.

Levin, D. M. (ed.) (1993), *Modernity and the Hegemony of Vision*, Berkeley and Los Angeles: University of California Press.

Lewis, L. (1890), *The Bells*, New York: J. F. Wagner. Available: https://archive.org/details/bellsdramainthre00lewi [20 January 2018].

Lewis, R. (1994), *The Life and Death of Peter Sellers*, London: Random House.

Lindley, D. (2006), *Shakespeare and Music*, London: Arden Shakespeare.

Lingis, A. (1994), *The Community of Those Who Have Nothing in Common*, Bloomington: Indiana University Press.

Litman, J. (2010), 'The Invention of Common Law Play Right', *Berkeley Technology Law Journal*, 25(3), Summer: 1381–426.
Logue, C. (2001), *War Music*, London: Faber and Faber.
Luhrssen, D. (2013), *Mamoulian*, Lexington: University of Kentucky Press.
Lyon, J. K. (1983), 'The FBI as Literary Historian: The File of Bertolt Brecht', *The Brecht Yearbook*, 11: 210–32. Available: http://digital.library.wisc.edu.
MacDonald, I. (2008), *Revolution in the Head*, 2nd edn, London: Random House.
Macpherson, I. (2011), 'The Electric Ear, Part Two', *The New Soundtrack*, 1(2): 113–32.
Maeterlinck, M. (1897), *The Treasure of the Humble*, London: George Allen.
Mayer, D. (1976), 'Nineteenth-Century Theatre Music', *Theatre Notebook*, 30(3): 115–22.
Mayer, D. (1980), 'The Music of Melodrama', in *Performance and Politics in Popular Drama*, Cambridge: Cambridge University Press.
Mayer, D., Jones-Evans, E., and Lewis, L. (1980), *Henry Irving and The Bells*, Manchester: Manchester University Press.
Mayhew, E. (1840), *Stage Effect*, online edition, London: C. Mitchell. Available: https://babel.hathitrust.org/cgi/pt?id=mdp.39015091113038;view=1up;seq=45 [24 March 2019].
McCann, G. (2006), *Spike & Co.*, London: Hodder & Stoughton.
McGillivray, G. (2008), 'The Picturesque World Stage', *Performance Research: A Journal of the Performing Arts*, 13(4): 127–39.
McNeley, J. K. (2003), 'Holy Wind before Emergence', in J. K. McNeley (ed.), *Writing on Air*, Newark: Terra Nova/MIT.
Meisel, M. (1983), *Realizations*, Princeton: Princeton University Press.
Milne, T. (1969), *Roubden Mamoulian*, London: Thames and Hudson, with the British Film Insitute.
Mitchell, H. (2006), 'Help! I'm Surrounded', *Scope: An Online Journal of Film and Television Studies*, 5(5). Available: https://hydra.hull.ac.uk/resources/hull:12446 [6 February 2018].
Murray Schafer, R. (1994), *The Soundscape: Our Sonic Environment and the Tuning of the World*, Vermont: Destiny Books.
Nancy, J.-L. (2007), *Listening*, New York: Fordham University Press.
Napier, F. (1936), *Noises Off*, 2nd edn, London: Frederick Muller.
Novack, D., and Sakakeeny, M. (eds) (2015), *Keywords in Sound*, Durham and London: Duke University Press.
O'Callaghan, C. (2011), 'Lessons from beyond Vision (Sounds and Audition)', *Philosophical Studies*, 153(1), March: 143–60.
Ovadija, M. (2013), *Dramaturgy of Sound in the Avant-Garde and Postdramatic Theatre*, Montreal: McGill-Queen's University Press.
Partridge, A., and Bernhardt, T. (2016), *Complicated Game: Inside the Songs of XTC*, Kindle edition, London: Jawbone.
Payne Knight, R. (1805), *An Analytical Inquiry into the Principles of Taste*, 2nd edn, London: T. Payne and J. White. Available: https://play.google.com/books.
Picker, J. (2003), *Victorian Soundscapes*, Oxford: Oxford University Press.
Plumptre, J. (1798), *The Lakers*, London: W. Clarke. Available: https://archive.org/details/cu31924104104223 [11 January 2018].
Popular Science Monthly (1926), New York: Modern Publishing, 105(1), January.

Price, U. (1810), *Essays on the picturesque, as compared with the sublime and the beautiful; and, on the use of studying pictures, for the purpose of improving real landscape*, London: Mawman. Available: https://archive.org/details/essaysonpictures01priciala [11 January 2018].

Punter, D. (1994), 'The Picturesque and the Sublime: Two Worldscapes', in S. Copley and P. Garside (eds), *The Politics of the Picturesque*, Cambridge: Cambridge University Press.

Pyne, W. (1823a), *Wine and Walnuts; or, after Dinner Chit-Chat. By Ephraim Hardcastle, Citizen and Dry Salter, Vol I*, London: Longman, Hurst, Rees, Orme, and Brown. Available: https://archive.org/details/wineandwalnutsor01pyneuoft [12 January 2018].

Pyne, W. (1823b), *Wine and Walnuts; or, after Dinner Chit-Chat. By Ephraim Hardcastle, Citizen and Dry Salter, Vol II*, London: Longman, Hurst, Rees, Orme, and Brown. Available: https://archive.org/details/wineandwalnutso01pynegoog [17 January 2018].

Radio Times (1935), 'The Cenotaph Service', 10 November: 7.

Rancière, J. (2009), *The Emancipated Spectator*, London: Verso.

Rancière, J. (2004), *The Politics of Aesthetics*, trans. G. Rockhill, London: Continuum.

Rebellato, D. (1999), *1956 and All That*, London and New York: Routledge.

Roesner, D. (2017), 'Sound (Design)', in A. Aronson (ed.), *The Routledge Companion to Scenography*, Abingdon, Oxfordshire: Routledge.

Ross, A. (2009), *The Rest Is Noise*, London: Harper Perennial.

Ross, A. (2010), 'Nowehere Bound', *New Yorker*, 4 January. Available: https://www.newyorker.com/magazine/2010/01/04/nowhere-bound [24 March 2019].

Ruskin, J. (1865), *The Seven Lamps of Architecture*, New York: Wiley. Available: https://archive.org/details/sevenlampsofarc00rusk [11 January 2018].

Russolo, L. (2009), 'The Art of Noises: Futurist Manifesto', in C. W. D. Cox (ed.), *Audio Culture: Readings in Modern Music*, New York: Continuum.

Schnupp, J., Nelken, I., and King, A. (2011), *Auditory Neuroscience: Making Sense of Sound*, Cambridge, MA: MIT Press.

Scott, C. (1890), 'The Judge (review)', *Illustrated London News*, 2 August: 131.

Scott, C. (1897), *From The Bells to King Arthur*, London: John McQueen.

Serres, M. (1995), *Genesis*, Ann Arbor: University of Michigan Press.

Serres, M. (2016), *The Five Senses: A Philosophy of Mingled Bodies*, London: Bloomsbury.

Shelley, M. W. (1831), *Frankenstein, or the Modern Prometheus*, London: H. Colburn and R. Bentley. Available: https://archive.org/details/ghostseer01schiuoft [12 January 2018].

Shepherd, S., and Wallis, M. (2004), *Drama, Theatre, Performance: The New Critical Idiom*, Abingdon, Oxfordshire: Routledge.

Sieveking, L. (1934), *The Stuff of Radio*, London: Cassell.

Skinner, J. (1931), 'Seeing What You Hear', *The Brooklyn Daily Eagle*, 23 January: 24. Available: https://bklyn.newspapers.com/image/59904145/?terms=seeing%2Bwhat%2Byou%2Bhear [9 March 2018].

Smith, B. R. (1999), *The Acoustic World of Early Modern England: Attending to the O-Factor*, London: University of Chicago Press.

Smith, J., and Verma, N. (eds) (2016), *Anatomy of Sound: Norman Corwin and Media Authorship*, Oakland: University of California Press.

Southern, R. (1962), *The Seven Ages of Theatre*, London: Faber & Faber.
Stafford Clark, M. (2002), 'The Man Who Saved the Stage', *Guardian*, 5 October. Available: https://www.theguardian.com/stage/2002/oct/05/theatre.artsfeatures [10 January 2018].
States, B. O. (1985), *Great Reckonings in Little Rooms: On the Phenomenology of Theatre*, Berkeley: University of California Press.
Stark, S. D. (2006), *Meet the Beatles*, New York: Harper Collins.
Sterne, J. (2003), *The Audible Past*, Durham and London: Duke.
Sterne, J. (2012), 'Sonic Imaginations', in J. Sterne (ed.), *The Sound Studies Reader*, Abingdon, Oxfordshire, and New York: Routledge.
Sterne, J. (ed.) (2012), *The Sound Studies Reader*, Abingdon, Oxfordshire: Routledge.
Sterne, J. (2013), 'Soundscape, Lansdscape, Escape', in K. Bijsterveld (ed.), *Soundscapes of the Urban Past*, Bielefeld: Transcript Verlag.
Stoever, J. L. (2016), *The Sonic Colour Line*, New York: New York University Press.
Stoker, B. (1897), *Dracula*, New York: Grosset & Dunlap. Available: https://archive.org/details/draculabr00stokuoft [13 January 2018].
Sully, J. (1881), 'George Eliot's Art', *Mind*, 6(23), July: 378–94.
Swainson, D. (1931), 'The Voice of the Machine', *Music and Letters*, 12(4), October: 393–7. Available: https://www.jstor.org/stable/726486 [7 September 2018].
Tan, M. C. C. (2012), *Acoustic Interculturalism: Listening to Performance*, Basingstoke: Palgrave Macmillan.
Tennyson, A. (2004), *The Works of Alfred Lord Tennyson*, Kindle edition, C. Ricks (ed.), Spanish Fort: Packard Technologies.
Thackeray, F. (2015), 'Shakespeare, Plants, and Chemical Analysis of Early 17th-Century Clay "Tobacco" Pipes from Europe', *South African Journal of Science*, 111(7/8): 5–6.
Toop, D. (1999), *Exotica: Fabricated Soundscape in the Real World*, London: Serpent's Tail.
Townshend, P. (2012), *Who I Am*, London: Harper Collins.
Verma, N. (2012), *Theatre of the Mind*, Chicago: University of Chicago Press.
Vincent, H. (1904), 'Stage Sounds', *The Strand Magazine*, vol. xxviii, October: 417–22.
Voigt, P. G. A. H. (1932), 'Lecture Demonstration on Sound Reproduction', *Proceedings of the British Kinematograph Society*, 1(7).
Welton, M. (2012), *Feeling Theatre*, Basingstoke: Palgrave Macmillan.
Whitehead, G. (1996), 'Radio Play Is No Place: A Conversation between Jérôme Noetinger and Gregory Whitehead', *TDR*, 40(3): *Experimental Sound and Radio*, Autumn: 96–101.
Whitley, W. T. (1915), *Thomas Gainsborough*, London: John Murray.
Woodruff, J. (2013), 'A Voice in the Dark: Subversive Sounds of the Living Newspapers and the Flint Sit-Down Strike of 1936–37', *Interference Journal*, Noise. Available: http://www.interferencejournal.org/a-voice-in-the-dark/ [11 March 2018].
Zegura, E. (ed.) (2004), *Rabelais Encyclopaedia*, London: Greenwood Press.

Index

3D audio 69, 70
3D movies 78

academia xiv, xvi, xvii–xviii
acousma 157
acousmaître 157
acousmatic sounds 44
acousmêtres 135, 157, 158, 181, 182
acoustemology xx, 28–30, 39, 133, 193–4
Acoustic Interculturalism (Tan) 133
acoustic space 32–4
advertising 123
aesthetic 48. *See also* Picturesque
aesthetic dissensus 18, 19, 61–2, 121, 133
aesthetic regime 18–20, 60–2, 94
aesthetic state 60, 98
Age of Anxiety, The (Auden) 166
Ahbez, Eden 132, 133
Amazon Alexa 79, 80
America 123–4, 170–1, 173
amphitheatres 51–2
amplification 145–6, 152–5, 189
Anatomy of Sound, The (Corwin) 183–90
anechoic chambers 37, 68
animal sounds 129
Appia, Adolphe 18, 19, 41–2, 60, 61
    paradox of Appian scenography for sound design 43–6
    scenographic metaphor 43
Applause (Mamoulian) 160, 161, 163, 164
art 18
Art of Noises (Russolo) 124
art pop 123–5

Artist, The (Hazanavicius) 154, 164, 165–6
Asteroid (Pearl and Dean Advertising theme) 4
Astley's Circus 85
asyndeton 37, 54, 60, 154, 162
Atkins, T.R. 151
atmosphere 37–8
Attali, Jacques 30, 31, 39, 46, 55
audibility 20–1, 197
audience xiv, 47, 49, 51, 58, 167
    aesthetic dissensus 62
    The Bells (Lewis) 147–8
    The Encounter (Complicité) 68, 69
    interactive audio drama 171–3
    No Thoroughfare (Dickens and Collins) 140
    prologue 53
    scenic reconfiguration 96, 97
audimus xx, 5, 27, 30, 53, 123, 195–7
audio drama 165–6
    The Anatomy of Sound (Corwin) 183–90
    interactive form 171–3
    kaleidosonic form 170–1
    mono loudspeakers 179–80
    On a Note of Triumph (Corwin) 173–7
    symphonic form 166–9
    theatre of the mind 179
audio memes 5–6
audio technologies xv
Audio Transformer 145–6
Audion 145, 195
audio-visual litany 33–4, 39–40, 41
auditorium 20–2, 47–62
    fictional ontology 60–2
    immersive theatre 74
    picturesque 75

as space in process 47–60
    listening versus hearing 56–9
    prologue 53–4
    rhetorics of the auditorium 48–52
    silent listening 54–6
auditory/audibility xix
auditory dispositive 73
auditory field 25
auditory imagination 177–9
auditory scene 34–6
auditory space 34–8
  as inscape 67–72
Augoyard, J. and Torgue, H. 37
aural/aurality xix, 15–16, 34
aural representation 20–2
aurality of the contrived gaze 104–6
baby-boomer children 3–5, 13–15

Backus, Georgia 170, 171
Baird, Logie 86
Barenboim, Daniel 50
Barthes, Roland 20, 45, 46, 193, 194
Baudouin, Charles 150, 162
Baugh, C. 103, 106, 111–12
Baxter, Les 130, 131, 132
BBC 161, 166–9
BBC Radiophonic Workshop 122
BBC Year Book 1931 36, 76, 168–9, 170
Beatles, The 13
  A Day in the Life 121
  'Revolution 9' 123
  Sgt Pepper's Lonely Hearts Club Band 10, 121, 132–3
  Yellow Submarine 121
beauty 102–3, 107
Becvar, William 160
Bells, The (Lewis) 146–9
Berendt, E.J. 41
Bermingham, Ann 110
Berry, Cicely xviii
Beulah Spa 85–6
Big Bang 27, 65–6
Blackburn, Tony 119, 121
Blue Peter 3
Blumlein, Alan 76–7

Boethius, Anicius 39
  De Institutione Musica 27–8, 30–1
  as acoustemology 28–30
Boulez, Pierre 43, 59, 193
Brecht, Bertolt 57, 58, 89–90, 172–3, 180–1
Bregman, Albert 34
Briggs, Asa 153
Broadley, A.M. 87
Brooklyn Daily Eagle 171
Burke, E. 102
Burris-Meyer, Harold 181, 182
Burton, Decimus 85
Busby, Thomas 138
Byron, George Gordon 107–8

Calling All Cars 11
Carpenter, E. 32, 39, 67, 133
Castle Thunder 5, 6
Cathode, Ray 14. *See also* Martin, George
Cazeaux, Clive 179
Central School of Speech and Drama xvii
Cherry Orchard, The (Chekhov) 149
children 3–5, 6–9, 13–15, 121–2
Chion, Michel 157
Chronegk, Ludwig 136
Cibber, Colly 47
cinema 3–4, 73, 77, 78, 195
City of Glass (Kenton) 130
City Slickers 11–12
City Streets (Mamoulian) 163
cocktail party effect 37–8
Coelina (Pixérécourt) 138–9
Coleridge, S.T. 26, 42, 102, 128, 129
colonialism 127, 129, 133
Columbia Experimental Dramatic Laboratory 170, 171–2
Combe, William 108
comedic sound effect 12–15
common sound 185
communication 32
composition xix, 24, 43–4, 103–4
concept album 10, 130, 133
conceptualization 24
Confessions of an English Opium-Eater (De Quincy) 125–6
Connor, Stephen 34

Corwin, Norman xxii, 173, 180–1, 182–3
  The Anatomy of Sound 183–90
  On a Note of Triumph 173–7
coup de théâtre 98, 147
Cowper, W. 91, 93–4
Crystal Palace 86
Curtin, Adrian 15

Daniel Deronda (Eliot) 149
Day in the Life, A (Beatles) 121
De Forest, Lee 145
De Institutione Musica (Boethius) 27–8, 30–1
  as acoustemology 28–30
De Loutherbourg, P.J. 109
  Eidophusikon 110, 112–15, 119–20, 121
De Quincy, T. 125–6
Dekker, Thomas 53
Designing Sound (Farnell) 6
Dickens, Charles 101, 139–41
Die Ahnfrau (Grillpanzer) 136
Die Musik und die Inscenierung (Appia) 43
diegesis 138
diegetic forms xix, 73
digital revolution xv, xvi
disembodiment 157
Disney, Walt 77
dispositions xix, 22, 43
  auditory space 34–8
  god sound 23–34
  scenography of sound 38–46
dispositive xix, 48, 73, 75, 172, 194
dissensus 18, 19, 61–2, 121, 133
Doctor Faustus (Marlowe) 53
Dolby, Ray 78
Dracula (Stoker) 134–6
drama 30–2, 55, 94, 197. *See also* audio drama
  New Drama 144
  university study of xvi–xviii
Dramatic Literary Property Act 1833 56
dramaturgy xix, 34–8, 98–9
drugs 125–6, 128
Drury Lane 94, 95, 96–7, 111
du Noyer, Paul 13

Eden's Island (Ahbez) 133
Edison, Thomas A. 83–5
Edison Company 86
Edison Electric Light Company 88
Edison-Bell Company 86
Effect 98–9, 104, 169
effects 146–8. *See also* cocktail party effect; sound effect
Eidophusikon (De Loutherbourg) 110, 112–15, 119–20, 121
Electric House 85, 86–7
electricity 88
electro-acousmatic being 155–7
Eliot, George 122
Elizabethan acoustemology 29
Elizabethan theatre 53–4
Encounter, The (Complicité) 21, 37, 67–74, 191–2
Enlightenment 33
'Eolian Harp, The' (Coleridge) 26
Epidaurus 51–2
Erlmann, Veit 42, 54
escapism 129
Essays of Elia 55
exclusion xx, 31. *See also* exoticism
Exeter Exchange 110, 111
Exotica 110, 111, 129, 129–33
exoticism 32, 126–7, 129

Fagandini, Maddalena 14
Fantasia (Disney) 77
Fanque, Pablo 85
Fantel, H.H. 78
Farley, Paul 161
Farnell, Andy 6, 65, 72, 74, 81
Faust (Goethe) 54, 88, 143
Feld, Stephen xx, 28–9
Film Journal 151
Fleming, John Ambrose 145
'Flowers in the Rain' (The Move) 119
Fogerty, Elsie xviii, xxii, 86
Frankenstein (Shelley) 5, 107
Freud, Sigmund 150

Gable, Martin 175
Gainsborough, Thomas 119–20, 121
Garrick, David 94
gaze 45, 104–6

gender 75–6, 78
Generation Game, The 17
Gielgud, Val 167–8
Gilpin, William 101, 103–4, 105, 106
god sound 23–5, 38
    acoustemology 28–30
    acoustic space 32–4
    music 27–8
        and drama 30–2
    totality 26–7
Goons, The 12–13, 122
gothic 5, 32, 100, 113–14, 125, 134
    Dracula (Stoker) 134–6
gothic melodrama 137–8, 139
Gouraud, Charles
    Electric House 85, 86–7
    sound recording 83, 87–8
    Terry's Theatre 88–9
gramophones 89–90
Grossman, Rudolph 73
Guthrie, Tyrone 166–7, 168, 171

hallucination 146–8
Harari, Yuval Noah 68
harmony 27–8, 29
Hartley, David 42
Harwood, R. 148–9
headphones 67, 68, 69, 72–4, 75
hearing 20, 25, 33–4, 34–6, 38, 155
    unhearing 36–7, 154. *See also*
        psychoacoustics
    versus listening 56–9
heartbeat 151–2
Henry V (Shakespeare) 89
Hermann, Bernard 175
hi-fi 75–6
    Spike Jones Demonstrates Your Hi-Fi 124–5
    stereo 76–9
hi-fi exotica 129–33
Hi-Fi Review 78
higher education xiv, xvi, xvii–xviii
Higher Education Act 1992 xvii
hip-hop 9–10
hippy culture 132, 133
Holcroft, T. 137, 138
Home-Cook, G. 41
House of Wax (Price) 78
Hughes, David 153

Ihde, Don 24, 25, 178
I'm the Sound Effects Man (Davis) 11
immersive cinema 78
immersive theatre 72–4, 192–3
inclusion xx, 31
inscape 67–72, 192
interactive audio drama 171–3
interval music 14

Jekyll and Hyde (Stevenson) 150–2
Johnson, S. 94, 95–6
Jones, Spike 11–12
    Spike Jones Demonstrates Your Hi-Fi 124–5
Judge, The (Law) 88–9
Justice (Galsworthy) 160

Kahn, Inayat 40
kaleidosonic audio drama 170–1
Kaluli people 29
Keightley, Keir 75–6, 79
Kendrick, L. 15
King Lear (Shakespeare) 106
knowing, way of xx, 6, 10, 13, 28–9, 30, 55, 56, 156
Koller, A.M. 136
Kornhaber, David 114

La Main Passe (Feydeau) 89
Laker, The (Plumptre) 104–5
Lamb, Charles 55–6, 58, 125
landscape composition 103–4
Laughton, Charles 181
Lefebvre, Henri 47
Lehman, Rudolf 150
Lehmann, Hans-Thies xiv, 99
Lennon, John 13, 123
light 27, 42
Lindley, David 29–30
liquid metaphor of sound 40–3
listening 54–6
    versus hearing 56–9
literary theatre xv
Little Menlo 85, 86–7
Living Newspaper, The 181–2
logos 26, 156
Logue, Christopher xxi–xxii
London Illustrated News 89

London Magazine 55
'Lotos-Eaters, The' (Tennyson) 128–9
loudspeakers
    'Loudspeaker' as voice 180–2
    mono loudspeakers 179–80

Macpherson, I. 156
Maeterlinck, Maurice 160–1
Mamoulian, Rouben 158–9, 162–3, 168
    Mamoulian's sound stew 150–2, 150n
Mandelstam, Osip 144
Manhattan Tower (Jenkins) 130
Martin, George 13, 14, 123
Mayer, David 139, 147–8
Mayhew, Edward 98
McBurney, Simon 37, 67, 68, 191–2
McDonald, Ian 123
McGillivray, G. 103
McLuhan, M. 32, 34, 39, 67, 133
Meddle (Pink Floyd) 10
Meisel, Martin 97, 99, 107, 139
melodrama 137–9, 140
melodramatic farce 159
Merchant of Venice, The (Shakespeare) 29
meta-dramaturgy 98
metaphors 41–2
microphone effect 153
microphone signals 152
Miller and His Men, The (Pocock) 139
Milligan, Spike 122
mimetic forms xix, 18
minimalism xvi
Mitchell, Helen 77
Mitchell, Katie 80
modernism, popular 162–4
mono loudspeakers 179–80
Morning Chronicles 111
'Murder in the Studio' (Backus) 171–2
music 15, 44–6, 193–4
    children 6–9
    Confessions of an English Opium-Eater (De Quincy) 126
    De Institutione Musica (Boethius) 27–8, 30–1
        as acoustemology 28–30
    and drama 30–2
    Exotica 129–33, 130
    interval music 14
    picturesque 106–7
    political economy of 55–6
    pop music 9–12, 122
        art pop 123–5
    Rouben Mamoulian 163–4
    versus sound 43
    versus stereo 78
    Tempest, The (Shakespeare) 127
    totality 41–2
Music and the Art of Theatre (Appia) 43
music videos 11
mysticism 40–1
mythology 26–7, 34

Nancy, Jean-Luc 57–8
Napier, Frank 162, 166
narcotics 125–6, 128
New Drama 144
New Romanticism xiv–xv
No Thoroughfare (Dickens) 139–41
Noakes, John 3
noise xix, 37–8, 54
Noises Off (Napier) 162, 166
North American Review, The 83
'Notes on the Early Progress of the Picturesque of Sound' (Le Bruit) 120
'now hear this' xxi–xxii
Nowhere Bound (Mitchell) 80

O'Callaghan, Casey 40
On a Note of Triumph (Corwin) 173–7
Ong, Walter 33
Ongian litany. *See* audio-visual litany
ontology xix–xx, 21
opera 19
opium 125–6, 128
overture 3

Parkinson, J.C. 87
Parlophone 13
Partridge, Andy 13–14
Passions, The (Baxter) 131
Pavis, Patrice 41
Payne Knight, Richard 34
personal audio 72–4
Pet Sounds (Beach Boys) 10
phenomenology 24
phonography 83, 86, 87, 88–9
Picker, J. 56, 57, 149, 150
Picturesque 99–100, 194
   gothic melodrama 137
   parodies 109
   of sound 101–15
      aurality of the contrived gaze 104–6
      Eidophusikon (De Loutherbourg) 110–15
      modern stage thunder 106–9
      'Notes on the Early Progress of the Picturesque of Sound' (Le Bruit) 120
picturesque auditorium 75
picturing 39–40. *See also* audio-visual litany
   scenic reconfiguration 93–100
Piscator, E. 89–90
Pithecanthropus Erectus (Mingus) 130
Plumptre, James 104, 105
Polish Jew, The (Erckmann and Chatrian) 149
pop music 9–12, 122
   art pop 123–5
popular modernism 162–4
Popular Science Monthly 145
popular science of sound 148–50
Porgy (Heyward) 162–3
Pride and Prejudice (Austen) 101
privilege xx
prologue 53–4
psychoacoustics 34, 35–6, 37–8, 74, 76, 154, 197
Punter, David 115
Pygmalion (Rousseau) 138
Pyne, William 109, 110, 111, 112–14, 119
Pythagoras 27–8

Quiet Village: The Exotic Sounds of Martin Denny 131–2

race 127
radio xxii, 11–12, 57, 123
   BBC Radiophonic Workshop 122
radio drama 165–6
   The Anatomy of Sound (Corwin) 183–90
   interactive form 171–3
   kaleidosonic form 170–1
   mono loudspeakers 179–80
   On a Note of Triumph (Corwin) 173–7
   symphonic form 166–9
   theatre of the mind 179
Radio London 120–1
Radio One 119
Radio Times 161
Raikes, Cecil 87
rainforest 28, 29
Rancière, Jacques
   aesthetic 48
   aesthetic regime 18–20, 60–2, 94
   background noise 154
   community 172, 177
   music and drama 31
   theatre 32, 45
recognition 36
recording. *See* sound recording
Reis, Irving 172
representation 20, 31
resonance 26, 27
'Revolution 9' (Beatles) 123
rhetorics of the auditorium 48–52
Romanticism
   acoustic space 32–4
   aesthetic regime 60, 62
   aural subjectivity 72
   exoticism 129
   Faust (Goethe) 54
   literature 26. *See also* Coleridge, S.T.; Cowper, W.
   music 39, 41–2, 44–5, 193, 194
   New Romanticism xiv–xv
Ross, Alex 80
Royal Haymarket 97
Ruskin, J. 100

INDEX

Sardanapalus (Byron) 107
scenery 107
scenic reconfiguration 93–100
scenography 18, 19, 21
   of sound 38–46
      paradox of Appian scenography for sound design 43–6
      picturing 39–40
      stage design and liquid metaphor of sound 40–3
Schaeffer, Pierre 44, 157
Schopenhauer, Arthur 43
Schultze, Holger 73
Scott, Clement 88–9, 148
Sellar, Peter 17–18, 21, 44
sensorium commune 42
Serres, Michael 20, 24, 25, 38, 51–2, 58, 197
Seven Keys to Baldpate (Der Bigger) 159, 160
Sgt Pepper's Lonely Hearts Club Band (Beatles) 10, 121, 132–3
Shakespeare, William 29–30
   Henry V 89
   King Lear 106
   Merchant of Venice, The 29
Sieveking, Lance 167, 168, 169, 171
silence 3, 68, 159–61
   The Anatomy of Sound (Corwin) 186–8
   auditorium 51, 52
   Bishop Berkley 39
   The Encounter (Complicité) 37
silent films 76, 154–5
silent listening 54–6
Silly Symphonies (Disney) 11
Sister Beatrice (Maeterlinck) 160
situations 98–9, 146–8
Skiera, Helen 21
Skinner, J. 171
slapstick 11, 85
Smith, Bruce R. xviii, 29
Smith, Jacob 170
sonic comedy 12–15
Sonic Experience (Augoyard and Torgue) 37

sonic turn xvii–xix, 15, 17, 123
sound xxii, 22, 59–60, 168, 197. *See also* god sound
   acousmatic 44
   animals 129
   common 185
   liquid metaphor of 40–3
   picturesque of 101–15
      aurality of the contrived gaze 104–6
      Eidophusikon (De Loutherbourg) 110–15
      modern stage thunder 106–8
      'Notes on the Early Progress of the Picturesque of Sound' (Le Bruit) 120
   popular science of 148–50
   scenography of 38–46
      paradox of Appian scenography for sound design 43–6
      picturing 39–40
      stage design and liquid metaphor of sound 40–3
Sound (Tindall) 149
sound design xiv, xvi, xvii, 59–60, 140, 182, 193
   paradox of Appian scenography for 43–6
   total program of sound 17–18
sound designers 16
sound effect xvi–xvii, xxii, 16–17
   baby-boomer children 3–5
   comedic 12–15
   and music 6–9
      pop music 9–12
'Sound Effects Man, The' (City Slickers) 11–12
Sound in Theatre (Burris-Meyer) 182
sound location 35
sound operator 49, 50
sound recording 83–5, 86, 87–8
   gramophones 89–90
   Terry's Theatre 88–9
sound studies xvii–xviii, 15
soundie 11
Southern, Richard 96

space xxii. *See also* auditorium
  acoustic 32–4
  auditory 34–8
    as inscape 67–72
  auditory imagination 177–9
  hi-fi cell 78
stage design xvii, xxii, 41–3
Stage Effect (Mayhew) 98
States, Bert 144
stereo 76–9
Sterne, Jonathan 33, 39–40, 41, 47–8
Stoever, J.L. 127
Stoker, Bram 134, 136
  Dracula 134–6
stories 191–2
sublime 102, 107
Sullivan, Sir Arthur 87, 88
Sully, James 149
surround-sound auditorium 75
surround-sound systems 77, 78
Swainson, Dorothy 154
symbolism 150, 159, 161
symphonic audio drama 166–9
synecdoche 37, 60, 195

tableau curtain (tabs) 50
Taboo (Lyman) 132
Tale of Mystery, A (Holcroft) 137
telegraphy 153
television 14, 76, 86
Tempest, The (Shakespeare) 126–7, 128
Tennyson, Alfred 128–9
Terry's Theatre 88–9
test-cards 14
theatre 18, 32, 45, 46, 58, 197. *See also* amphitheatre
  auditory configuration 178
  scenic reconfiguration 93–100
Theatre Noise conference xviii–xix
Theatre Noise (Kendrick and Roesner) xix, 41
theatre of the mind 177–8
Theatre Royal Drury Lane 94, 95, 96–7, 111
theatre sound. *See* sound design
Theatre Studies xviii
theatrical turn xiv–xvii, 95

theatricality 103
Theory of Sound (Rayleigh) 149
This Modern World (Kenton) 130
Thompson, H.H. 161
thunder 121–2, 194–5
  Castle Thunder 5, 6
  Dracula (Stoker) 134–5
  Eidophusikon (De Loutherbourg) 113–14, 119–20
  modern stage thunder 106–9
Tijuana Moods (Mingus) 130
tinging 105–6
Toop, David 130, 131, 132
total program of sound 17–18, 21, 44
totality 26–7, 29, 41–2
Tour of Dr Syntax in Search of the Picturesque, The (Combe) 108
Townshend, Pete 40

unhearing 36–7, 154. *See also* psychoacoustics
United States. *See* America
university courses xiv, xvi, xvii–xviii
Upanishads 41
Upper Norwood, London 85–6

Verma, N. 170, 177
Verve 124
Vincent, Harley 89
virtual audio reality 21
vision. *See* audio-visual litany
Voigt, P. G. A. H. 86, 180
von Sömmerring, Samuel Thomas 42

Wagnerian opera 19
War of the Worlds (Welles) 171
waterfall 140–1
Waves (Mitchell) 80
ways of knowing xx, 6, 10, 13, 28–9, 30, 55, 56, 156
we xx, 5, 6, 25, 52
Welton, Martin 178
What's Going on (Marvin Gaye) 10
Wheatstone, Charles 153
White Album (Beatles) 123
Whitehead, G. 169, 171

Whitley, William 119–20
Wilson, Brian 132
Wonders of Derbyshire (De Loutherbourg) 111–12

Yeates, Edmund 87

Yellow Submarine (Beatles) 121
'Ying Tong Song' (The Goons) 12–13
Young Person's Guide to the Orchestra (Britton) 7–8

Zappa, Frank 124

www.ingramcontent.com/pod-product-compliance
Lightning Source LLC
Chambersburg PA
CBHW052037300426
44117CB00012B/1861